The Man Who Cycled the Americas

www.rbooks.co.uk

Also by Mark Beaumont

The Man Who Cycled the World

For more information on Mark Beaumont and his books, see his
website at www.markbeaumontonline.com

The Man Who Cycled The Americas

Mark Beaumont

BANTAM PRESS

LONDON · TORONTO · SYDNEY · AUCKLAND · JOHANNESBURG

TRANSWORLD PUBLISHERS
61–63 Uxbridge Road, London W5 5SA
A Random House Group Company
www.rbooks.co.uk

First published in Great Britain
in 2011 by Bantam Press
an imprint of Transworld Publishers

A CIP catalogue record for this book
is available from the British Library.

ISBN 9780593066980

Addresses for Random House Group Ltd companies outside the UK
can be found at: www.randomhouse.co.uk
The Random House Group Ltd Reg. No. 954009

The Random House Group Ltd supports the Forest Stewardship
Council (FSC), the leading international forest-certification organization. All our
titles that are printed on Greenpeace-approved FSC-certified paper carry the FSC logo.
Our paper procurement policy can be found at
www.rbooks.co.uk/environment

Typeset in 11/15.25pt Times New Roman by
Falcon Oast Graphic Art Ltd.
Printed and bound in Great Britain by
CPI Mackays, Chatham, ME5 8TD

2 4 6 8 10 9 7 5 3 1

The Man Who Cycled the Americas

Acknowledgements

When I wrote the acknowledgements for my first book, *The Man who Cycled the World*, I didn't know if it would be my only chance to write down such thanks for a lifetime of help and friendship. So I thanked everyone, and rightly so! Second time round I thought I could be more concise, but this section has once again run to an impressive tally of names. Expeditions like mine don't happen without a great wealth of support and kindness. Reading these few pages will give you a better understanding of the depth of logistics involved.

I would like to give first thanks and to dedicate this book to David Peat, a great friend. David was the man who first believed in my ability to bring expeditions to screen, introduced me to the BBC and has been my constant mentor. We have shared great adventures.

If you have followed my expeditions from the start you will know of the great family team that I have with my mum, Una. She has supported me since I first pedalled across Scotland at the age of twelve, and continues to be my number-one supporter and adviser. This is more than a full-time job and I couldn't do what I do without her – thank you, Mum!

Individual and huge thanks also go to Nicci Kitchin who has given me endless support, both through the expedition and writing the book. Her brilliant patience and good humour during my long absence and long hours of work have been so important. The writing took about five months and in many ways felt like an expedition in itself!

I think I write the way I speak, and it takes a hard-working team to check and shape that lengthy manuscript into the book you are now reading. I am pleased that they changed remarkably little, but the devil is in the detail and it is a vital process. Thanks to Giles Elliott, my editor, Mark Stanford (Stan), my agent from Jenny Brown Associates, Daniel Balado-Lopez, Madeline Toy (Mads), Phil Lord and Nick Avery. Congratulations also to Mads for winning Best Publicity Campaign at the National Sporting Club's Book of the Year Awards for *The Man who Cycled the World*.

This expedition was a BBC project shown afterwards as a three-part series, as well as broadcast during the journey across radio, TV and online, including at www.bbc.co.uk/cyclingtheamericas. It was the first time such a long, mainly solo journey had been shared across so many BBC platforms. Special thanks to my production team of Andrea Miller, Neil McDonald, David Peat, Tony Nellany, Nick Schoolingin-Jordan, Jenni Shaw, Dominique Middleton, Graham Gillies, Craig Frew, Shona Kyle, Michelle Knight, Wendy-Ann Dunsmuir, David Devenney, Adam Spencer, Lesley Smith, Eileen Maguire, Therese Lynch and Jonathan Seal. Further essential input and support came from Dave Chalmers, John Carmichael, Keith Wood, Matt Barret, Jim Gough, Nick Roxburgh, Craig Summers, Iain McVie, Claire O'Neill, Anne Heining and Bill Paterson. For the great coverage from BBC Radio 1 thanks to Greg James, Neil Sloan and Piers Bradford. At BBC Radio Scotland thanks to Fred MacAulay as well as Lindsay Gillies, not just for their regular updates but also for creating a brilliant series of radio documentaries afterwards. The BBC Radio Scotland Newsdrive team and the BBC TV Reporting Scotland team also gave very generous coverage to the expedition.

Names that may be familiar from the book are the escorts who met me in Mexico and Central America. Many thanks for the support from Julian Cardona, Jose Avilez, Roberto Zavala, Julian

Rolando Ruiz and Jose Soto Rivera. To arrange these and many more logistics took BBC fixers and local contacts, including Lara Rodriguez Warmington, Gregg Koenigsberger, Marthmaria Morales, Brian Bonilla, Mario Carmona, Dan Collyns, Gabriel Padilla and Macarena Gagliardi. My special thanks also to Claudio Flores for his help throughout the Spanish-speaking world.

I have worked with my personal trainer, Craig Ali (www.total-health.uk.com) for a number of years and can always rely on his expertise and friendship. Val Vannet, my geography teacher from school days, gave considerable help with route planning. Bruce Murray (www.bcgwebdesign.co.uk) has always built and maintained my website. Jim Kerr in Chamonix taught me the essential skills to climb Denali and Aconcagua. Steve Cook and the team from AKA Training & Consultancy took me through the excellent Surviving Hostile Environments training course. Thanks to you all.

Social media has now connected many long distance cyclists and adventurers, and I am amazed by how many like-minded people I have come to know in recent years. Many of them have contributed to my Americas journey and I am very grateful for their time and enthusiasm. If you don't already know these names I would recommend looking up the expeditions of Scott Napier, Alastair Humphreys (www.alastairhumphreys.com), Dominic Gill (www.takeaseat.org), James Hooper (www.james-hooper.com) and Tom Kevill-Davies (www.thehungrycyclist.com). Thanks also for the valuable input from Oli Bray and Simon Jenkins.

In nearly nine months, from Alaska to Tierra del Fuego, I met so many interesting and kind people. I can't mention many, but would like to thank especially Melis and Joey Coady for their great leadership, and Johann Van Zyl for his friendship on Denali. My best friends from the road were undoubtedly Mike and Alanna Clear (www.goingthedistance.org.uk) apart from the fact that I met them five times between America and Argentina, they also helped me out hugely and were great fun. The journey from Central to South America wouldn't have been possible without the support from

Beverley Waring, Kenneth Ross, John Fitzsimmons of Star Reefers and the owners of the Crown Opal at Nky Reefers. I was the first passenger that the Crown Opal crew had ever welcomed aboard, so many thanks to Captain Evseev and his men for looking after me. On Aconcagua, Damian Benegas and Sebastian Ezcurra formed the best team I have climbed with. They were inspiringly positive and fun to be with. Thanks also to Harry Kikstra (www.exposed-planet.com) for his advice, Fernando Grajales for logistical support, Martin from Mendoza, Oksana Chekulaeva and Alice Dixon.

Other friends from the road who I would like to mention and thank are the British Embassy throughout North, Central and South America, Alan Klerc (www.velomech.net), Mona Welborn, Allan and Pat Poertner and Heidi (www.solfun.com), Jack Brennan (www.gilahikeandbike.com), Steven Walker and family, Xavier Romero, Angelino Abad Flores and family, Miguel and Francisco Rendon (www.escoffee.com), Alan Paredes Arce, Percy from Arequipa, Sarah Green and Stewart Starrs from Pisco (www.piscosinfrontcras.org) and Liz and Phil Bingham (www.pedallingnorth.com).

So far I have managed 'to thank' in fairly ordered groups, but I'm now left with a number of equally deserving people who have less in common, but who are just as deserving of a mention! Firstly, my family has always been there for me, especially my sisters, Heather and Hannah. It was brilliant to see Heather in Alaska and for us to share a part of the journey. Dad, Granny and Grandpa are keen supporters as well and I am very grateful for their encouragement. David Fox Pitt (www.wildfoxevents.com) was hugely important at the start of my career and continues to be on hand to help whenever needed. Rob Pendleton and the team from LDC (www.ldc.co.uk) have been equally supportive and it has been a great pleasure to share my journey over the last four years with them. Thanks also for the support from Brendan Keller, Jim Munroe, Trish Peat, Laura Turner, Tim O'Donovan, Andy Barlow, and Kev and Harry at Footprints (www.footprintsglasgow.com), Brian Tinsley at Yellow Ltd (www.yellowIimited.com), Chris Tiso at Tiso's (www.tiso.com), Pieter Jan Rijpstra at KOGA (www.koga-signature.com), Martin Kirton at Lyon Equipment (www.lyon-outdoor.co.uk) and Michael Atkinson at High Five (www.highfive.co.uk).

My friends have always supported my expeditions, albeit some with perplexed enthusiasm! You all know who you are and my great thanks for the wonderful send-off party and regular messages of support.

As this expedition went on, the online following grew until the army of support on Twitter, Facebook and the website felt like a virtual peloton. I may have been out there on my own, but I never felt alone with the quite amazing level of feedback, questions and constant enthusiasm. Thanks to everyone who was a part of this. I can't thank you all, but I'd like to mention in particular Stuart Fairley, one of the most dedicated supporters. I was thrilled to fly back into Edinburgh Airport and see him there to shake my hand.

To everyone who I met on the road and everyone who has been involved in this journey, I hope you remember it fondly. I certainly do.

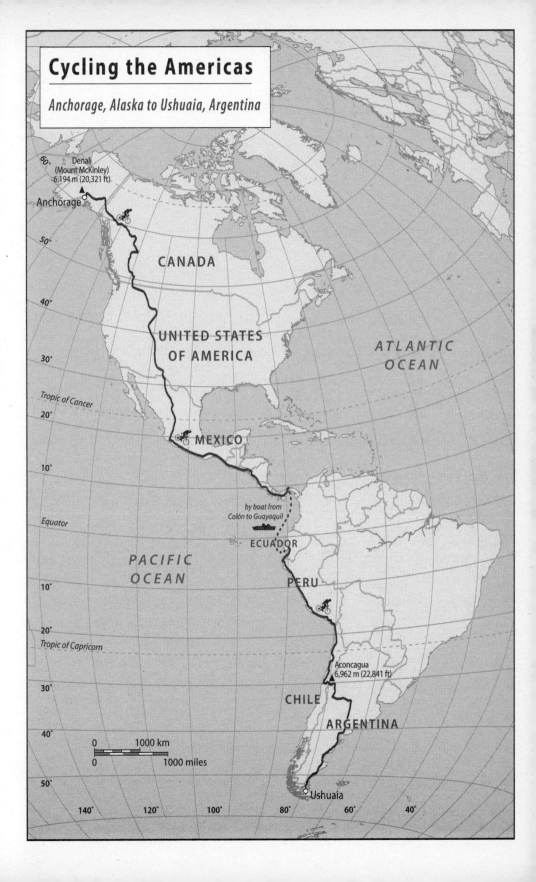

Cycling the Americas

Anchorage, Alaska to Ushuaia, Argentina

Denali
(Mount McKinley)
6,194 m (20,321 ft)

Anchorage

CANADA

UNITED STATES
OF AMERICA

ATLANTIC
OCEAN

Tropic of Cancer

MEXICO

by boat from
Colón to Guayaquil

Equator

ECUADOR

PACIFIC
OCEAN

PERU

Tropic of Capricorn

Aconcagua
6,962 m (22,841 ft)

CHILE

ARGENTINA

1000 km

1000 miles

Ushuaia

Prologue

The dull, deep ache in my calves was unbearable. I stretched up, arced my right axe hard into the flaky ice, then lifted my left crampon and kicked the two toe points back home a little bit higher. Glancing up, I saw there was still a long way to go. I had absolutely no choice but to keep tiptoeing my way to the top, muscles screaming. The alternative was to fall.

Nothing in a decade of endurance cycling had prepared my legs for this.

It was April, but it didn't feel like springtime on the high peaks above Chamonix. Half an hour later I had cleared the steep ice and started along a very exposed rock-and-ice arête towards the top of the Petite Aiguille Verte. It was pea soup; I couldn't see more than 20 metres, which I didn't actually mind as it hid the stomach-churning drops on both sides. In double-shell plastic boots and crampons I felt very cumbersome. The feeling and sound of metal spikes on rocks are very unnerving. I felt that a pair of skin-hugging climbing shoes would have been far better in such extreme terrain, but I needed to learn this new art form, and learn it fast.

I watched Jim effortlessly shimmy around boulders, walk the line along a ridge and secure the rope around another rock. In comparison I was all arms and legs, no longer trusting my sense of balance and the forces of gravity to keep me from falling. To tease me further, just as I edged along the tumbled obstacle course, the thick cloud drifted effortlessly away for a brief minute, exposing a few thousand feet of fresh air to my left and another sheer drop to my right. Nothing had changed, the climb was no harder than it had been a few seconds earlier, but my body involuntarily tensed.

The top was too small for two men to stand on, or so I thought. Come on, Jim gestured as he stood easily on the summit, no hand-holds in sight. It was only another few metres and as high as the rock I had just passed. I'm already at the top, I reasoned, so I held on where I was. I felt no need to do a Man on the Moon pose, having already pushed well beyond my comfort zone. Thankfully Jim agreed, with a laugh – another thing I was unable to do until I was back on terra firma a few hours later.

By the time of that climb in Chamonix just over a year had passed since I broke the world record for the fastest global circumnavigation by bicycle. The original plan for a BBC2 Scotland half-hour documentary on that expedition had blossomed into a four-part national series on BBC1. It was the launch pad into the expedition world I had hoped and worked for. However, not everything since that cycle had gone to plan.

For half a year I had trained to row the North Atlantic as part of a twelve-man team. My motivation for committing to this challenge was straightforward: after the solitude and landlocked efforts of cycling around the world, I had been dreaming of doing something very different. I had secured my place on the expedition after an inclement and insanely tough selection week based around Loch Tay in the Scottish Highlands. That boyhood excitement about world firsts and fastests had not left me and I couldn't wait to be part of the world record attempt to row the 3,500 miles from New York to Falmouth in less than fifty-five days. As ocean rowing records went, it was as coveted as they got. The legendary crossing of Harbo and Samuelsen in 1896 had stood for 106 years. Our departure date was set for 5 June 2009.

In January that year, Leven Brown, the team leader, took a

different crew for a crossing of the mid Atlantic in our 55-foot rowing boat *La Mondiale*, both as a crack at that record but mainly to test some new onboard systems we would undoubtedly need in the much colder and stormier north. Reliable and well-tested water purification systems and a self-righting mechanism were high on all our wish lists.

A week into the crossing the rudder broke in high seas; *La Mondiale* carried no spares. After three days of being tossed around like a cork, the crew, very shaken but unscathed, were rescued by a passing cargo vessel. *La Mondiale*, broken during the rescue by the crashing hulls, was never recovered.

I was writing my first book so was unable to go on this ill-fated test run, but I was following closely online from the comfort of my flat in Edinburgh. I watched, concerned, as the boat's daily average went from over 100 nautical miles to nothing, before news reached me that *La Mondiale* would not be coming back.

I now wasn't going to be rowing anywhere in a hurry and had no concrete plans. There were plenty of ideas, but I spent a few weeks resigning myself to the fact that it was too late to organize another major expedition that year. It had, after all, taken over a year to plan and train for the 18,296-mile pedal around the globe.

However, at the end of the previous year the BBC had come back enthusiastically with the viewing figures and feedback from *The Man Who Cycled the World*. We'd brainstormed a few other ideas and had agreed to put one particular expedition on the backburner while I attempted the North Atlantic. Six weeks after the loss of *La Mondiale*, I received a phone call from my friend David Peat, the BBC director who had championed the world cycle documentary and first given me a camera. After catching up briefly, he cut to the chase. 'Seeing as you have nowhere to go this year,' he began . . .

David explained that when BBC Scotland heard I was no longer rowing, they had put forward to the commissioners my proposal to cycle the Americas from top to bottom. I understood that this was on the basis of nothing ventured, nothing gained, as documentaries normally needed a much longer commissioning period. But I could tell this call wasn't just a catch-up. I remember standing up and starting to wander quickly and aimlessly as David continued, 'If you can go this year, then BBC1 are able to commission.'

Three months later I was on a flight to Anchorage, Alaska.

1

My personal motivations are tricky to pin down, but I feel it's important to try to explain what I was about to attempt. While publicly I may be regarded as a cyclist, full stop, my main idea has always been to find journeys that haven't been tried or certainly haven't been documented. Great endurance journeys give us a unique chance to explore the world and to learn about ourselves. So I have no interest in racing around the world again, and when I did the bike was simply the best choice of transport rather than a late bid on my part to become an elite cyclist. I hope this sentiment makes some sense, as it will shape the way you read this book and help you see the journey the same way I did.

More people have cycled down (or up) the Americas than have cycled around the world, and the attraction is fairly obvious. It's the ultimate top-to-toe journey that this world offers, a John O'Groats to Land's End on a much bigger scale. If you ignore the formidable, roadless Darien Gap between Central and South America, the Americas can be seen as the longest unbroken land journey on planet Earth.

I had always looked longingly at this part of the world on the wall chart, but I'd never felt any desire to race it, especially after racing around the world. This would have felt like more of the same, and in terms of a documentary might well be seen as less of the same; it was certainly shorter. My interest lay in the formidable mountainous spine that joins the northern, central and southern parts of the Americas. Mountains were one of the main features to avoid on the world ride as they rarely provide the fastest route; here was a chance to create a journey that followed the longest mountain ridge on earth – the American Cordillera. And as I now had the opportunity to undertake a journey down the world's longest mountain ranges, I decided it would be appropriate to crown this at either end with the summits of the highest peaks in North and South America. The more I considered this, the more it seemed like the perfect mountain journey. Maybe not the simplest to explain, but essentially a very pure journey.

Within the climbing world, the Seven Summits – climbing the highest peak in each of the seven continents – has in recent decades become a popular amateur ambition. It's mainly a pastime for the very few rich, free and fit enough to be able to commit to such a huge task. While elite mountaineers sometimes frown at taking the easiest route on any mountain just to be able to reach the top, avoiding the skill and endurance necessary for new and more technical routes, the Seven Summits is not to be underestimated. High-altitude climbing is always unpredictable, unforgiving and, for any living being, unnatural.

The two peaks I was intending to climb are the second and third highest of the Seven Summits, after Mount Everest, which at 29,035ft (8,850m) is well known as the king of mountains: Aconcagua (22,841ft/6,962m) in Argentina and Denali (20,320ft/6,194m) in Alaska. Due to the jetstream at altitude, the daylight hours and other seasonal effects, each mountain has a different and limited climbing season. Winter ascents have been attempted on each mountain but this is the realm of the very experienced, and sometimes the foolhardy. The fact that I was to travel north to south was decided for me: the BBC wished me to start as soon as possible and I was reluctant to be climbing in or cycling through either Alaska's or Patagonia's winter. So although cycling the Americas may not ever have been planned as any kind of world record attempt, there was time pressure. I needed to climb Denali around June time and Aconcagua in January 2010, and between the two mountains lay thirteen countries and 11,000 miles (17,700km) of mountainous cycling.

My early enthusiasm for the expedition overlooked two glaring facts. By the time I made it back to Paris at the end of the world cycle I had taken eighty-one days off the old world record, but just eight hours off my personal target of 195 days. After all the trials and delays over 18,296 miles through eighteen countries, this was an unlikely small margin. And in the days after finishing I soon found that I had physically paid the price for such specific endurance. The truth was that I had barely walked anywhere for half a year and I suffered from pains in my lower back and shins when walking, as well as discovering that my back had rounded off considerably. With the help of hydrotherapy, massage, physio and gentle cross-training I managed to normalize my fitness over the following months, but it had come as a shock how maladjusted my body had become.

Sixteen months later, just before setting out for Alaska, I realized that this all-round endurance fitness would be one of the attempt's greatest challenges. This time round I needed to climb for weeks in Alaska, then spend half a year on the bike before hopping off and going straight back into a climb of the western hemisphere's highest peak. This would be a far greater test of my physical and mental stamina than anything before.

I was not much of a climber, either. The scale of my new project hit me at Seattle airport as I studied a vast picture of Mount Rainier on the wall, the highest mountain in Washington State (and also of the mainland forty-eight states). It looked huge, beautiful and intimidating. I examined it over a cappuccino, trying to bury my concerns as I realized that many climbers used Rainier as a warm-up for where I was going. I hadn't even climbed Ben Nevis. My five-day crash course on mountain skills in Chamonix was the first time I had ever felt the effects of altitude, albeit at only

3,500m (11,500ft), and the first time I had done any ice climbing.

Aboard the flight from Seattle to Anchorage, I spent much of the time staring out of the window at the seemingly endless peaks, glaciers and snowfields of the Rocky Mountains. The rest of the flight was spent marvelling at Alaskan Airways' unique take on luxury travel. The seats were extraordinarily large. I am 6ft 3in and I wallowed in luxury. On the carpeted walls of the plane were dated paintings of the wilds of Alaska. I had never really seen either carpeted walls or paintings on planes before, and it gave the impression that I was not just flying five hours north but also three decades back in time.

Adventure and Alaska are synonymous to all. Even to live and work in 'The Last Frontier' was in my imagination a pretty wild experience. Then again, what did I know, apart from what I'd picked up from *White Fang* and *Into the Wild*? Still, it seemed a wonderful place to start any expedition.

On the morning of Friday 29 May 2009, after briefly meeting a small hustle of Alaskan TV and newspaper reporters in downtown Anchorage, I headed out of the suburbs to find a suitably iconic official starting point. But Anchorage is like any other US grid town and doesn't particularly reflect the wilderness of the north or the setting I'd imagined leaving from. I was surprised by the gated communities and incredible mansions that jostled for a Pacific view – not at all matching my mind's-eye image of the place. I had hoped to start on a beach, just like I hoped to finish on a beach near Ushuaia, the southernmost city in the world. However, the only piece of semi-wilderness I could find without travelling too far in the wrong direction was about 300 metres above the water's edge on steep grassy cliffs.

It was also a very grey day, and while I could see over the water for miles, a thick bank of cloud started at a few hundred feet and shrouded the entire coastal range. David Peat was with me, and these inclement conditions posed more of a problem for him than for me. It was near-perfect cool cycling weather, but David was with me for just four or five days to try to capture the essential opening sequences for the documentary series. And while I stood on the edge of the grassy cliff trying to describe the mountainous view you couldn't see behind me, if you had swung the camera round you would have seen a group of increasingly impatient motocross bikers whom we had asked to cut their engines so we could film for a few minutes.

I wouldn't have wanted to miss leaving from the Pacific, but it felt like a bit of a false start. The pedal up from the coast to the Denali National Park was the only time I planned on going north, and my focus the entire way was on the climb ahead. Also, although fit, I felt cumbersome. I had spent the previous six weeks feeding up as much as I could, consuming a number of liquid meals a day between my regular big diet, as I was keen to start what promised to be a gruelling expedition with weight to lose. The consequence of now being heavier was that I didn't feel completely comfortable on the bike.

Talkeetna lies 130 miles (210km) north of Anchorage, and is a small town at the end of a road in the foothills of the Alaskan Range. Officially it has about eight hundred inhabitants, but how anyone can carry out an accurate census in the wild forests of Alaska where some people just don't want to be found is a mystery to me. In 1919, the year when the town was established, you could get change from $15 for a town centre plot. Now it's a summer mecca for tour buses, fishermen and climbers. Apart from passing Sarah Palin's estate entrance there hadn't been a lot on the road north so I was surprised to pedal into such a hive of activity. A dozen short and mainly unpaved streets make up Talkeetna, whose airport is almost as big as the town itself. Along the main street lies the 'historic' heart with Nagley's Store, the Fairview Inn and the West Buttress pub. Scattered in the wooded surroundings were all shapes and sizes of house, all looking like they were built out of the trees that once stood on the same land, often with a big truck parked outside.

I had a few days to meet my team and prepare for the climb, but I also wanted to explore this amazing little town. The entrance to Denali National Park lies a good 100 miles north, on a different road, but for the majority of tourists content with taking a picture from afar, and maybe a sightseeing flight, Talkeetna offers one of the best views of the park's namesake, the highest peak in North America. As I stopped my bike outside Nagley's and looked around, I could see that most people were either wiry climbers or plump tourists, and it was amusingly obvious that each group acted like the other wasn't there.

There was another difference between them. The word 'Denali' is a native Athabascan word for 'The High One'. In 1896 a gold prospector renamed it Mount McKinley after William McKinley, a US presidential candidate of the time, and ever since there has been a fairly heated debate about the correct name. I found that climbers and Alaskans called it Denali whereas other tourists usually referred to it as Mount McKinley.

Denali is also often talked about as one of the coldest mountains in the world, among many other endearing properties. Its summit may stand a long way shy of Mount Everest's and other great Himalayan peaks, but it actually has a longer ascent, due to how low you have to start, which in turn is dictated by a no-landing zone within Denali National Park. In fact, it's the longest ascent of any of the Seven Summits. What is more, whereas in the Himalayas climbers use sherpas, and in the Andes they use mules, in Alaska you and your team are on your own in terms of carrying enough supplies to last up to a month in a polar climate.

Denali's unique character is mainly due to its northerly latitude. At 63°N it lies about 200 miles (320km) from the Arctic Circle. This is why it is so glaciated, so cold, has such a short climbing season and, less predictably, more extreme altitude effects. Put simply, the barometric pressure at more northerly latitudes affects acclimatization, so climbers will tend to suffer from the effects of altitude more on Denali than at the same altitude on a mountain nearer the equator. Oddly, this meant that while Aconcagua, my second climb, would be 2,519ft higher, the effects of altitude on both summits, assuming the same conditions, were likely to be similar. This surprising effect is caused by the troposphere (the lowest portion and 75 per cent of the entire atmosphere) being thinner at the poles – about 4 miles thick compared to 12 miles in the tropical regions.

I felt more like a tourist than a climber that first day in Talkeetna, but my thoughts were consumed by where I was about to go. Perhaps luckily, the cloud remained low so I couldn't see the mountain.

By the time I reached Talkeetna, on 31 May 2009, my body clock had just about adjusted to being nine hours behind UK time. The next day I had an eight a.m. till six p.m. induction and skills course with my new team. Having almost always been on solo expeditions, meeting the team was a moment I was a bit apprehensive about. And I had reason to be concerned.

The Alaska Mountaineering School was leading the expedition and putting together the six-strong team plus two guides. When I read their guidelines and prerequisites, I realized that they had made a serious exception allowing me to join. 'Denali requires a significant amount of prior climbing experience,' it said, 'and applicants should have climbed mountaineering routes that require roped glacier travel and winter snow camping. The mountain is too severe to be learning these skills for the first time.'

Also, a few weeks earlier AMS had sent out an email introducing Mike, Johann, Peggy, Hiroko and Denis to me. After a few days with no replies from my new teammates I imagined them as a hardy group of mountain characters, people of few words and deep contemplation who would see straight through my inexperience. So I felt it right to instigate a dialogue and I introduced myself, explaining that I would be keeping a video diary of the climb as part of a BBC series. A few more days passed, and I received just one reply, from Johann. To my great relief it was friendly and enthusiastic.

Then came a call from AMS to say that they were in the middle of
some serious damage control. One member had freaked out about
my filming plans and was threatening to pull out of the team. This
came as a shock as I had been told that everyone was in the loop
and understood that the filming needn't involve them unless they
particularly wanted it to. However, with no response at all from the
other four, I had left for Alaska with the impression that I would be
starting the expedition both out of my depth and deeply out of
favour.

For these reasons I asked David to leave me to it as I made my
introductions, and the cameras were kept well out of sight to begin
with. Thankfully, most of my fears were unfounded. The team,
diverse in age, background and character, seemed to gel well. As the
day went on I also realized we all had vastly different levels of
experience. It was like a first day at school: I could see that my own
trepidation was matched, if not exceeded, by that of some of the
others.

Mike, a doctor from America, was the oldest in the group. He
had spent years ticking off the highest peak in each US state. With
forty-nine in the bag, this was his ultimate and toughest mountain
yet. Denis was from Quebec. It was unclear what he did for a living
or had ever done in terms of climbing, mainly as his English wasn't
great. This surprised and concerned me: clear communication
would be of huge importance during the climb. Hiroko was a tall
but slightly built lady from Japan who smiled constantly and per-
formed a very slight bow every time she laughed or answered a
question. I wondered if she would be strong enough to carry and
pull 80lb of gear. Peggy was from Switzerland. As soon as I'd
parked my bike and walked up to the group I'd read her body language. She was short, well built, with long plaited blonde hair. Her
greeting was civil enough but I sensed a slight frostiness, and she
spent most of the day watching me quietly. I reflected thankfully on
my last-hour decision not to walk in for our first meeting with a
camera behind my shoulder. It would have added unnecessary fuel

to this unnecessary fire. I didn't meet Johann, my only known associate, until the following morning.

During the day a number of guides came in to meet us, each more bearded and wilder than the last. These were the sort of men I had imagined climbing with, as opposed to our group of what I considered to be slightly unlikely suspects.

The key lessons started with how to rope up as a team of four (we would be two groups of three with a guide each). This entailed running a 50-metre rope through both a waist and chest harness while also securing a sled. Next we mocked an exercise in moving up a section of fixed line rope. In just over a week we would be moving up to 16,000ft on a headwall of ice at 50 degrees using a fixed line for running protection. However, on the flat woodland floor, dressed in a T-shirt, it was hard to relate the skills as we ran our 'ascender' gear between sections of climbing rope tied to trees.

The last major skill to learn, and the one we hoped never to need, was how to survive a crevasse fall. Apart from a few ridgeline sections, the entire 16-mile climb on Denali is on glaciers – all moving, all fractured, melting and freezing, and all constantly unpredictable. Hanging from the roof of a barn, it was painfully slow and tiring work to 'prusik' our way up a hanging rope, which involved making a foot loop and handhold on the rope and transferring weight from one to another using knots that slide when unweighted but grip when pulled. As I observed the level of strength and dexterity in the group, I struggled to imagine us doing this confidently in full puffy down gear with big mitts in minus 20-degree conditions. Everyone had more climbing experience than I did, but it was clear that Denali required specific polar skills none of us had, and great endurance. I was confident that I would be physically stronger than most of the group members, so while I couldn't fall back on experience, I should be able to hold my own.

The following day we were due to fly out to our starting point, and over breakfast I met Johann, our final member. Originally from South Africa, Johann lived in California and had climbed a number of high peaks including Aconcagua. In his late thirties, he was very outgoing and immediately likeable. I could see he would be an important link in keeping the team together.

This was the day. You could feel the nervous energy of the team as we laid out and repacked our gear for the last time.

2

Unlike the wild mountain men I had met the day before, our guides were introduced as the young husband and wife team of Melis and Joey. Melis, our lead guide, was now the new smallest member of our team, and if it hadn't been for the obvious respect she commanded among the other guides, I might have thought we'd got the short straw. To answer any doubts, she pointed out that being big and strong wasn't the key to a successful climb.

Because of cameras, spare batteries and solar panels, I already had a weight handicap over the other team members. In addition, being six foot three means that everything from your sleeping-bag to your underwear is that bit bigger. A bit of extra material per item doesn't sound like much, but the grams add up, and my most pressing task at this time was trying to cut weight. Starting off with a pile of absolute essentials, I managed to get rid of another few kilos until I was under the 80lb (36kg) limit, but still with the heaviest pack.

The small bush planes that populated the airfield in Talkeetna split their time between sightseeing flights and acting as a taxi service for climbers, taking off on their wheels then landing on their skids on the ice. Denali has been climbed from Talkeetna itself, but this involves about ten days' hiking through forests, fording rivers and climbing lower glaciers before getting anywhere near the mountain. Over 99 per cent of people who have attempted and ever will attempt Denali fly to the edge of the Denali National Park, the furthest point planes are allowed to land, from where it is still the longest climb on earth.

Overheating in heavy double-shelled climbing boots and thermal layers, we piled out of the van that had taken us and our bags from AMS to the airfield. From there, with the help of a quad bike and trailer we shifted our 480lb of kit – enough to survive life in the freezer for up to a month – nearer to the planes. We were ready early for our scheduled five p.m. flight, and we sat about chatting in the sunshine outside the log cabin that was the airfield HQ waiting for news of conditions on the mountain, which were worsening despite it being a warm summer's day in Talkeetna. It had been a frantic but enjoyable day. All my initial fears had been put into perspective by the realization that we really were all in the same boat. The nervous anticipation of all was clear. There would be no gradual introduction to gain our bearings. We would soon be dropped in a sterile, glaciated world and left to our devices.

After a long wait, Melis rejoined us and broke the news: there would be no flying today. I was surprised to feel slightly relieved. One more night in a warm bed, one more shower. We bundled back into the van and returned to base, talking mainly about how we would find a hotel booking at this late hour.

As we pulled up and started unloading the bags, Harry, one of the lead guides, came sprinting out. 'That's the air taxi on the phone. Change of plan. They can take you if you hurry.' No one celebrated. I could see I hadn't been the only one who was quietly relieved about the delay, although there would have been considerable loss of face to admit to it.

It was a pretty bumpy ride inside that small prop plane. The huge pile of gear was kept in place with cargo mesh and we were all buckled in, earmuffs on. It had felt more like stepping into an old car than a plane, with its poorly sealed doors and tattered upholstery. For the first half-hour we swept low over a sea of forest and I stared down in awe at some remote huts, serious miles from anywhere, some with their own small airstrip that left a scar in the greenery. After crossing a few meltwater rivers we soared high across the first of the glaciers. Most looked completely impassable, with frantic crumple and fracture lines running their length and breadth. They were as stunning as they were intimidating. Higher still we crossed very close to a ridgeline the sight of which would have been exhilarating on its own without the small plane repeatedly falling into pockets of lesser air pressure before stabilizing with a shudder. It motored on determinedly, sounding and feeling like an unsilenced Land Rover going where no vehicle had gone before.

The lower Kahiltna glacier landing area is at about 7,200ft (2,200m). It's actually on a small spur glacier off to the side, and I say 'about' 7,200ft because these lower glaciers melt every year as the summer progresses and the planes are forced to land higher and higher up the spur to find firm ice, instead of slush. Landing higher is not as helpful as it may sound, as the only route is to descend to the main glacier before the real climbing up can begin. Luckily it had been a cold year so far, so we landed relatively low on 'Heartbreak Hill' and cleared the planes for a quick take-off. It was getting late.

I could see that time would seem different here. For one thing, it never got dark in June, and it was obvious that we would be climbing at odd times of the day to minimize the chances of falling through weak snow bridges. I was surprised to find the glacier very bumpy and rough, giving excellent grip even without crampons on. However, the freeze/thaw action at this altitude had also compacted the top layer to the hardness of a brick. It took some serious shovelling to bury the snow parachutes, which took the place of the traditional pegs that would be used on greener camp spots. That done, we bedded down for the night.

Four hours later, at three a.m., I woke up. The tents were soon down and just after five we were off. It was light but the sun wasn't yet on us and it was pretty cold. Compared to the day before, down the valley, it was very cold, but on the grand scale of coldness it was only relatively cold. Denali is a mountain where the Fahrenheit and Celsius ranges often meet at night, at around minus 40.

Forget fancy polar fibreglass enclosed sleds, ours were big rectangular plastic sledges, the sort kids use, the perfect size to carry a large duffel bag. The sled and my 80-litre rucksack together was about 80lb of gear. It was a weight that would take some getting used to, as would the technique of hauling it. As we crunched out of camp, snowshoes flapping rhythmically like massive flip-flops, each of us was kicked in the heels by our sleds as they tried to over-take us. It took the coordinated pace of all four in each team to keep the sleds from racing freely on downwards and from flipping over on camber slopes.

Once on the body of the mountain, we would be using the standard mountaineering technique of carry gear high, then sleep low. This would allow us to split the weight of our gear on tougher parts of the climb while also helping us acclimatize by being more active while spending time at each altitude level. If all went to plan then today and summit day would be the only parts of the climb when we wouldn't travel twice.

At five and a half miles, it was the longest day on the climb, and by far the heaviest while we had everything with us. Later on we would be storing unneeded gear in snow caches, to be collected on our return. But covering a third of our total climb distance on day one was a bit of a false victory as it was altitude gain which counted up here. Camp two was at 7,870ft (2,400m), just a few hundred metres higher than where we'd started, and from this point the climbing really would begin. It would be quite a few days until, having crossed Kahiltna Pass, we were actually on Denali. This commute from the outskirts of Denali Park was also the access route for any other number of climbs.

By ten a.m. it was insanely hot. I had been warned that at low altitude, walking through this ultra-reflective world was tough, but

I hadn't imagined being stripped down to a base layer, dripping with sweat under a baseball cap and glacier-rated sunglasses. Forget frostbite, the greatest evil for climbers low on the mountain is often heatstroke and sunburn. Time really did slow down as we wove our way around vast open crevasses on an indirect course up the very wide valley. We had to take a pace for the whole team, but I would have loved to up the ante and get it over and done with a bit faster. Progress was painfully slow, and after a while the dull ache in my shoulders and back was too great for me to be distracted by the breathtaking summit views left and right. I simply walked along staring at my snowshoes, trying not to trip on the rope whenever the person in front slowed momentarily.

By two p.m. we had the tents up. Despite the weight limitations, Johann, Mike and I had the luxury of a four-man tent between three. Denis was sharing with Hiroko and Peggy while Melis and Joey had their own smaller tent. It didn't take long for the tents to get even hotter inside than it was outside, so we set about building our kitchen tent. This needed to be a 10-foot-wide circular hole in the ground, about 5ft deep, with bench seats cut in the sides, and some snow steps down into it. Once dug, a long central pole was covered with a pointed section of parachute fabric and weighed down at ground level with snow on all sides. It was hot work, but it made for a surprisingly large and cool snow bunker. The fact it was mainly underground meant it was a key skill to learn for higher up where the winds would flatten a similar-sized above-ground structure, not to mention saving us from carrying the extra materials such a structure would have needed.

The first job had been to carefully stake the whole area for crevasses and 'wand' the edge of camp with thin bamboo poles. After the tents were put up, with every conceivable guy rope anchored, basking in T-shirts we set about upturning our sledges and securing all unused gear, storm-bounding the whole camp. Many of these routines seemed rather pedantic, but Melis made it clear that most of these tasks needed to be second nature by the time we got higher up, where conditions often change so quickly there is no time to react.

From camp we had a clear and quite staggering view of the summit over 13,000ft (nearly 4,000m) above us. Despite the calm at camp and the clear view, I could see spindrift whipping off the top. Another impossible summit day. It would be the last time we saw the top before our own summit bid, as we would soon be underneath the mountain on its vast flanks.

The following morning started very early again. For two days and two nights we had now lived in the same clothes; it would be about another twenty days and nights before the next wash. Ahead lay the aptly named Ski Hill, which, if I was skiing it, I would have graded as a red (quite difficult), but only in gradient. It was wide, smooth and a few hundred metres long, and even if you were to pick up too much speed, you had a five-and-a-half-mile run-out, albeit slightly crevassed. Skis would have been welcome: the snowshoes felt like they were on their grip limit as we marched upwards, pulling lighter sleds and packs than before. From there it was a flatter but much longer plod up the glacier to 9,500ft (2,900m) where we dug a big snow hole, buried our loads, and stuck some long bamboo poles on the top. It would be a few days before we came back to retrieve this gear. Everyone felt fine and seemed to be coping well as we retreated back down the Ski Hill with empty bags.

This season's even fiercer than usual conditions had been the talk of the town in Talkeetna. I had learned that in the month prior to my arrival – keeping in mind that May and June is the whole season – there had been only two possible summit days. With a season summit rate of 48 per cent, our chances of getting anywhere near the top were not to be taken for granted. Melis raised this over dinner as she read out the bad news. The high pressure was moving on and a snow storm was expected in the night. She added that this year there had rarely been a day with winds less than 20mph. Certainly for the next few days, summit winds were forecast at nearer 55mph – an impossible task. There was no point in worrying about the long-term forecast so we busied ourselves in camp storm-bounding, this time in anticipation of bad weather rather than just out of good routine.

Mike, as first impressions had suggested, turned out to be a fairly quiet but good-natured teammate while Johann bordered on the boisterous with his quick wit and loud South African drawl. Despite eating together and sometimes being part of the same roped team, I hadn't yet had the chance to get to know the rest of the team.

I woke at midnight to the sound of pouring rain. I sat up slowly. I and my tentmates were top to toe and I was the filling in the sandwich. I am so used to waking to the sound of rain on my tent that it didn't seem that odd until I completely came to and put it into context.

At 3.30 a.m., when Mike, Johann and I got up, it was still raining. Not even the guides were prepared for this. It doesn't often rain on one of the coldest mountains on earth so no one had rain gear. That is, no one except me. Accustomed to the wet Scottish hills, I was ready in my head-to-toe Gore-tex. It was all I knew in terms of outer wear. During packing I had felt like the odd one out and then had been left sweating feverishly inside my trousers during the long glacier march as everyone else sported top-of-the-range, ultra-breathable, super-flexible mountaineering trousers. My ignorance was now paying off as I ran about taking down tents as happy as a duck in a rainstorm, as everyone else got wet through.

As the rain eased a thick fog rolled in, denoting a sharp change in the temperature. It was about two and a half miles back up to where we had cached the gear the day before and during that undulating journey I saw almost nothing. It was like walking inside a ping-pong ball. There was zero distinction between the snow and the sky, which made navigation painfully slow. The bamboo wands we had laid down in perfect visibility the day before were now our only way of avoiding the countless crevasses on all sides. Barely being able to make out the climber just 10 metres ahead meant that the few narrow crevasses that needed stepping over appeared quickly out of the whiteout and gaped menacingly for a few seconds before disappearing again into the gloom.

The cache point was a pretty open spot, so by the time we got there Melis had decided to keep moving. The next protected area was over a mile away at an altitude of 11,000ft (3,400m). While shorter than the first leg, it took longer to climb up, around a long right-sloping section called Kahiltna Pass. In such visibility no one seemed to be able to keep the rope tension sufficient to stop the side slope pulling the sleds over to the left, and therefore we were constantly being tugged down the mountain.

The last hour was tough. The wind blew hard, stinging exposed bits of my face until they went numb. Some of the team were having issues with fogging goggles, which slowed us further, and despite being on a well-used path we were breaking trail through the fresh and drifting snow. Hour upon hour of walking straight up steep gradients was taking its toll on me. Using snowshoes meant that I could not do the natural thing of placing my feet sideways across the hill when it steepened. The weight on my back while pulling against a heavy sled also kept my balance into the hill, pivoting forward on my increasingly stressed Achilles tendon.

By half past three we had arrived at the next camp and I could immediately see why we had carried on. It was blowing a gale, and we all huddled together as we coiled the rope team into camp hand over hand. All around were high snow walls, built by other teams. Some spaces had a tent in them, but many didn't. We quickly chose three abandoned shelters as our own. Even then, in the howling winds and bitter cold it took two hours to put up tents and repair the snow walls before we could get inside and start to thaw out with the help of some watery soup. If we had stopped at the cache point, on the open glacier, it would have taken us far longer. We also had strength in numbers here, and benefited from the honeycomb effects of other snow walls dotted around the nearby area, cocooning fragile fabric and cowering climbers from severe wind-chill.

A few hours later the storm cleared and within minutes the view down the glacier and of the sky was crystal clear. The virgin layer of snow was the only evidence of the recent ferocity. The scene was utterly breathtaking. The mystery of Motorcycle Hill, which we had just climbed, was now unveiled: a wide glacier with a backdrop of broken seracs, ridges and pinnacles of ice that towered upwards to the left like organ pipes in a cathedral. The fresh snow blew off them in wisps that caught the sunlight. Off down to the right, the far side of the valley rose up to meet Kahiltna Dome, one of Denali's foothills but still an imposing peak from where I was standing.

The next day began with a short five-hour journey back to pick up our cached gear. It stayed clear and bright and I relished revisiting this section of the mountain and being able to see it. By midday we were back in camp at 11,000ft and now had the afternoon and following day to relax and acclimatize. It was a hive of activity, each group on a similar schedule but at a different stage of the ascent, so while we went about some daily chores I watched as some arrived and left, and others dug up or buried gear. Firstly, the snow walls needed to be reinforced after being eroded by the storm. The fresh snow was abundant and appealing but being light and powdery made poor bricks so we set up a bit of a mining operation, cutting older bricks from deeper down and passing them up to the designated wall builders. It was hot work, but I enjoyed the activity. I hadn't actually realized until now how much time on a climb you spend inactive.

Life in an ice camp takes getting used to. To my surprise, so far I was finding the simple housekeeping tasks far tougher than the physical or technical demands of the climb itself. I am used to being on expedition alone, pushing on constantly and being my own boss. Mountaineering in a group, especially in glacial conditions, works by different rules, and I found myself growing increasingly frustrated. The irony was that I was in one of the greatest natural expanses on earth yet felt cabin fever, being unable to move out of the small tented area. I had been mentally prepared for a tough daily routine and focus, but soon found myself to be the only one who hadn't brought a book to relax and unwind with. I simply hadn't realized that high-altitude mountaineering involved so much of doing nothing, just passing time to allow our bodies to acclimatize. I needed to start thinking differently to stay focused because I didn't feel like I was dealing well with the lack of control and regular action. The fact was, life was pretty uncomfortable, and my usual coping mechanism of 'keep moving, keep thinking, keep active' wasn't an option here.

At night the temperature dropped to below minus 20. By high camp, we knew, this could be below minus 30. And yet by day it got surprisingly warm, the sun radiating off the ubiquitous white. Everything that could freeze needed to be put inside my sleeping-bag at night, including a few water bottles and all electronics and toiletries. I had customized a skin-tight base layer top by sewing on a dozen small pockets to store batteries. This way my body warmth would stop them from draining.

It was now day six since flying into Kahiltna Glacier and our second full rest day. Acclimatization affects everyone differently, and sometimes can affect the same person differently at different times. I could understand the temptation of pushing on faster than your body can adjust. Going by my own frustrations, I could also see why it was often the younger, fitter but less experienced climbers who suffered the most. Not because they aren't as good at acclimatizing, but because they are physically stronger and maybe less patient, so they feel they can push on. After all, life in the freezer just isn't very comfortable, so why hang around? But climbing at this level is more of a waiting game than an athletic challenge.

There was again a lot of activity in camp during the day with groups coming and going while much of our time was spent preparing food, repairing snow walls and practising techniques for the upper sections of the mountain. Melis and Joey were obviously well known and there was a regular flow of visitors to the kitchen tent with news from up and down the mountain. Later on a team of four arrived looking very weary, and they gratefully accepted a bowl of soup. They had made the summit late the day before, making that only the third possible summit day in the last month. Their arrival brought an awed response from most of the amateur climbers in camp, each with their own hopes and fears. Seeing these sun- and wind-battered men returning from the very top gave everyone a glint of hope. Everyone knew the long odds of ever reaching the top; there was nothing to say that all this preparation would pay off.

Over the previous months I had often thought about the prospect of not summiting Denali and what it would then feel like to get on my bike for about half a year to reach a mountain that had an even lower success rate. I imagined it would be tougher to stay focussed and optimistic, but there is no way that the journey wouldn't continue. I always pictured myself summiting, but rationally I knew this was far from certain.

Each night I woke a few times to my tentmates kneeling beside me, peeing awkwardly into a Nalgene bottle that then needed to be cuddled all night to stop it turning into a block of yellow ice. Going outside was not an option once you were warm in your sleeping-bag. Thankfully I had a more reliable bladder.

My first morning at 11,000ft camp had been accompanied by a cracking headache. Most of the team had some degree of headache and a few had struggled to sleep above 9,000ft. During the night, as your breathing slows, it's common at altitude to wake up feeling anxious, gasping for air as your body struggles to adjust to the diminishing amount of oxygen. Arriving at this altitude had felt fine, and while active my body compensated well, but after about twelve hours the sustained effort of functioning at a lower oxygen level was very noticeable. We were all suffering from mild altitude sickness, and it was a constant reminder not to move on too fast. Acute Mountain Sickness can develop into cerebral oedema (swelling of the brain) and pulmonary oedema (fluid in the lungs) which can easily kill the fittest of climbers if they don't descend fast and seek urgent medical attention.

By day eight we planned to be at the main Basin Camp at 14,200ft (4,200m), less than two miles away but a tricky route. None of Denali is rated as very technical, but the relative risk is still high. Denali's long and extremely cold winter means that fresh snow on top doesn't semi-thaw then weld together, which makes for a constantly high avalanche risk and weaker snow bridges over often unseen crevasses.

The immediate task out of camp was a very steep climb up Motorcycle Hill, before a traverse around Windy Corner, one of the major potential stumbling blocks on a climb up Denali: when the weather closes in, teams of climbers can get trapped above or below it for long periods. Melis reminded us that her last team had failed to summit and been forced to spend eleven days at Basin Camp before the weather allowed them to descend. Before the corner we stopped the rope team for a rest and I sat on my rucksack, looking back over a staggering view below. Six out of Denali's seven glaciers are on its south flank, and the sea of ice flowed in all directions. Mount Foraker and Mount Hunter were still higher than us, but I already had the impression of being on a vast mountain among relative foothills.

Climbing again, the crunch of metal spikes rhythmically breaking into polystyrene snow was mesmerizing. The Northwest Buttress flattened out as it curved to the right but you could see the effects of the regular 100mph winds, with half a mile of blue ice shimmering in the sunshine. This bulletproof terrain was far less enjoyable and I gingerly transferred weight from one crampon to the other, trying to keep my balance as centred as possible. Not only was it hard to grip, but any fall would be far harder to catch. Normally you would fall on your ice axe, dragging the tip deep into the glacial slope until you slowed. Here, you would do little more than draw a shallow jagged line down the ice, like nails on a blackboard. It was always tempting to kick your toes in when you fell, but here, more than ever, that would simply cause you to flip head over heels. Better simply not to fall.

Windy Corner was the only reason we carried helmets on the climb, and as we crossed its narrow apex and started a long traverse, I could see why. The glacier was peppered with small rocks, some of them not so small, that had been frozen, then thawed and blown off the cliffs that towered to my left. It's very hard to look around, up or down for anything more than a glance while walking along a very narrow route. But it's essential to keep the same pace as the team, because if there was ever slack in the rope when someone fell through a glacier, they would fall much further and you would be pulled after them much faster, lessening your chances of being able to react. Standing on loose rope with crampons was also a sure way of breaking it. For this reason I was kept fairly tunnel-visioned, but I saw enough to appreciate that even a small rock falling from that height would kill you whether you had a helmet on or not.

As the climb toughened, the differences in the group began to reveal themselves. On the second climb around Windy Corner, this time moving all the way to Basin Camp as opposed to caching some gear, Joey, Hiroko, Johann and I arrived a full hour and a half ahead of the other team of Melis, Mike, Peggy and Denis. For Johann and me in particular, the fine balance between making the ground safely and staying warm meant progress was slightly on the slow, cold side. However, still aware of my relative inexperience, I certainly wasn't willing to make any suggestions. Privately, however, I could see the obvious: Denali is not for everyone. Even with the best winter camping skills, physical strength and techniques, it is a place that can easily defeat those unused to the mental stamina necessary for such harsh climates. One definite benefit of my solo endurance trips was an ability to deal with this slog privately, whereas others burdened the group with doubts and insecurities. I was concerned we were heading for a much tougher place with some people who weren't tough enough.

My personal concern was my damaged Achilles tendon, which I had kept Melis in the loop about in case it got worse. With more acclimatization days ahead I hoped it would relax, but having suffered from tendonitis before, I remained concerned.

Basin Camp was by far the biggest yet, acting as an advance base camp for the West Buttress route of Denali. It sits on a wide plateau and is a village of a hundred or more tents nestling behind high snow walls. It also hosts the main National Park Service Ranger station on the mountain and is the highest point helicopters normally fly for rescues. A few hundred metres to the south of my tent, behind the rangers' tents, was 'the edge of the world', a 4,700ft (1,430m) sheer drop to the north-east fork of the mountain. To the north and east the mountain reared up to a horizon a few thousand feet above us at its lowest point. This is where the real climbing would begin on a snow and ice face at about 50 degrees known only as 'The Headwall'. Once there, the route followed the horizon along a rocky, icy and exposed ridgeline for nearly a mile to High Camp at 17,000ft (5,180m).

I soon got to know Basin Camp very well. It was quite amazing to see so many colourful tents and different climbers from all over the world (I was one of about four hundred people dotted around the great mountain). Like any community it had well-trodden paths between dwellings, and some real estate was obviously better maintained and more valuable than others. Luckily no avalanches had made it as far as camp recently so some sections of 'town' were established, with double-block-deep snow walls. The community even had a few toilets. My favourite was out towards 'the edge of the world', a plastic seat over a very deep crevasse, kept in place by a piece of chipboard. A snow wall on three sides provided some privacy, but the whole camp could still see you on the throne as you looked out over Mount Foraker – the best toilet view in the world. It certainly beat the routine of using a bucket then throwing biodegradable bags of waste in crevasses. Glaciers move over time, crevasses open and shut, and this was the same glacier we were melting for drinking water and to cook food. It was all a bit too interrelated for my liking.

Denali, and I assume any of the world's high mountains, are funny places in that they attract, for the most part, wildly adventurous people who crave the challenges remote places offer. Then, when they get here, they find it's a short climbing season and everyone else with the same ambition is jostling for the same few safe camp spots. This creates a strange atmosphere about camp, especially among the amateurs who don't really know anyone else. I got the distinct sense that everyone was in the place of their dreams, and was trying to act as if everyone else wasn't crashing their party.

Now that the terrain was much steeper, we decided to leave the sledges behind, which made our rucksacks much heavier. For the first twenty-four hours at Basin everyone suffered from the altitude. The main test of acclimatization was a pulse oximeter, a small machine that pinched your finger and measured both your heart rate and blood oxygen saturation level. We all struggled and needed time to adjust. My headache came back strongly and I felt slightly nauseous. I was relieved when these passed.

After another day fetching the last of the cached gear up to Basin we were ready to attempt the Headwall for the first time. All along I had been calling home (and Radio 1) on my satellite phone to give updates, but at this point I struggled to find the words to describe either what I saw or how I felt about what lay ahead. It was making that final practice climb in Chamonix look like child's play.

Fortunately, many people had climbed the route recently and it was fairly clear where to start. The slope began gradually in soft snow but then steepened, and the final 2,500ft was a steep, icy face. The trudge up to this took hours. I was amazed how long it took to climb this gradient, in this deep snow, at this altitude. Looking up, I could see a fixed line of rope had been secured with deep ice screws up the face, giving us some running protection. It wouldn't help us climb much, but it would save our lives if we slipped and fell. A risk of icefall under the bergschrund (a crevasse at the head of a glacier) kept us moving as I clipped my ascender gear into the rope and started methodically inching my way upwards. A deep crevasse cut across the lower end of the Headwall, and it was a short vertical climb to step up and over it. I hurled my ice axe as high as it would go and pulled up for all I was worth. Looking up or down did me no favours, so I focused on the ropework and each foothold, kicking heavily into the ice. Moving was nerve-racking but fine. Having to stop and wait for slower teammates up here was not fine. Looking down made my calves start to shake uncontrollably, so much so that my toe grip would work loose; so I faced the ice, with four points of contact, waiting for the call to carry on.

On the saddle of the ridgeline, where we topped out, the view back down the Kahiltna Glacier was staggering and we all sat there in silence, eating and drinking, soaking up the scene. Digging a snow cache in this exposed spot was hard work, and it was nearly an hour before we were all ready to descend again. The main headwall was tricky but went well. There was a flurry of light-hearted banter as our tensions evaporated and we unclipped to start out on the long but less steep snowfield to Basin Camp.

Rockfall and avalanches are a big problem on Denali. Normally alerted by a deep rumbling, we had all seen a few huge avalanches at Ski Hill, and also at 11,000ft camp. The speed and force of such an explosion of snow has to be seen to be believed. We had also learned to be alert to the distinct sound of rocks skipping over rocks.

About an hour out of camp I heard just that. Up to my left, as I climbed down, the even snowfield we were on was broken by seams of rocks forming lots of couloirs (steep, narrow gullies) and outcrops coming down from 16 Ridge. 'Stop!' I shouted. I still couldn't see anything and wanted to check they weren't coming our way. Melis was behind me and hadn't heard anything, but wasn't surprised that I'd shouted for us to stop: we had done so times to sort out rope problems. Someone else had heard it, however, and the other team stopped.

I saw them. There were two of them. Within a few seconds everyone was looking and had spotted them. Small black dots bouncing downwards, about 1,500ft to our left. I said nothing, but immediately realized the black dots weren't rocks. Down past a long shoulder of rocks I saw the climbers tumble, arms and legs limp. Once on the lower snowfield they simply slid. A rope I couldn't see was obviously keeping them a measured distance apart. I stood rooted, unable to look away. They had fallen well over a thousand feet.

Assuming we were the only witnesses, Melis immediately used her radio to call the ranger station at Basin Camp and Joey and I took it in turns to call across the valley to the climbers to tell them help was on its way. There was nothing more we could do. We were a long way across a crevassed snowfield from where the climbers had ended up. However, within ten minutes we saw three skiers descending fast on a very steep glacier opposite. One was a good distance ahead. When that skier reached the two climbers there was a short pause and then a loud scream. We all hoped it had come from one of the climbers. It would at least mean one of them was alive.

I felt pretty numb as we moved off again. The team climbed down slowly but everyone kept looking off left towards the rescue as rangers climbed up from camp. Tears flowed freely inside my goggles for a while. I knew there was no way they could have survived that fall.

They hadn't.

3

That evening the mood in camp was subdued. While the others wanted to talk it through and sought the company of the kitchen tent, I spent a few hours on my own in my tent. Nothing had changed in terms of our climb. The weather was still good, everyone was climbing well, and we were on schedule. Yet things had changed for me. The mountain had shown me what I already knew was possible. Seeing men pay the ultimate price for taking on a dream shared by me was a stark reminder.

I hardly slept, and I could tell that Mike and Johann were restless as well. Whether it was the altitude or their thoughts keeping them awake I don't know, but it was a long, light night for us all. Sunset was at 11.30 p.m. and sunrise was at 12.30 a.m. so it never got even slightly dark. There was simply one hour when the sun wasn't visible.

The following day was another acclimatizing day, and I wished it wasn't. I struggled with thoughts of carrying on. The fallen climbers' empty tent was still pitched near ours, and from conversations with the guides I learned that they were both doctors from the US, and realized that we had shared camps in the last week. As one of the only witnesses to the fall, I was summoned to the rangers' tent where I described what I had seen, but no one got any closer to figuring out what had gone wrong. They had been on another route when the accident took place but it was unclear what exactly happened to cause their fall down near Messner Couloir. It had been a bad week, with two other accidents on the mountain just two days before. Both those climbers had survived their falls but one had needed a helicopter rescue with a crampon through his knee.

There was never any real option of turning back, but I saw the mountain differently now. Though I'd been alert before, I was now fairly obsessive about my ropework and climbing. I also noticed that I was becoming less tolerant of lethargy and self-pity in the group. Lack of commitment and focus was asking for accidents. Most of the team were self-controlled and diligent but there was a certain amount of unnecessary drama. We were each here out of our own choice so I struggled to be patient with such slacking. There had already been occasions when Johann and I took heavier loads to help the group, which I was very happy to do, as long as the whole group was giving their all.

The day of the climb back up the Headwall was clear and bright. It was now two days since the accident. Peggy's pulse oximeter reading had been too high to continue after one day and Melis was on antibiotics for a bug she was fighting. It was a much-needed rest for my Achilles, but it had been the slowest forty-eight hours and I was relieved to be moving again. It was to be a big day. We were going to High Camp and gaining nearly 3,000ft (900m) of elevation in one move.

Once at the cache point at the top of the Headwall we had 16 Ridge to negotiate. It was relatively stable and easy to navigate the rock-and-ice ridgeline so the chances of slipping were low. However, with a several-thousand-foot drop on both sides, the consequences if you did slip were very serious. It was a case of walking with cat-like balance not just for your own path but to react to any slips by the person in front or behind you on the rope. On a couple of occasions we passed descending teams. Some places could allow a few climbers side by side, but I felt distinctly uncomfortable when fast-descending climbers pushed past our slow ascent. This section is almost impassable in high winds and I could see how many accidents, especially while descending, had happened here.

Apart from that, it was the most breathtaking section of the climb yet. The rocks provided some interest after almost two weeks on ice and the views down were vast. My favourite was a 20-metre vertical rock feature called Washburn's Thumb (Dr Bradford Washburn and his team were the first to climb Denali's West Buttress route in 1951). A steep section of fixed line was required to negotiate this striking landmark, not to mention some tight manoeuvring to get our heavy rucksacks round while hugging the rock.

At the easterly edge of the ridge we walked out on to a small barren plateau. It was relatively calm but the furiously funnelled hard-packed snow suggested that this was often a windswept and inhospitable spot.

We were now breathing about half the oxygen we were used to at sea level. The effect was alarming. It took conscious effort to slow down everything to prevent yourself from being constantly breathless. As we erected the tents and built yet more snow walls I would keep forgetting, so after a minute's activity at a normal pace I would have to sit down quickly, slightly dizzy, with my heart pounding at 180 beats per minute. To start with it was quite funny, simulating the life of an incredibly unfit person, but after a few hours my limbs felt leaden and I was exhausted.

We all were. Life at this altitude is hard work, and as a general rule most summit bids are abandoned after a number of days here due to a loss of energy. Even at 14,200ft camp it had been difficult to eat much as the body slowly shut down what it considered to be non-essential functions to make better use of the limited oxygen supply. Here, even the sweetest of treats, which we had kept for high altitude, were hard to stomach. There was no pleasure to be had in eating.

By the time camp was storm-bound I had a fierce headache. At each altitude I had suffered a little, but this was a skull-cracking, behind-the-eye pain that was harder to bear. I wasn't alone: after just a few hours above 5,000 metres, all of the team was suffering.

It was another restless night. A small section of my face was the only part of my body that was out of the sleeping-bag and for the first time that got so cold that I slept in a balaclava. The temperature outside the tent had plummeted to minus 33 degrees. Under the shadow of Denali Pass, the ridgeline to the east, there was no direct sun to start warming things up properly until nine a.m.

I woke to find that I had left my small contact lens case outside the sleeping-bag by accident. The small tubs of saline solution were blocks of ice. After a few minutes in my mouth the tubs defrosted and I was amazed to find that the lenses seemed OK. A bit stingy and cold to the eye, but I could still see. My only spare pair had also been frozen so I was very relieved. I could barely find my way out of the tent without contact lenses, let alone negotiate an icy ridgeline.

The cold was also playing havoc with the film gear. I had now drained four out of my five battery packs for the camera. As soon as the battery was attached and the camera taken outside you could see the power draining away. The satellite phone was also experiencing cold-related battery issues and none of the solar panelling, which had worked so well at sea level, seemed to provide even a trickle charge. It meant that I needed to ration my filming and photography. I could imagine the horror of my production team if I told them I'd filmed the whole two-and-a-half-week journey but run out of battery for the summit piece to camera.

A rest day at this altitude was not very restful, but we continued to hold on to a great weather window. Mid afternoon we all walked to the ridgeline, just 50 metres from our tents, and looked down over Basin Camp nearly 3,000ft below us. Looking back along the

broken and undulating basin rim we could see another team of
climbers ascending 16 Ridge, silhouettes above a blanket of clouds.
In the middle of our section of ridge was a 10-metre rock jutting
out into the abyss, fondly referred to as the 'Diving Board'. A few
of us walked gingerly out as far as we dared for a brave-faced photo
before scurrying back. Melis then showed us all up by going right
to the edge and standing there on one leg. Without a rope in sight,
and with memories of the American doctors' fall near here still
fresh, my stomach did somersaults just watching.

Everyone was still feeling the altitude, and the lack of sleep and
food was taking its toll. I spent most of the day simply lying in my
sleeping-bag, listening to music. For no particular reason Jon
Mayer's 'Belief' and Creed's 'One' had become my songs of the
climb. This often happened on tough stages of an expedition: I
would find a few songs, often ones I wouldn't normally listen
to, and play them over and over, as a kind of therapy. It was a
comfort.

Summit day started clear with a dry, cold wind. In the grey shadow
of Denali Pass I got up at seven a.m. and pulled on three thinner
layers, then my primaloft jacket, then my huge down jacket. My
body was warm but the still air stung my face; I was glad of my
three-week beard. Our night-time breathing had formed frozen
condensation on the inside of the tent so when anyone moved we
were dusted with fine snowfall. Pulling on my climbing boots was a
sensitive task for cold fingers as the inner laces needed to be pulled
very tight before tying the outer plastic shell. I wandered over to the
yellow man-made crevasse for a moment before scurrying back into
the tent.

At 7.30 I called Scotland to confirm we were going for it. I was
given a list of radio programmes and journalists to call when I
reached the top. Laughing, I assured my production team that if we
reached the top I would not be hanging around for long chats to
news desks.

By nine we were roped up and ready to leave. Our tents remained pitched, but our packs weren't as light as I had hoped. We still had to carry enough emergency supplies to spend a night higher up, dug into a snow hole, if the weather closed in. Denali rarely has clear, stable weather for more than twelve hours and our summit attempt was expected to take at least that long.

Johann and I were put at the back of each rope team, with Melis and Joey leading. Mike and Peggy were the weakest so they were put second in each team. Mike had been suffering quietly all along. In his early sixties, he got more tired and took longer to recover than the rest of the team. He therefore never helped much with team jobs like building the kitchen tents and collecting snow to melt, but everyone excused this because he was great company and we could see he was giving his all.

Relations with Peggy were more strained. She had burst into tears at the base of the Headwall, stalling the team on a dangerous section, and at other times had dragged down the pace to as slow as she could walk. I felt sorry for her. I felt she was physically out of her depth and mentally unprepared. There had been a number of opportunities for her to go back down with other teams and I grew increasingly concerned and surprised when neither she nor the guides made that decision.

Hiroko on the other hand, despite her tiny frame, had proved herself a resilient mountain goat. Determined, hard-working and always smiling, she was the only one of us who had ever been to 8,000 metres before. Denis was also a determined climber. Peggy had taken a disliking to her tentmate, but the rest of us valued his even temper and good sense of humour. There had been a few examples of miscommunication, much to the frustration of the guides, but he was fully committed and predictable, and I liked him for that.

The steep traverse of Denali Pass took about two and a half hours. Kicking the uphill edge of my crampons into the icy path, I stepped foot over foot, sidestepping upwards. Even at this snail's pace and still in the mountain's shadow, I was soon very warm. Every so often we would stop for a minute or so while Mike got his breath back. Down the steep and increasingly long slope to my left was a series of deep cuts. A fall from this delicate perch would mean a fast slide followed by a long drop into any number of waiting crevasses. To limit this risk, a number of snow pickets had been placed on the high side of the traverse, giving running protection along the most exposed parts of the pass. I hooked into the first of these with some relief. Purist mountaineers might call this cheating, but the experience was full enough for me. I don't believe an expedition is worth losing a single digit for. At the top, I sheltered behind a cluster of large rocks and tried to eat something, anything. We had topped out into brilliant sunlight, but it did little to temper the sharp wind-chill which cut through my layers.

The next third of the climb was easier as we followed the ridge-line south. As we started out, the long, domed summit appeared far off to the front left. I hadn't seen it for nearly two weeks as we had been ascending the mountain's considerable flanks. Now, as we passed 18,000ft, I got a closer look, and was encouraged. From the Kahiltna Glacier the top had looked ragged and steep, but from here, with about 2,300 vertical feet to go, it looked smooth and gradual. Down and to the left, Harper Glacier sparkled amber and turquoise in the sun, while to our right the stunning black and grey 'Zebra' rocks marked the edge of the ridgeline. I was thankful for having been trusted at the back of the rope and for being the second team as it left me right at the back of the group. On the safer sections this allowed me to close the gap on Mike and get snatches of steady filming before the rope caught up with me. From any other position in the group it would have been impossible to film.

Simple and obvious to say, but it was a case of one foot in front of another. I was amazed at my breathlessness and how heavy my boots felt. One step, gasp, pause; another step, gasp, pause. My throat felt dry and raspy in the cold and very dry air and I breathed through my buff for a while to encourage moisture. Then I took it off, dropping it back around my neck, and the condensation quickly froze. At lower altitudes each team had tended to set its own pace but up here we were sticking together, which meant going at the speed of the slowest climber. I found it tough. We were all finding it tough. Nevertheless I felt well within my limits.

By 2.30 p.m. we were at 18,600ft and heading for Archdeacon's Tower, a rocky outcrop that we would skirt to the right of, before our final unbroken view of the summit. The wind had now dropped and I was surprisingly warm. My down jacket was stowed and I climbed in the thinner layers. I also packed my thick woolly hat and replaced it with a baseball cap to limit the sun's glare. I was closer to the sun than I had ever been, and it felt like it; a full nose guard and white zinc cream stopped my face from burning.

I plodded along, happily chatting to my camera as the summit came into sight: 'I think we are within half an hour from the top now.' I felt confident. Apart from being painfully slow, we were doing well. We stopped for five minutes every hour and the team was holding together, the weather was completely clear and our guides were confident. So was I. As we crested the thin windswept snow and ice beside Archdeacon's Tower I looked up to see a few dots standing on the summit. A team had already made it. It looked spectacular. I wished I was with them. Considering the odds with this season's conditions, we had been very lucky to get this break. A number of teams were making the most of it and were pushing for the summit today.

Between us and the final ascent was a wide flat plateau which we needed to descend slightly to reach. The aptly named 'Football Field' was easily big enough for an eleven-a-side game but you would have done well to make a break down the wing in this thin air.

As the slope started to turn up again, Melis stopped us for a final briefing. The weaker members of the team were given the option to leave their bags here as we made a return trip up the summit ridge,

but the most essential kit was still needed so a few of us ended up
with a bit more group gear. My bag was the lightest it had been on
the whole climb, yet it dug into my shoulders as if it had 40kg in it.
While lying in my sleeping-bag that morning having just woken up
my heart rate had been about three times what it normally is. Just
standing up sent it to high exertion levels, so labouring slowly under
weight and up steep slopes felt like a sprint.

We were now at 19,500ft and within a thousand feet of the
summit. It looked tantalizingly close. However, there was no
straight route towards it. First we needed to climb the oddly named
Pig Hill to a rocky outcrop called Kahiltna Horn, which meant a
sharp swing to the left to the start of Denali's summit ridge. The
final quarter of a mile was a long, exposed ridgeline to the South
Summit.

Mike was always quiet, but he had been particularly reserved all
day. I was two behind him on the rope and could see he was
dragging his crampons a bit and his head was constantly down. I
felt concerned, especially when I saw that Pig Hill was much steeper
and longer than it had looked from Football Field.

About halfway up the wind started to pick up and within minutes
wispy clouds had blanketed out the sun. I hoped they would blow
past, so we would get a view from the top. A little higher up large,
fluffy flakes of snow started drifting on to us. The main telltale sign
of a major storm on Denali is a lenticular cloud, like an atomic
mushroom cloud, on top of neighbouring Mount Foraker. One of
those would have prompted an immediate descent. However, this
pocket of weather hadn't been predictable, and the visibility was
quickly dropping.

It was hot work and I gasped and sweated, using my ice axe as an
uphill walking stick. Just as we reached the turn at Kahiltna's Horn,
Mike fell to the ground. He didn't slip further so we all paused for
him to recover. After a minute he was still down. Through the snow
my vision was blurred but I could see Joey backtracking to his side.
Another five minutes passed and my calves began to protest at

having to pause on such steep terrain. It was usually dangerous to pull the roped team together due to crevasse risk, but the chances were very low just here and Joey signalled for us to coil ourselves together; Melis did likewise.

Mike was not looking good. Pale and getting very cold, he was worse than we had all thought. The altitude had taken the last of his strength. His dogged determination had fooled us all, including himself, into believing he had a bit more in the tank. With only 300 metres to go to the summit, he could go no further.

I assumed our climb was over. The only option was to get Mike back down to a better supply of oxygen as soon as possible. I didn't have time to be disappointed, it was too real and dangerous a situation for that.

There was no way Mike could be carried down; it was too far and far too technical. Melis's only option was to give him a shot of drugs that would hopefully give him enough legs to retreat slowly to High Camp. At that moment another group appeared out of the veil of snow. It was the climbers I had seen on the summit an hour before in clear weather. We knew them well, having shared most of our camps with them, and they gave us a golden offer: they would descend slowly with Mike, letting us carry on; in his weakened state we should easily catch them up again and be able to take Mike with us. At this altitude, people can develop selfish streaks, as they fear for their own lives too much to care for others. Taking Mike would considerably slow down these climbers, but it was a risk they seemed happy to take, so we quickly made ready to carry on. I could see that Melis and Joey were both very concerned about the weather. Thankfully it wasn't all that windy, but the visibility had now dropped to less than 10 metres and we were about to move on to a narrow ridgeline.

The drops down left towards Football Field and right facing the South Buttress were considerable – not that we could see either of these features. What had started as a wide snowfield was now a narrow arête. To start with, where the terrain allowed we walked along the left side, on a shoulder of hardpack. It was steep, but not too steep to self-arrest on. Then, as the shoulder disappeared we were pushed on to the arête itself, first walking one side, then the other, before starting on a section right along the top, straddling the arête and digging the inside edge of each crampon into the mountain-top. The 'what if' theory had been explained carefully, and it made sense – in theory. If anyone tripped and fell, which is easily done when oxygen-deprived, wearing bulky high-altitude gear and following a rope, it was now too steep to catch yourself so it was up to your rope-mate to balance a fall. Quite literally, this could mean throwing yourself off the left side of the arête if your ropemate was to fall off the right. If two of you got pulled off the same side of the mountain, then there was every chance you were all going.

One step, slowly, in front of another step. I was consumed by the placement and crunch as each boot settled for grip, only glancing up whenever the rope tension changed – to find I could barely see anyone in front of me. That final push was the most focused half-hour of my life. All natural emotions of fear and doubt were overridden by thoughts of balance and control.

From the side, Denali's summit had looked like an easy plod, a wide dome like that of Mont Blanc. In fact it was an exposed ridge, and due to the weather I couldn't see how far it went. We could have been anywhere; the ground and sky were all white.

I was last on the summit. Melis was already shouting orders. We needed to descend as fast as possible. I didn't know what to think. We had made it. 20,320ft. North America's highest point. But there was none of the relief and sense of completion I had expected. My greatest motivation was to descend, to seek safety.

Gathering my thoughts, I did look around, searching for a view. I then gave Johann and Denis a hug; the others were too far away. After a minute I cracked a smile, following Johann's example. We had made it.

In camp I had heard climbers contending that the highest point was actually a cornice of snow now a good few metres higher than the round, metal summit marker. Safe inside the kitchen tent I had happily debated this fact, but now I didn't care how old and strong that cornice was, the summit for me was that summit marker. Any more was asking for trouble.

Once the rope was sorted, Melis shouted that there was no more time for photos. However, I was at the back of the rope team and it took a few minutes for everyone to spread out along the ridge so I managed a five-second piece to camera: 'This is the summit. It's too cold and blustery to say any more. I will explain later.' Later, I was glad I'd done it. It would have been a tricky situation to describe well afterwards, especially as by the time we got back to Football Field the storm had passed and I chatted again to camera, this time with the summit clearly behind me, framed in a blue sky. The mask of snow still clinging to the side of my beard and my face told another story, however.

It was already getting late by the time we caught up with Mike near Denali Pass. We had summited at 9.15 p.m. on Tuesday 16 June, nearly eleven hours after leaving High Camp. Some groups complete a round trip to High Camp in that time, but we weren't so lucky. We still had a few hours to go, but I called home with the news. I had reached North America's highest peak.

The descent of Denali Pass was slow and dangerous as we helped Mike down, no longer trusting his legs. A trip at this point, we knew, would be hard to recover. It was clearer than ever why the descent of Denali Pass is historically the most lethal section of summit day, as tired bodies and minds push towards the welcoming sight of tents far below.

By the time I crawled into my tent, we had been on the go for nearly sixteen hours. I had a cracking headache and didn't feel the least bit elated. Despite the altitude and lack of food all day, I immediately fell asleep.

Descending 16 Ridge with tired legs proved trickier than the ascent. Just above Washburn's Thumb Mike slipped again and fell badly, this time on a steep, icier section, and he started to slide. Hiroko was in front of me, behind Mike, and she immediately fell on her ice axe, digging it as deep as she could. On the ridgeline I was pulled over, but just had time to throw the handle of my axe deep into the far side of the ridge. It was a stunning display of strength by Hiroko: she held almost the full weight of Mike and his bag for a few long minutes before he was able to recover.

Then, as we descended the Headwall for the last time, it started to snow. They had had a lot of snow lower on the mountain, and once clear of the fixed lines it was great fun storming through knee-deep fresh powder. Any falls now would stop where you landed.

That night it kept on snowing, and we woke to another foot of powder. The orange and yellow circus of tents was now buried in a bumpy white world. By mid-June the weeks of summer sun had completely changed the look of the lower glaciers. What had been a vaguely meandering route was now a very indirect squiggle through a crevasse minefield. We set out from 14,200ft camp late in the afternoon on what would be an eleven-hour march through the night. As we turned Windy Corner, walking through knee-deep snow, the clouds cleared and the sun came out. It was the most per-fect wonderland. Yellows and golds streaked the sky and were reflected by the sparkling snow as the sun set.

We paused at 11,000ft camp to dig up our cache and find our well-buried sleds. We then loaded them up and walked on into the night. Our snowshoes and sleds were the only noises in this still world. One o'clock came and went, three o'clock, and I was still in my own world of memories. I had made it. I laughed aloud a couple of times as I thought the climb through.

The last drag lived up to its name, and by the time the mountain's shadows were lifting off the lower Kahiltna we were sweating our way up Heartbreak Hill. Planes were now taking off about a kilometre higher than they had been, which made arriving back at Base Camp a short-lived victory. Joey, Denis, Johann and I were the first team back by a long stretch and we laughed and joked until we collapsed on to our sleds, content to do nothing until a plane arrived for us. Elated and exhausted, we chatted and reflected on how Denali had shown us only some of her great character. For me, it had been enough.

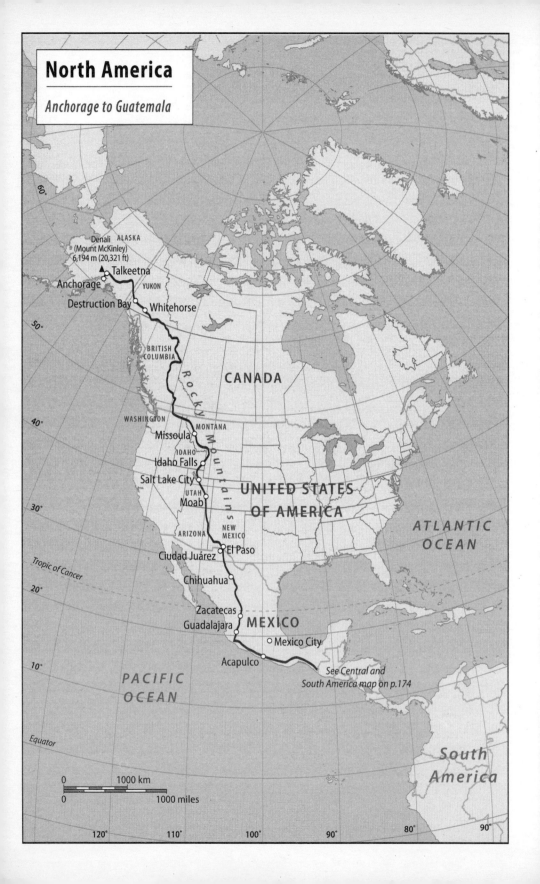

North America

Anchorage to Guatemala

Denali
(Mount McKinley)
6,194 m (20,321 ft)

ALASKA

Talkeetna

Anchorage

YUKON

Destruction Bay

Whitehorse

BRITISH
COLUMBIA

CANADA

WASHINGTON

MONTANA

Missoula

IDAHO

Idaho Falls

Salt Lake City

UTAH

Moab

UNITED STATES
OF AMERICA

ARIZONA

NEW
MEXICO

El Paso

Ciudad Juárez

Chihuahua

Zacatecas

MEXICO

Guadalajara

Mexico City

Acapulco

See Central and
South America map on p.174

ATLANTIC
OCEAN

Tropic of Cancer

PACIFIC
OCEAN

Equator

South
America

0   1000 km

0   1000 miles

60°

50°

40°

30°

20°

10°

120°   110°   100°   90°   80°   90°

4

A few hours later, at midday, we flew back into Talkeetna.

I could have shouted for joy as the plane bumped its way down the glacier and eventually lifted off, though it was slightly disconcerting being on a downward runway. When collecting snow to melt for drinking we had often dug through layers of ash dropped by a neighbouring volcano. When it lies fresh, climbers have to sweep the entire glacier as it causes too much friction for planes to take off. I was very relieved to have been excused this final feat of endurance. We were all utterly exhausted.

When flying in, there had been too much cloud cover and too many nerves to really appreciate the view. Now I stared out of the window in utter awe. In the midst of countless peaks, broken ridges and a labyrinth of ice, Denali stood centre stage. She looked massive, a giant among hundreds of impressive mountains. It was hard to imagine that just days earlier I'd been standing on top of what I was staring at.

As I jumped out of the small bush plane and started walking across the runway, the air bowled me over. I actually stopped. It was thick and sweet, with a base line of heavy woodland, and lighter flowery scents wafting through it. This was the most vivid I could remember smelling anything. I guess our senses are so bombarded every day that they are dulled and you aren't conscious of all that's going on. But for nearly three weeks we had been living in a frozen, sterile world where the only thing that really smelled was us.

Then there were the colours. At the risk of sounding like a complete tree hugger, it was truly amazing to see so much vibrant life. I was reminded that it is always easier to prepare yourself for changes when going away somewhere new than it is to prepare yourself for finding things unfamiliar when you come back home. Not that rural Alaska was like home in Scotland, but it had the similar raw ingredients.

It was 20 June, the day before summer solstice. We dumped some gear back at AMS then went our own ways, having agreed to meet for dinner. After a day and a night awake and active, everyone was now running on vapours. I checked into Swiss Lodge, a very basic hostel, and stripped off fully for the first time that month. Standing in the middle of a mess of stinking kit, it felt very odd being naked again. I looked very odd as well. Having lost 7kg (over a stone) in weight, my lower ribs stuck out even more than they usually did, and my unwashed skin looked clingy and dehydrated. I was too tired to wash properly; I just stood in the shower for a while, dozing on my feet. After doing most of the scrubbing with the towel, I fell on top of the bed and slept.

When I woke it was already late and I thought I had missed dinner, or at least I had missed the time I was meant to meet the others for dinner. As I scrambled into some clean clothes I realized I had the appetite of a bear coming out of hibernation, which was appropriate as I soon found that the main food on offer was either moose or caribou. I raced over to find the team were still feasting and well settled for the long haul. Everyone was in high spirits. All the guys apart from me had shaved and all the girls now had make-up on. The smell of deodorant and perfume was overpowering to my renewed senses. It was odd seeing the team I had come to know so intimately back in their everyday gear, relieved of the pressures of the climb.

Joey had fallen ill and hadn't made it out but everyone else looked and felt very much rejuvenated after an afternoon's sleep.

They were about as diverse a group of climbers as you could imagine, and we had shared a unique and privileged experience together. It was wonderful to sit with them, laughing and recounting stories, each of us flushed with the indoor heating and excess of food. In my heart I wished that Mike had been strong enough to make the summit. He'd certainly deserved to. He would now have to be content with having climbed forty-nine out of the fifty highest peaks in each US state. Without thanks Johann and I had carried enough of Peggy's gear to allow her to summit. However, that was all behind us now, and I sat back in the knowledge that we had all survived and that I had learned a great deal.

The conversation soon turned back to Peggy. She had spent a lot of time in Alaska and I was fascinated to hear about her work helping with the Iditarod 1,000-mile husky race. It sounded as wild and utterly beautiful as a race could be, man and beast pitched against nature as much as each other. Her plan was somehow to move to Alaska, a place she felt far more at home in than her native Switzerland. I could certainly see the attraction. However, the US immigration authority was playing tough hosts and her search for a way to stay was ongoing. This conversation amusingly and logically led on to her other great quest: finding a husband. The widely held opinion, it seemed, was that finding a man in rural Alaska was a tricky business. Melis commented that while the odds were good, the goods were mainly odd. Everyone, including Peggy, rolled around laughing. I learned how every winter the Talkeetna Bachelor Society hold a Wilderness Women Contest, which is open to all single women over the age of twenty-one and consists of timed events that are meant to highlight the skills an Alaskan bachelor would find desirable in a woman. These traits include (but are not limited to) hauling firewood, harnessing a sled team and shooting a moose. The conversation moved on, so it remained unclear what the lucky lady stood to win. I can only assume it's something odd.

*

Once again I arranged to meet the team for a meal the next day, and once again I slept through. After thirteen hours' slumber I woke groggy around midday, wallowing in the luxury of a bed and sheets. It wasn't freezing, and I didn't have to stagger outside to pee in the snow. But I had properly missed breakfast this time and had to start the day with a couple of caribou burgers instead.

A few hours later Heather, my big sister, drove up. I had long been looking forward to seeing her. The team was great, but they were familiar strangers. Seeing family after such an intense experience was wonderful.

Heather was to be with me for a week while I transferred off the mountain and got back into the swing of things on the bike. It had turned out that having her fly out to take all my climbing gear back home cost not too much more than sending it all back by courier. At the same time Heather also brought the twin benefits of being a qualified masseuse and a great hugger on behalf of all the family. And for her it was a birthday trip to Alaska.

Back at AMS, I caught up with everyone. After sorting through climbing kit and swapping photos, Melis asked if Heather and I wanted to join her at a solstice party. Alaskans have good reason to celebrate midsummer, as for much of the year it barely gets light. The plan was to go to a party in the woods before joining everyone else at the Fairview Inn, where there would be a live band. As she described the first of the two events, I wondered if we were being taken for the experience or for her protection.

I knew from flying over Talkeetna that there was much more to the community than initially met the eye. However, travelling by car to a house at the end of a long dirt road brought a new understanding to the term 'remote living'. It also wasn't much of a house, by most standards. We pulled up in what looked like a farmyard, except there was no farm around, only dense forest.

The huge barn was home to a man called Yukon. Yukon and Melis weren't obvious friends, but since she had successfully guided one of his sons up Denali, he was her biggest fan. Yukon was a big

man with a big mullet and beard. He wasn't big in an overfed, soft
way, but big in a rugged way that made him look more closely
related to bears than humans. He wrung my hand mercilessly and
beamed keenly at Heather.

I didn't say much for the next few hours, unsure what to talk
about. Yukon didn't notice, holding court with story upon story
about many things. By his own accounts, Yukon was an all-singing,
all-dancing Alaskan action man. The barn was filled with every
conceivable toy for land- or water-based adventure, which usually
meant catching or shooting something. Yukon thrust a big rifle,
which had been slung across the bars of a quad bike, into my hands
in order to describe how he had taken down a running bear with it.
It sounded like he had killed many bears, and one big grizzly stood
at the bottom of a flight of stairs. It was the biggest piece of taxidermy I had ever seen. Around its paw was draped a fine ornament.
I took a closer look. It was a thread with what looked like a tooth
on it. Yukon laughed. In response he showed me his collection of
bear-claw necklaces, all procured and then made by the man himself. His other favourite jewellery medium was bear penis bone. I
didn't know that any animal had anything which truly justified the
term 'boner', but Yukon explained that walruses, raccoons and
bears all have a phallic skeleton. He had a fine collection to prove
it, too.

He then led us into another room to show us an even more
surprising possession. On the wall was an old and faded photo of a
much younger man, unsmiling and staring out from under a bear's
skull. He looked like a chief out of a cowboys and Indians film,
albeit a white one – maybe called 'Sitting Bear'. It was an impressive pose, wonderfully passive-aggressive. It came as no surprise
to learn that this was a young Yukon with one of his first kills,
donned in its cured hide, head still attached. And there it was,
draped over the back of a seat. It now looked brittle and moth-
eaten but it was still intact, though obviously not an everyday
working garment. I am not a fan of fur or taxidermy, but there was

no point in climbing on to the moral high ground here, and whether I agreed with its existence or not, it was definitely interesting. Yukon lifted the bear cloak proudly and placed it over my shoulders. It was heavier and warmer than I had expected, coming down to just above my knees. The bear's nose jutted out from my brow so its head made a full hat. As an Ice Age man I'm sure I would have been delighted, but in 2009 it was about as far from en vogue as anything I had ever worn, which is saying something, and I was glad to take it off.

It turned out that Yukon lived up the stairs in a flat within the barn, but the solstice party was happening outside, and it was in full swing by the time our tour was over. There were at least three of his sons there, but also a number of other friends and girlfriends. It was unclear who was family as most of the men spoke the same, sported the same big anchor tattoo on their arm, and looked similarly big. They were an intimidating group in their thirties and forties. It became clear that all the men knew each other from time spent in the US Navy, which seemed to be their rite of passage to manhood. According to the stories, their role as proper Alaskan men now mainly consisted of drinking lots of beer and fighting. Yukon was definitely still head of the pack, but as Melis, Heather and I stood there quietly, it was fascinating to watch the younger 'dogs' practising their 'barks' and baring their 'fangs'. It was the first time since school days that I had seen guys actually flexing their muscles in a serious display of peacocking. The one exception was the youngest son, the one who had climbed Denali. He was thinner, smarter, quieter, and introduced himself and his girlfriend with a smile. It was clear that he now lived a very different life to his family, and he wore an expression of long-practised tolerance in the face of their showboating. In return they poked fun at him.

The focus of this odd evening moved back on to Yukon when he decided that it was time to get a haircut. No one was going to argue that his well-seasoned mullet shouldn't go, and one of the girlfriends stepped up to lop off huge tufts of hair to an accompaniment of cheers and shouts from the ring of spectators.

It was time to go.

The party at the Fairview was also in full swing by the time we got there. A local band, Matt Hopper and the Roman Candles, were excellent, and it was great to chat aimlessly with everyone, but after our warm-up gig it seemed rather tame. I learned that Yukon and his extended family were banned from the Fairview, though no one was prepared to turn them away when they arrived en masse a few hours later. Heather is usually more than capable of taking care of herself, so I was surprised to see her mouth 'help me' when Yukon grabbed her roughly for a dance. Fighting isn't in my repertoire, and diplomacy definitely wasn't in Yukon's, so I felt fairly helpless. I watched closely, and once she had prised herself away we agreed to keep a wide berth.

Despite Heather's jet lag and my continued exhaustion it was a night that was hard to end. The team gradually headed off as the party wore on into the small hours, and it was then that I realized this would be the last time I would ever see most of them. By closing time Heather and I were left with a motley crew of young guides, still toasting the climb. One of them suggested that there might be a bit of an after-party down on the banks of the Talkeetna River so we wandered off until the road ran out on to a dirt track through the woods. There were a few groups dotted around, drinking beer, playing music on the stony banks, but no one we knew so we passed some time skimming stones, enjoying the three a.m. daylight.

Todd, one of the guides, stopped to point out to Heather the direction of Denali. On the far bank there was a wall of trees that continued for many miles until the mountains started, but a thick layer of cloud had formed a deep blanket in the background so nothing was visible. We peered across for a good few seconds until Larry, another of the guides, pointed up, well above where Heather and I were looking. A dark shape peeked out from above the clouds. It was the very top of Denali. Even from this far away, she looked so much bigger than I'd imagined. It was a magical, unforgettable way to see 'the Great One' one last time.

The deep exhaustion took a few days to pass, and there was a lot to be organized in that time. Still, I was back in fully oxygenated air, which to my acclimatized body felt like wonderfully enriched fuel. I functioned in short bursts of great energy between prolonged periods of sleeping.

On my second day of recuperation and preparation I was in my room when I felt a sudden jolt. Everything shook as if a dumper truck had just driven by right outside. Back in the brick-built UK it would have had little effect, but the Lodge was mainly made of plasterboard so it continued to shake noticeably for a few seconds. It wasn't until later that I was told this was an earthquake, measuring 5.4 on the Richter scale; the epicentre was about 50 miles back down the road near the town of Willow. It was my first earthquake, and a relatively big one at that, but for all I knew it could have been stampeding moose.

In the outside world, it wouldn't stop raining. I would undoubtedly have to cycle through weeks of rain before this expedition was out, but it would have been masochistic of me to look forward to starting in the rain. Fortunately, the morning of 24 June was stunningly sunny. I retrieved my bike from the stable where it had spent the past three weeks under a plastic tarpaulin alongside a beautiful grey horse and got everything ready to start pedalling south. Physically I knew it would be an odd transition, calling on a totally different fitness, but it was the mental game I was more distracted by. On the mountain, the climb was my sole focus; for the rest of my team it was their entire expedition. To come back after that success, leave the team behind and focus on a half-year commute to another climb was a daunting task. Aconcagua, the highest peak outside Asia, which lay about 11,000 miles down the road, had an even lower average summit rate than Denali, so it wasn't exactly a light at the end of the tunnel to try to focus on.

The willow trees were in full bloom and their huge fluffy pollen filled the air like snow, collecting along the verges. It was well after lunchtime when I at last clicked into my pedals, cycled past the airstrip, turned left and headed out of town. Fortunately I'd planned to cycle only 50 miles (80km) that first day back to Willow, to stay with Jim and Kathy, a local couple I had met on the cycle up from Anchorage. There would be plenty of time for living wild, and I planned to take the offer of hospitality while it was possible.

I spent those first miles lost in thought about what lay ahead, through Alaska, Canada, the USA, Mexico, Central and then South America by Christmas. After the climb in Argentina there was the smaller but not insignificant task of the final few thousand miles in the saddle to Tierra del Fuego. I wanted to finish in Ushuaia, the most southerly city in the world. At that point I was at 62°N; by the time the journey was over I would be at about 54°S.

I had spent half a year alone on a bike before, but as I've explained, I wanted this to be a very different expedition. As far as the geography went it would certainly be more mountainous, and on the physical side I had the significant task of keeping myself in shape to climb as well as cycle. More fundamentally, however, I wanted to experience the whole journey differently. The world cycle had been an out-and-out record attempt, my secondary focus being to make a successful documentary series out of it. This time there was still a demand to stay on target but I wanted to make time to explore more of the countries I was travelling through, see more of what was around me, meet more people, and tell that story better. I would still be filming for a documentary, but I was now also carrying the technology to share the journey as it happened. The plan was for the BBC to research some stories and locations while I would find others on the road. I didn't yet know how much of a daily task that would be, but I did know how much heavier the bike felt for carrying three cameras, a satellite dish, a laptop, solar panels, a satellite phone and chargers, to mention just some of the gear. My own essential personal kit took up very little space and weight in the five stuffed pannier bags.

This first day back on the bike is best summarized by that evening's diary entry: 'Some sunshine, a hailstorm, some big trucks, lots of trees . . . hey, it's Alaska!'

Jim also had an impressive collection of taxidermy and furs in his house, including a corner display of a stuffed grizzly bear appearing out of a wall that was painted to look like a river salmon hunt. However, unlike Yukon, Jim was the perfect host and was visibly relieved to see that I'd come back safely off Denali. He had vast knowledge about historic Alaska and we chatted into the evening. A pioneer's pride in living in such a harsh climate was obvious, as it had been in many people I had spoken to. Jim concluded the evening meal by insisting that if I wanted to see the real Alaska I should get off the highway and take one of the old roads. Logic dictated that I take it easy, get used to a bike again before taking on anything over-ambitious. However, I also realized that I wouldn't ever be here again, and Jim was very insistent. The winning ticket was that to take Hatcher Pass was much shorter than following the main highway, saving two sides of a triangle. There was obviously a reason why the highway followed the long way round, but this wasn't dwelt on.

So, the following morning I left, after a hearty breakfast of moose sausage with blueberries – both from the garden, so to speak – and pedalled north again. Backtracking was a bad habit that I wanted to avoid, but it was only 4 miles to the turn-off. Jim had called a friend for news on the pass and seemed pleased to confirm that while it wasn't officially open until 4 July, it had been cleared of snow and recently graded and I should have no problem getting through on a bike. 'Graded' meant that it was untarred, and it hadn't even occurred to me that there would still be snow on the passes in late June. I was alarmed, but far too committed to back down.

In Willow I passed a shop with a huge ice-cream cone outside. On my pedal north to Talkeetna, the owner had got news of my story and taken it upon himself, along with his younger brother Bob, to spontaneously burst into prayer for me, clasping my shoulders, heads bowed. Regardless of my personal views, it was a kind gesture, but I didn't have the confidence to go back in and face a re-run. Instead I looked for the small turn-off Jim had described. Then I came across a large fluorescent yellow sign that said ROAD OVER HATCHER PASS CLOSED. In case you missed this, a tattered red flag hung from each corner.

The first 10 miles were easy cycling on an empty double-lane tarred road, winding slowly up the valley bottom, following a meandering river. Heather had been keen to see the route, but when the road ran out and it started to rain she decided not to get her small hire car stuck in the Alaskan interior so turned round, wished me well and headed for the highway.

The rain didn't come to much but was enough to keep it very cool. The road went from well compacted and fast to broken and jarring. It was a good but unexpected initiation for the new bike. I had thought about bringing my round-the-world bike, which was still in perfect working order, but had opted for a newer version of the Koga Signature, with a few improvements. One change was disc rather than standard rim brakes, which immediately came in useful as the bike soon became muddier than my world bike had ever been.

The road's main function was as access to a few remote gold mines. The valley had become very steep to my left and high up on the scree slopes I could see shaft entrances dotted about. Over a few hours I tackled a number of steep, loose climbs, all the time look-ing ahead, trying to figure out where the actual pass was, and wondering at what point I would start to descend. It was much further than I thought; my large-scale road map didn't do justice to the contours of this off-road section.

By early afternoon the road had stopped hugging the valley side and turned right. A white pick-up pulled up, a couple of big diesel drums rattling noisily in the back.

'Where you heading?' the driver yelled, smiling.

'Over Hatcher Pass, I hope,' I replied.

'Jeez, man, good luck,' he laughed, and drove off. Not a hint of encouragement.

As I passed the large entrance and compound of Lucky Shot Mine, I briefly entertained the thought of turning back. By this stage the day would be a write-off but it looked like more rain and I wasn't prepared for anything to go wrong and to have to spend a night on a high pass.

The road was now constantly steep, which was tough going with a fully laden bike on loose stones and dirt. I then reached a locked gate. It was easy enough to push the bike around this and I found myself on an almost virgin road. It had indeed been recently graded so it was perfectly level, but it hadn't been compacted so was soft and wet. With my set-up, with skinny road tyres, it was impossible to cycle on. Once the gates opened it would take only a dozen cars to create a smooth pavement, but as it was I was left with no option but to push.

As I climbed, remnants of deep snowdrifts lined the road, up to 6 feet deep. I could see where the snow blower had sliced through, creating vast banks of compacted snow that never melted. After about 4 miles of very slow uphill pushing I reached a gradient where I could cycle; a small strip down the roadside where the grader hadn't reached allowed some traction. The view down the valley was vast and beautifully empty. I passed a small lake near the summit which was a brilliant turquoise, and relished the final hour's efforts to the top. A tourist plaque sat at the side of a small car park. I didn't bother reading it, keen to keep going – it was now very cold – but it did remind me that this would be a very different experience once the pass was open, with other tourists around. The magical part was the solitude.

The road from the top hadn't been graded, so while it wasn't nearly as smooth it was rideable, at very slow speeds. There was nothing exhilarating about those miles of descent, but it was fun.

My forearms burned from the bumps and constant braking, but on such a heavy bike I couldn't risk going fast and breaking anything. This bike hadn't been built for such abuse.

Once I reached the main road again, past another closed gate, it was a fast and very cold descent for another 10 miles or so to the town of Palmer. I was glad to check into a motel and find Heather again. I had travelled a total of 52 miles. While unforgettable and brilliant, it left me shattered. In this fashion it would take a few years to reach Argentina, and undoubtedly a number of replacement bikes.

I was now heading east and slightly north for a while towards the Canadian border. In a couple of days I would be across the Alaskan Mountain Range and I'd have a week or so of mildly undulating roads before reaching the Rocky Mountains. At the start of any long cycle, days two to four or five are the toughest as your legs adjust, but this time the issue was compounded by my basic cycling condition having been shot by the climb. I felt out of shape for the bike, and I noticed my pedalling grew asymmetrical as each day wore on. I knew I'd be back to strength within a week or so, but for now I felt lethargic and uncomfortable.

It was about 700 miles to Whitehorse, the next big town, and apart from that it would remain very remote for the next 2,000 miles (3,200km). Within a few hundred miles I would join the infamous AlCan highway that would take me the length of the Yukon Territory. It was a part of the world I was fascinated, excited and slightly intimidated by. Bears, bears, and more bears. It was always the main topic of conversation once someone learned what I was doing.

The day after Hatcher Pass, I followed the Matanuska Valley over a spectacular road. I didn't care how hilly it was, still relishing being back on smooth tar and making fast miles. There wasn't much choice in terms of a camp spot. Wild-camping anywhere in the USA has to be among the trickiest in the world. I learned on the world cycle to be incredibly careful and to make sure not to be seen if jumping behind a wall or into the trees to sleep. Another deciding factor in taking refuge in the only campsite I found all day was my overactive imagination about the ubiquitous bears. There was no fence or obvious deterrent, but I took comfort from the knowledge that there were other humans within shouting distance. I had plenty of time to meet bears, mountain lions, wolves and the other characters of all the scare stories.

I woke with a start and, realizing what had woken me, wrote, 'It's midnight, bright as midday, and raining on my tent.' In the morning I woke again to pouring rain. I was doubly thankful for the campground so I could have a warm breakfast in the dry. In the last 20 miles the previous day I had passed vast Matanuska glaciers tumbling on the valley's right. The moraine shaped the tree line, but the ice had now shrunk a good way higher. Back on the bike I kept climbing, wearing all my cycling layers. Eureka Summit was only a few hours away but in the stingy cold rain this time passed slowly. Half an hour from the top the temperature had dropped to 2 degrees and the rain had turned to hail. I was glad of my helmet, not to save me in a fall but to buffer me from the icy deluge. The hail was carried in the wind so it fell on me in waves, hitting every few seconds, with moments of calm. I put my sunglasses back on; I saw even less but at least my eyes were protected. If it hadn't been so cold it would have been funny to get pelted with thousands of big icy bullets. But my clothes were wet through and my fingers and feet were pretty numb.

At the top, to my surprise and utter joy, was the Eureka Café, a small hut on the opposite side of the road. Without a thought I bombed across the road and stomped inside. Everyone else on this lonely highway was also sheltering from the dangerous conditions. Some bikers, truckers and RV drivers occupied the tables. Apart from a few odd looks no one paid any attention as I entered looking frozen and drowned. I was going to get even colder before I warmed up now I was off the bike, but this still seemed preferable to going another round with the charming Alaskan summer.

My second breakfast was a few burgers and coffees, which I could already see would be my main lifeline in North America. Before cycling around the world I had been a vegetarian. I was back in a part of the world where such a life choice would have been frowned on even more than wearing figure-hugging lycra.

The rain continued until I was off the mountains and into the tree line, then things warmed up as I dried out and sped up. Later on I caught up with Heather who had been on a road trip to see the glaciers. She had heard the severe weather warning on the radio, including hailstorms and lightning. I could easily confirm that.

The forest was dotted with lakes and beaver clearings. Passing one of these, I spotted an animal wading through the shallows, grazing on water plants. I stopped as fast as I could and back-tracked. About 40 metres away, knee-deep in the water, was a large female moose. It was years since I had seen a moose. They are odd-looking animals, like an overgrown deer with an oversized head. Their muzzles and ears look especially outsized – all the better for grazing while listening out for bears, I guessed. This fine lady gave me a moment of her time before striding quickly into the trees and disappearing in seconds.

Reaching the little community of Glendale was a great relief. Camping would have been heroic but I just wanted to get everything dry and warm so I opted for a room. The previous night's couscous over the campfire had been delightful, but it had nothing on tonight's 16-inch pizza.

Next day I set out refreshed. The road's undulations were now shallow enough for me to spin out a great average speed and I was starting to love the bike again. The scenery left a bit to be desired, but I needed to get used to that. These trees would be with me for a long time yet.

I stopped at a petrol station mid-morning to be given some unexpected news from a complete stranger. A young local working on his car stopped to tell me that Michael Jackson had died. 'I thought he was on tour,' I replied dumbly. If I had heard this in the wilds of Alaska then I guessed it was massive news around the world. I also heard that UK diplomats had been arrested in Tehran and that Honduras's president had been deported by the military to Costa Rica. The Iranian situation was very sad; I had nothing but fond memories of the country from cycling there. The developments in Honduras were a more immediate concern: in a few months I was due to be cycling through the country.

At a place called Gakona Junction I turned right on the road that would take me to the Canadian border. I had arranged to meet Heather here so was delighted to find a tiny coffee kiosk sat off the road. It was a remote spot to set up such an enterprise, but being on the main Canada–Alaska commute it probably saw a lot of seasonal trade. The only other customers were two bikers on McGregor- and Boorman-style BMWs. Alone, I doubt I would have warranted enough interest to cross the biker/cyclist divide, but as I was with Heather they were happy to converse. They were from Anchorage but had been biking in the Yukon, which sounded like an annual pilgrimage. They were big gruff chaps but friendly enough. The bigger of the two had introduced himself as 'Fighter'. It was too odd to have been his mother's idea, and I wondered at what point in his life it had seemed like the right idea.

Before leaving, Fighter gave Heather a business card, of sorts. It was black and bright green, and on the front the title read TEAM PTERODACTYL – COMBAT TOURING. On the back he scribbled 'Note for Dawson Dick, Take care of these two. From Fighter and Carmo.' It was a kind gesture, but neither Heather nor I had the heart to tell Fighter that neither of us was going to Dawson City so were unlikely to run into Dawson Dick. They struck me as characters straight out of a comic book and it was fun talking to them, but they didn't seem to engage very well with the fact that I was cycling to Argentina. As an idea, that obviously trumped their adventures, and they simply ignored it. I decided not to ask about their names or what Combat Touring involved, though Heather and I debated the options afterwards for some time.

The only other characters I encountered that afternoon were another moose and a bald eagle, the US national symbol and a stunning bird. As I passed St Elias National Park the clouds started blackening. The road steepened at the end of the day and I finished in another frantic hailstorm. I raced into Grizzly Bear RV park still being battered by the falling ice balls and was quickly hustled into a cabin inhabited by a family of Australians who just laughed kindly at my miserable state. Once the storm had passed I left reluctantly to cook more couscous and camp out.

As I lay in my tent that night I heard an eerie howling from the forest. It was impossible even to guess which direction it was coming from. I had never heard wolves before, but I guessed that's what the sound was.

The Glenn Highway, which would become the AlCan Highway at Tok before the border, is the main artery for road goods and summer holidaymakers to the north. I had been looking forward to meeting people who managed to live on its route, sustaining and being sustained by the travellers, and early the next day I met a lady called Mary Francis De Hart. At milepost 59.8 she ran a post office, RV park, food and art store. Now in her sixties and alone, Mary wanted to leave. Back in her youth, her husband had been a bear-hunting guide and writer, which had brought them a small ranch and an exciting life. Now that was impossible to sustain. I was only with her for an hour, enough time to stock up and have a look at her tapestries and sculptures. Hers was a lovely but sad story. The wilderness that had once attracted her now kept her trapped. There aren't many people who would commit to a life here, even as an important community link in a very long chain. She hinted that many other links had already been broken, and that the road was not what it once had been.

Cycling was proving a monotonous task, even more than usual.

The scenery is your greatest distraction when sitting in the saddle for most of the day, and although I had expected trees in the far north, I hadn't planned on this many. The forest seemed endless, and I soon realized that in fact I knew nothing about this part of the world. I had absolutely no idea why I was now in an ocean of fairly stunted pine trees.

That night was my last camp with Heather, and I was glad to find another official site. Campsites in North America need some introduction if you have never been to one. Most campsites cater predominantly for families and the army of retirees travelling in their motorhomes, known regionally as recreational vehicles, or more commonly just RVs. Like America's cars, these motorhomes tend to supersize their European cousins by considerable margins. To actually set up a tent in a campsite is always the minority option, and in many places there are no longer tent spaces. Fortunately, in the wilds of the north campsites weren't yet bold enough to exclude those odd pioneer spirits who were willing to live without a microwave and satellite TV.

It was a manic evening of packing and repacking, desperately trying to save weight on the bike. With all the film and communications equipment it was the heaviest bike I had ever ridden, and I was yet to experience the real mountains. The only diversion came after dinner when the whole campground got mustered for the weekly pancake-throwing competition. My pitcher's arm has never been great, and it certainly didn't adapt well to throwing small rubbery discs into a tin bucket, but it did provide a wonderful insight into the competitive nature of even the least sporting of tourists. The cheering and applause grew as everyone queued up for the chance to win a free breakfast at the camp diner.

Heather had been great company and had made the transition off the mountain much easier to face in terms of logistics and moral support. However, in truth I was keen to be alone now, so I could really focus on the cycle. The scale of what lay ahead was daunting me and I needed to zone out to find my rhythm.

The following day Heather road-tripped till lunchtime, and her parting present was to give me a haircut, with a very small pair of scissors, on the roadside in the middle of nowhere. I knew it would probably be my last trim for the next six or seven months.

Though I had quietly been looking forward to going solo, that afternoon I felt uneasy, very alone in my own company. I already knew there was little in this part of the world to entertain my senses, but it had felt different when I knew I would be meeting Heather in the evenings for a meal cooked around camp together.

Slightly alarmingly, my first night on my own was at Dead Man's Lake campground. Thankfully it seemed to be a misnomer: apart from being eaten alive by mosquitoes and pestered by over-tame squirrels, it was a stunning spot. It was also free, which excused the fact that there was no water. However, it was obviously too wild for more modern 'campers' and was mainly empty. A young and very energetic park guide came by to give a talk to anyone who was interested and a group of about five of us learned more than we needed to know about what looked like not very much.

She explained that the never-ending forests were mainly black and white spruce which could be found at similar latitudes in a band that circled the globe. So I could easily have been in Russia, Sweden or, as I would soon find, Canada. It all looked the same. The main player in this weird world was the permafrost, a constant layer of frozen ground that could start at some depth and at other times was right up to the surface. Like all ice, it changes with the seasons, so this freeze/thaw action causes havoc with anything trying to grow or to be built on it. It explained the stunted and sometimes weirdly angled trees, as well as the cracks and creases that plagued the roads.

Billions of trees combined with my northern latitude were also playing havoc with communications. The plan was to have a regular Twitter feed, upload photos and blogs, have a once-a-week call with Radio 1, plus sporadic Skype calls with BBC Breakfast News. However, the geostationary satellites are all on the equator, and the already weakened signal was almost impossible to find through dense branches. Save from sitting in the middle of the road, it was an ongoing challenge to find anywhere I could broadcast from, and I had absolutely no idea how long I would be trapped in this evergreen tunnel.

5

Dead Man's Lake was just 30 miles (48km) shy of the Canadian border, and I pedalled into the Yukon on 1 July. Unlike the world cycle, when I was travelling as a tourist, my current task required work visas, therefore I needed carnets for all the equipment I carried. This bureaucracy was meant to ensure that I took into each country and left each country with the same kit. Everything I had was detailed down to its serial number. However, as a solo touring cyclist, not a touring band or large film crew, neither the customs and excise people nor I had any idea what to do, so it took a while.

The US and Canadian checkpoints are about 20 miles apart, and I had passed the US customs house, passport still in hand, before I remembered about the carnets and had to cycle back. Fortunately, they saw it as as much of a faff as I did and spared me unpacking everything to actually check what they were signing for. The Canadians were equally dismissive, even going so far as to tell me that I didn't need the carnets. I tended to agree, but knew that it took just one jobsworth to make it his pleasure to stop the journey or charge me extortionately if each little memory card and individual power cable wasn't accounted for.

A short distance past the border flags I cycled into the village of Beaver Creek which had many more of the red maple flags flying. A proud border town, I concluded as I looked for a place to stop for supplies. This was by far the biggest community for a long way in any direction. It even had a tourist information office, and inside was a very friendly lady and a huge half-eaten cake. 'Free cake,' she beamed. I have never had a better welcome to any country, and I tucked in happily. The lady went on to explain that it was in fact Canada Day and that I had just missed the 'Big Parade'. In a one-street town with about a hundred residents, I realized that she meant Relatively Big. Still, I was disappointed to have missed it.

Before leaving town I was hailed to stop by a lady in a bashed-up red pick-up. She was very enthusiastic and very American – I am not being nationally insensitive to Canadians, she was actually American. It seemed that she simply wanted to know what I was doing, and she laughed loudly with excitement when I explained. She insisted that I must come back and stay at her archaeological dig and meet her friends. It was tempting, but it was 6 miles back and I was keen to set a good pace.

There weren't many camping places shown on the map, and the tourist office thought the only site in range, at White River, was closed. It was too early to stop so I carried on, hoping they were wrong. It was immediately clear that the Canadians were having a tougher time maintaining their permafrost road than the Americans, and by the day's end I had already cycled long stretches of gravel.

White River camp was indeed closed, but the large open space remained so I approached the only cabin to ask if I could stay. Before I could reach the door a lady appeared. She seemed slightly edgy but agreed that I could camp. I didn't have time to question her Irish accent before she disappeared just as quickly. It was a stunning spot and I basked in the space, freed from my prison of trees. A few hours later I walked over to ask about charging some batteries, but when I got to the door the same lady rushed around the building as if to stop me knocking.

A while later she walked over to my tent. She was probably in her late thirties, naturally pretty but with a reluctant smile. We sat at a picnic table and chatted for over an hour. It wasn't the fast and bright conversation of many meetings, and her speech was punctuated with long pauses. I felt she wanted to talk to someone and that I was a window to the outside world for her. She mentioned that she had left her stockbroker husband in Ireland over a year ago to move to the Yukon and live out her dream in the wilds. Her young son was also here and she had grand plans to install solar panels, rebuild the place and reopen. However, she admitted it was going to be tough. 'These days everyone drives RVs and huge trucks. Their diesel tanks can take them from Whitehorse straight through to Alaska, where they race for the fishing. All the supply stops on the AlCan are disappearing now.' She was admitting to me that her plan wasn't a sensible business venture. It was an investment of the heart, and I could see her quiet determination. It still took a pioneer's spirit to settle here.

Eventually she explained that she was off to find mushrooms, and a few minutes later I watched as two quad bikes raced down the grassy runway (the field also acted as the only airstrip in the area).

The next day looked like about 80 miles until an opportunity for more supplies, so I was surprised and delighted to stumble across a dilapidated garage just a few miles out of White River. The two pumps were relics of yesteryear and it was unclear if the building was open. A lopsided sign by the entrance read HERE LIVES AN OLD BUZZARD AND A CUTE CHICK. I cautiously pushed open the heavy wooden door and paused as my eyes adjusted to the dark room. It was an absolute jumble, set up partly as a front room with a large round table and kitchen off to the back, and partly as a shop. But it was unlike any garage shop I had ever seen, more like a very old bric-a-brac sale. Odd ornaments, motoring parts and packaged foods were piled on tables around the room's edge, looking unsorted and certainly not dusted for months. It gave the impression of a shop where nothing was ever sold.

I no longer had any desire to buy anything, but an old man and woman were now staring at me, so I asked if they had any coffee. The lady was quite large and wore a dress which looked like a hospital gown. She told me to sit. They asked where I was cycling to, and I told them. They asked where I had cycled before and I mentioned a few countries I had pedalled across. This conversation ended quickly.

Then the most peculiar thing happened. The old man was standing, but he was very bent over and had a limp. Without warning or any obvious reason he started arguing with his wife. 'You old bat, I will run away,' he called out as he went about pouring my cup of coffee.

'You wouldn't dare, old man,' she replied, laughing until she coughed. 'Forty years here and forty years too long.'

I didn't know where to look, embarrassed at having walked in on a domestic. Then again, they were both laughing. I asked for a pastry whirl that was wrapped in clingfilm, as much to distract from their conversation as out of hunger. But it did nothing to divert their argument, and the comments flew back and forth as each recited how terrible the other one was.

'You see, in Iran women listen to their men,' he said at one point, referring to my comment about cycling there.

I sat in silence, sipping my coffee, which was pretty good, thinking I was in the middle of some kind of strange act that had obviously been played out many times before, to their amusement and to the horror of passers-by.

'So you must be the cute chick?' I asked, trying to change the tone again.

The old man laughed, but this one was more like a pantomime laugh than his own. Without warning he picked up a kitchen knife, walked up behind her and held it near her throat, saying, 'I will do it, I will do it . . .' She howled with laughter, which made her hack and cough alarmingly. He then broke into a song about running away, which made her cackle some more.

Thankfully a young tourist walked in. The look on his face was washed of emotion as he weighed up the scene. 'Do the pumps work?' he managed to ask.

'Yes sir, they do,' the old man responded promptly. But as soon as the door shut he started up. 'Do the pumps work? What's wrong with people these days?' He spat the word 'wrong' as if to suggest the world had gone mad.

The old lady addressed me directly. 'Where did you stay last night?'

When I told them about the closed campsite, they got very excited.

'You were lucky not to get shot,' the old man barked, still laughing. 'Bob is crazy.'

Pot, kettle, black, I thought, but stayed quiet.

The old man told me that they had reported Bob before for chasing cyclists with a baseball bat and pushing them in front of his car. One had turned up at the garage in floods of tears, scared witless.

'I didn't meet him,' I said, mentioning that I had met a friendly Irish lady.

This provoked some more chat between them. 'That is interesting. Amanda, his millionaire find . . .'

There were undoubtedly some grains of truth in their neighbourly gossip, but it was all pretty uncomfortable and I wanted to leave. The pastry was stale and inedible so I slipped it in my shorts pocket as subtly as I could and offered to pay.

It was a remarkable encounter, and I spent much of the day thinking back to that conversation with the buzzard and his chick, as well as about Amanda and her subtle efforts to keep me away from Bob, whom I had only seen from afar on his quad.

It was a day of tough cycling, with long stretches of gravel. At the edges the path was normally clear of deep, loose gravel, but I was nervous about passing trucks. The odd projectile of gravel spray really hurt.

On one particularly long stretch, the road narrowed to one lane. A stocky but attractive blonde lady was in charge of a start/stop sign but as there wasn't much traffic at all she was mainly playing solitaire on her laptop at the door of her pick-up. She insisted that I had to be taken through by pick-up and it would be about twenty minutes before that could happen, so I put the bike on its stand and went over to chat. Through her asking what I was up to, I ended up asking her where she had travelled. She replied that she had spent twenty years of her life working in a bar and being a mum so hadn't travelled much. Then, almost as an afterthought, she said that all of her travel outside Canada had happened as a result of competing in the World Arm Wrestling Championships.

'Amazing,' I said. I was genuinely impressed, so much so that I couldn't think what to ask next.

She went on to explain that she had competed in Russia, Europe and the USA.

'Amazing,' I repeated. 'How much training did that take?'

'Oh, I never weight-trained, except throwing the kids around.' She beamed at me. 'I came fourth in the worlds once, but the Russians and Eastern Europeans were always stronger.' She went on to say that she was too old for all that now and loved working outside on the roads.

I could have stopped there and chatted all afternoon, but an escort vehicle arrived in a cloud of dust and we threw the bike in the back. It seemed that everyone had a story worth telling in the Yukon.

By evening I had reached the small community of Destruction Bay – another wonderfully welcoming name. On the banks of Lake Kluane, the Yukon's largest lake, Destruction Bay is surrounded by reserve land for the First Nation People. I thought the hamlet itself would be First Nation, or what people used to call 'Indians': I had researched that the Southern Tutehone people have called the Shakwak Valley home for centuries. So I was surprised to pull up at the first building in the town to find a slightly drunk and haggard-looking white man called Loren. He had on a straw stetson and wore a Budweiser T-shirt under an open lumberjack's shirt, which went well with his scraggy grey beard. I then met an

Italian-Canadian called Lauren with a wide moustache and goatee, and a younger and much taller guy called Tim. The building was a bar, and behind it a large car park acted as the local RV site. This definitely wasn't a campground, but it was obvious that I was welcome to stay so I set up the tent on a tiny patch of grass at the back of a shed. I was pretty tired and pretty hungry.

To make up for having only thirty-eight year-round residents, it seemed that Destruction Bay welcomed all travellers as old friends. I try not to drink when on expedition, but a cold bottle of beer was thrust into my hand as I walked back over to find some food and saying no didn't seem the right thing to do. We were soon sitting around a large table inside the otherwise empty bar, telling stories.

'How long have you been here?' I asked Lauren, who sat at the end of the table, in denim shirt with a 'Molson Beer' baseball cap pulled low.

'Sixteen years,' he said slowly.

In response to my silence, he went on: 'I know . . . why? I don't know. It was just a bad decision I guess.' He laughed. 'Between the bank and the weather and the conditions and I can't think of anywhere else to go so I will stay right here, what the hell! I'm here now. I might as well retire here.'

'It's a beautiful spot,' I commented in agreement.

'Yeah, so that is what I do, fix and paint, sell a burger, buy a nail, sell a burger, buy a nail.' There was a long pause. 'People don't live in the north unless they like their own company,' he concluded.

Later, he gave me a poem he had written.

Secret of the Yukon by Lauren Maluorno

I came up to the Yukon not knowin' where I was goin'.
I needed a change, I had to rearrange.
So I said my goodbyes and had a few cries.
They called me crazy but they couldn't call me lazy, besides
I couldn't think of anything else to do.

I crossed the Yukon border, not much money, had no honey.

Didn't have a clue what I was going to do, well,

I had a friend, a room he'd lend,

but I didn't know that it would be 40 below,

he sort of forgot to mention that bit on the phone.

The Yukon sure is dark, mostly night, not much light.

I began to say of my friends far away that maybe they were right.

That gave me a fright, but not as much as it might

cause, you see, we still had three months to go.

Yikes, I am in the Yukon.

A few beers turned into a few rye and gingers, the national drink according to Lauren. Tim had once tried to make it as a musician, but now drove heavy machinery. At one point he picked up a guitar from a corner; along with Lauren's more amateur talents they made up quite a duo. Lauren tapped his beer loudly and nodded his head knowingly to each line, soaking up the impromptu entertainment. It was inspired, and I sat back just marvelling at the luck of finding such welcoming, wonderful characters. I had cycled in at about seven o'clock. By eleven, still sitting there in my lycras, I'd decided to stay a day longer. Hangover or not, I wanted to spend more time here.

The night went on till the early hours, singing, storytelling and laughing more than I had in months. I eventually crawled into my tiny tent, exhausted, but with the smug feeling that I wasn't cycling in the morning. I reassured myself that I would make up the miles.

I spent most of my day off with Lauren, who lived in a small house in the woods. He lived alone, grew most of his own food, and a lot of what he couldn't grow he found in the forests. In the morning I followed him on his battered old bicycle, whose tyres were so flat the rims clunked along the road, out of town for a few miles before continuing on foot so he could show me all the berries and fungi that were edible. It was fascinating, but I did feel slightly nervous being deep in the forest. Lauren spoke about bear encounters like I speak about going camping, as something one did quite often.

We got back to Destruction Bay after lunchtime, in time to get back on the beers. Sitting outside, he rambled on about life here. 'In the wintertime, for over two months we have no sunshine here, we are in the shadow of this mountain. But we look across the lake and we see the sun shining, on the other shore. So occasionally, even if it is fifty or below, I'll put on two pairs of coveralls and get my snow machine warmed up and putt-putt myself out there until I can actually turn around and look up into the sky and face the sun. And I spend ten minutes there shivering and then I come back.'

That night, near my tent I spotted my first coyote gliding across the road, before disappearing. For me, he symbolized this wild place.

In a car you would pass a place like this in a matter of seconds and never experience the spirit of one of the Yukon's most remote communities. The following morning it was hard to leave. Only was there to see me off. By his own account he was 'the Yukon's finest citizen', and by my account a wild but true gentleman.

Despite my overactive imagination, I was amazed how little wildlife I had actually seen; all I was seeing were trees and the occasional lake. With millions of acres of wilderness to call home, I concluded that while there were more bears than humans out here, there was also more space than I could imagine.

Then I nearly cycled straight into a bear. I was zoned out, on a long straight, when I became vaguely aware of a dark object at the side of the road ahead. It didn't alarm me as it just looked like a big rock in the long grass. As I cruised level, the grass revealed a black bear quietly grazing. I was too close to do anything but pedal on, but my stomach jumped and my heart raced and I had to suppress a shout of fright. It had been within a few metres of me. I looked back seconds later to see it had raised its head and was lazily staring at me.

No more daydreaming, I told myself.

It took two days of tree-lined cycling from Destruction Bay to reach the Yukon's capital, Whitehorse. It's a small town, similar in size to a small British market town like Cirencester. However, it's home to five out of every six people who live in the Yukon. That means that the five thousand people living outside Whitehorse share a space twice the size of Great Britain.

It had been a tough 100-mile day into Whitehorse and I was tired. A few miles from town, a car with a canoe on its roof had passed me. I'd noticed it going back a few minutes later, before turning again, pulling slowly past and stopping up ahead.

'Are you Mark?' a lady called out, walking across the road towards me.

Ange and her boyfriend Chris were from Edinburgh and were visiting friends. I had never met them before but she had recognized me. Before long I had pedalled into town and was camped in their friends' back garden, enjoying a generous dinner.

My GPS tracker wasn't working well so a smaller and lighter SPOT tracker was being sent out, along with a new VIO camera to film handlebar and helmet-view shots. They were meant to be waiting at the I Cycle Sport shop in Whitehorse, but were delayed. In the morning I got news that the package was arriving at the airport by two p.m. I Cycle Sport was a great find whose brilliant business model was to combine the best bike store for a thousand kilometres with a fine coffee store. The place smelled delicious, huge bags of quality coffee beans lying open everywhere.

Whitehorse was my first planned day off and in theory there was ample time to be interviewed by CBC radio and TV (the Canadian equivalent of the BBC), meet some locals and do some filming, but it was well into the following day by the time I was ready to leave town. My plan was still to make at least 80 miles to stay on target but it would mean riding into the night. So, while I sat outside the bike shop trying to make all the new kit fit on the bike, I drank a few big mugs of Colombian roast.

The effect was alarming. By the time I wheeled out I was completely buzzed. The coffee was more potent than I had anticipated and I was now set to ride happily into the night to make the miles – a good thing as it was nearly seven p.m. On the far side of town I passed a huge old paddle steamer on the river, then started a long slow drag to take me back up on to the AlCan.

About 10 miles on there was a sudden loud crack. It was a new noise, not the sound of a breaking spoke. Twisting my left heel outwards in order to release the cleats, I found that the whole pedal came away with my foot. Stopping quickly, I put my foot on the ground with the entire pedal still attached to the sole.

I'd used Shimano pedals for tens of thousands of miles and never broken them or even heard of them breaking. Somehow I had sheared the whole unit off the shaft and there was no way they would ever join again. It was a greasy mess. A few phone calls soon confirmed that the next bike shop was 1,130km ahead of me – seven straight 100-mile days. I had no option but to turn back to Whitehorse. I tried cycling a few metres just to make sure I had to. The pedal would stay on, but only if I constantly pulled my leg sideways as well as up and down. The effect was unbalanced and uncomfortable, and a week like that was out of the question.

Annoyed to be losing more time, and still hyped on caffeine, I retreated slowly back into Whitehorse. It was well into the night before I fell into a fitful sleep. The next morning, back at the bike shop, none of the mechanics had ever seen this failure either, so I took some small pride in my destructive talent for breaking new cycling ground.

The target of reaching Argentina by late December was always at the back of my mind. The season for climbing Aconcagua was not moveable. However, I was finding my daily targets hard to tally with the big picture. Because I wanted to meet people and get a good sense of the places I passed through, it was harder than any previous expedition to make the big miles as well. I was also amazed to find how time-consuming the storytelling was becoming.

There was no story to tell if the expedition didn't keep moving on, but every moment spent filming, writing, taking photos, online or broadcasting was time not spent turning the wheels, moving south. I was also finding that this level of communication both with people I met and people around the world who were following the expedition meant that I no longer had sufficient time to get lost in my own world. I no longer felt alone, blinkered by a singular focus to go fast; instead I felt like I was juggling, trying to fit more and more into each day.

Just a few weeks into the cycle, still with nearly half a year to go, I was keen to speed up and put some spare miles in the bank in case of further delays. Being in the far north I therefore decided to make the most of the long daylight hours and start riding late into the evening. Over the next couple of days I also started climbing, albeit gradually, crossing the Continental Divide for the first time. This mountain ridge runs from northern Alaska the entire length of the Americas to Tierra del Fuego and separates the watersheds to the west and east. My route would cross it at several points as I followed the mountains.

It was monotonous riding, but I loved the sheer scale of the wilderness. This lonely pilgrimage was broken one morning when a tourist called Roy excitedly told his wife to keep driving their RV after he'd grabbed his bike off the back. He joined me for about 50km. I could soon see that he was slightly frustrated by my slower speed, so I suggested we swap bikes for a bit. His race-spec mountain bike was a joy to pedal, while Roy wrestled awkwardly with my fully laden expedition bike. We soon swapped back.

Surprisingly, there was little opportunity to wild-camp, simply due to a lack of any clearings in the forests, so I had to reach designated camp spots, often big distances apart. I found a number of these snuggled into a lakeside, which was stunning but did come with plenty of mosquitoes. On the bike, the mozzies couldn't keep up with me, but cooking food over the camp stove in the evening was a constant fight, even wearing a head-net and repellent. They were often out in force during the day, too. While repairing my first puncture when I ran over a large nail, I collected an impressive spattering of red welts up my legs and arms.

Just before leaving the Yukon I reached the town of Watson Lake. With 1,700 residents it's the third largest community in the province. However, more oddly, it's also home to over sixty thousand road signs. Despite being forewarned by the BBC researchers I was still surprised by the sight as I pulled up at 'Signpost Forest'. A local lady proudly explained how in 1942 a young US Army GI called Carl Lindsay had been homesick so he made a sign pointing to his hometown with its name and the distance. In the nearly sixty years since similar signs had been added and they now covered a couple of square miles. I was amazed at the range, from hand-made messages to a six-by-ten-foot German autobahn sign. Borrowing some paint and a small plank I added mine to the forest. It was about 3,900 miles back home to Scotland and over 12,000 miles still to go until Ushuaia.

While the Yukon is one of the most monotonous and isolated places I have ever travelled through, it also ranks as one of the most hospitable. Almost everyone I had met was an adventurous spirit with an interesting story to tell, so my motivations weren't considered so wild here. I have had conversations the world over with people trying to justify my actions to themselves. 'So, you're not weird, running away from an issue or a job or a family? This is actually something you want to do alone, for the simple dream of it?' The words 'I am cycling from Alaska to Argentina' would often prompt a response of disbelief or a sentence with an excess of superlatives and sometimes profanities. In the Yukon, I would summarize the average response as 'fair enough, good luck'. Life off the grid was hard work, and it took a pioneer's spirit to survive. Everyone I had met, without exception, would be considered slightly eccentric in many circles, but here they fitted in.

6

Crossing into British Columbia coincided with my first 1,000 miles cycled, which felt significant. It was certainly easier to think about this than the distance still left to cycle.

At night it was now getting dark for a few short hours, but cycling into the late evening seemed to be working as a way to allow me to stop and explore while also covering about 75 miles (120km) a day.

Then I got a fright. I was pushing hard to reach a camp spot before nightfall, having been slowed by some rough sections of road. The AlCan was always pretty empty, but as it was nearly ten p.m. I was completely alone and hadn't been passed by any vehicles in over an hour. The foliage began fairly close to the roadside, certainly closer than normal, and I was flying along, only thinking about finishing for the day, when suddenly a dark object broke out from the cover on my right about 20 metres ahead and bounded across the road. It was a grizzly bear, much bigger than its black cousin, and stunningly fast. Thankfully it didn't even pause and effortlessly climbed a bank and disappeared.

I was carrying a big bottle of 'bear spray', which is a serious dose of pepper spray, and also 'bear bangers', which fired off a pen-style launcher and made a loud explosion. But there is no way I could have reached them quickly enough had the bear stopped; I'd've been on top of him in seconds. I was spooked and I redoubled my efforts, flying the last 10 miles, glancing around nervously all the while. I decided right then not to cycle into the night again.

Every night in camp I put all food, toothpaste and anything else that smelled in one sealed bag and pulled it high off the ground, using a rope thrown across a branch as a pulley. Apart from that, there was just my thin tent between me and the wildlife. If a bear did come pawing in the night there was little good a pepper spray or banger would do at such close quarters so I always slept with my knife open. However, having just seen my first grizzly bear, I now realized what a futile defence *that* would be.

I soon found that British Columbia had far more wildlife than the Yukon, or certainly far more visible wildlife. Black bears were a regular sight, grazing passively at the roadside. Only a few times did I feel the need to stop, once when a young male stood stubbornly on the road, and another time when I spotted a mum and her two cubs a short distance ahead. I was wary of startling a mum and had to wait for about half an hour until a pick-up appeared which I could flag down and ask to drive slowly alongside as a moving shield.

This tactic came in handy a few days later when I was on a very long straight but undulating road. From a long way off I could see black objects along the roadside. However, it wasn't until I got closer that I realized just how huge they were. The herd of twenty-five wood bison were grazing on the plentiful grass on the wide verges. I stopped for a long while, leaning on my handlebars, observing them and trying to work out what to do next. 'They are just big cows,' I tried to reason with myself. But there were also a number of calves, and the herd was on both sides of the road. Wood bison are bigger than their relatives who live on the prairie, and despite being vegetarian they have to be one of the most intimidating animals I have ever faced. The big ones looked to weigh about a ton, most of which was bulked in their front end. They had vast muscular shoulders and a thick neck balancing a head about four times the size of a cow's, crowned with black horns. Even with rolling security in the form of another RV which I had flagged down, it was exhilarating as I pedalled within a few metres of the beasts that were on my side of the road.

While being grateful for these bits of help, I wasn't the RV's biggest fan. Since Alaska they had been quietly terrorizing me. Many of the big motorhomes had a car in tow, so in total measured over 20 metres. The average occupant was a retiree couple. Therefore, my main road companions were elderly Americans driving something the size of a bus, after spending their lifetime driving cars. Though there wasn't a lot of traffic on the road, after a couple of close calls I started looking back every time I heard an engine, no longer trusting drivers to know how big their vehicles were and therefore pull wide.

Many supply stops along the AlCan now lie empty, abandoned. Apart from making it tricky for me to get supplies, the loss of livelihood was sad to see. I had many conversations with people about this problem. I stopped one night at Double G's, a surviving small diner, post office, motel and weather station. It proved to have some of the best food of the journey so far. Bob had run the place for decades, so was as old and worn-looking as the building, but charming and wonderfully welcoming. I shared dinner with a group of hunters who were heading into the Rockies with their horses for the season, and afterwards sat outside chatting with Bob. Every year he watched some of his neighbours leave, so that big gaps were left in the 1,422-mile AlCan community. He was determined to remain, but quietly accepted that the north's heyday, the gold-rush and fur-trading era, was long gone.

It was wrong to blame the RVs for this loss of livelihood. Developments and changes in technology and holiday styles are inevitable, but I felt a real connection with and respect for the people living here, so it was hard not to slightly resent the motorhomes as they thundered past, avoiding it all.

It had rained every day in Alaska, but now it was starting to get very warm. During one conversation with my production team back in Scotland I was warned of a heatwave in southern British Columbia and some serious forest fires. I thought I was being careful but had still managed to get pretty bad sunburn on my arms. More worryingly, I had a slight twinge in my left hamstring tendon, down the back of my knee. Having suffered from serious tendonitis before, I knew what this could develop into so I called home and reported it.

On my second night in British Columbia I reached Liard Hot Springs. Still deep in the forest I was surprised to find the busiest campground so far. In fact there were no camp spots left and I was told to pitch my tent at the side of the day parking area. I felt unused to so much company.

Apart from being interesting, I hoped the hot springs would help my strained tendon. A long hand-railed walkway led over the boggy ground deeper into the forest. Steam rose into the branches, a white mist in the cool evening air. The forest floor grew thick with human-sized ferns and thick mosses that you would normally expect to see only in tropical climates. The setting felt idyllically peaceful and health-giving, until I got near the first pool. Long before I could see it, I smelled it. The sulphuric stench was nose-curling. I still expected to see some idyllic natural spa, maybe with one or two young beauties swimming lazily, like in the shampoo adverts. However, the natural pool, maybe 30 metres long by 10 metres wide, had been built up like a swimming pool, with changing booths, steps in and a wooden border. What's more, it was crowded with about twenty children and many larger-than-is-healthy adults bursting out of skimpy swimsuits. All desire to get in evaporated, and I stood there looking on for a while, disappointed.

Then I noticed the path carrying on above the pool. With nothing better to do I decided to explore this. Ten minutes later I came out of the forest again to the edge of a second pool. This one was larger, maybe 30 metres round. Better still, it was completely empty and hardly smelled. It was too good to be true, and I hesitated before taking the plunge. Why was everyone crowded into the lower pool, which was smaller and stinking? There were certainly no signs to say it wasn't safe so I stripped off and waded in. The hot mud squelched between my toes until I started swimming. It wasn't very welcoming, and the murky waters prevented me from seeing anything beneath the surface, but I reasoned that nothing could live in such hot water. It was about as warm as I could take a bath. After a few minutes floating around lazily my head started to feel especially hot as I was perspiring profusely, trying to cope with the effects of being almost completely submerged. But it was blissfully relaxing once I got used to it. Half an hour later I emerged, hands and feet shrivelled like prunes, feeling like I had been given a massage, been exfoliated in a super jacuzzi and slept for twelve hours. Standing in the middle of the forest, air-drying, I felt reinvigorated, more awake than I had been in weeks.

If I was a bear, I thought to myself, I'd definitely be making more of this natural hot tub.

The next morning I called my production team at the BBC to catch up before setting off. My concern about my knee had been mentioned when they'd arrived at their desks at nine a.m. While I slept in my tent, eight hours behind UK time, they'd had a full working day to escalate the problem. For me, it was manageable; it was just something I wanted noted so that we had a full record of incidents. Alarmingly, as soon as I called, my series producer informed me that I wasn't to go anywhere. Furthermore, they had found out that the nearest hospital capable of knee scans was in Vancouver and they already had a helicopter and aeroplane flight plan sorted to get me from the depths of the forests in British Columbia down to the Pacific coast.

I was taken aback and slightly confused. To frustrate me further, the sat phone kept cutting out, so it took nearly an hour of broken conversation to talk the situation back into context. I felt fine to carry on, I'd just wanted to be careful. Their reaction certainly made me acutely aware of the pressures I was now under. This was far more than a personal ambition I wished to share. It now had all the hopes and budget of a major production.

We eventually agreed that I could carry on only if I got a doctor's sign-off. I was in a remote spot so the only option was to call one in London. The ensuing conversation was inevitably amusing.

'So, you have a slight strain to your Achilles tendon, but you have had it before and know how to manage it and are too remote and without supplies to stop and rest where you are,' summarized the GP.

'Yes.'

'Well, then there's not much I can say. You sound like you know far more about how to manage this where you are than I can advise.'

'Great. Well, please tell my team that so I can get back on my bike.'

The GP was probably used to people trying to persuade him that they needed sick notes, so seemed baffled by my insistence that I didn't want one. My knee wasn't better, but neither was it getting worse. I pedalled off, and agreed with the production team that it had probably been a good exercise for them in case I did get into serious trouble and needed to be evacuated.

The road, which had grown increasingly undulating since the Yukon, was now making a more concerted ascent as I found the top end of the Rockies. I loved it. These mountains were at the heart of this journey south and it was great finally to be in them. The scenery was becoming more varied too, with rivers and rocky valleys growing out of the carpet of trees. Some sections even justified crash barriers as the road hugged hillsides and made more turns. Caribou and stone sheep also started to make an appearance. The latter was a rugged but moth-eaten-looking animal which I wrongly took to be a goat for a while. Having grown up on a goat and sheep farm I should have known, but I remained confused until I managed to get within a few metres of some as they stood in the middle of the road, stubbornly licking salt residue.

The first real mountains I reached looked as if a child had drawn them. I pedalled between walls that seemed to be made of a single rock. Thick crayon-like marks appeared throughout them in parallel lines. The aptly named Folded Mountains were as bizarre as they were striking. It was as if molten rock had been laid down in neat layers, then kneaded into mountain shapes. Lost in my land-scape, it was one of those times when I had to remind myself to keep checking the road ahead as I cycled along looking up and around at everything but what lay in front of me.

It was never steep but kept on climbing for tens of miles until I reached Summit Pass, the highest point of the AlCan at 1,295m (4,250ft). Only a few trees survived up here and I flew along brilliant roads past Summit Lake, which sparkled turquoise in the afternoon sun.

As I started the long and fast descent, I heard a big engine behind me and glanced back to see a fully laden logging truck. I carried on as usual, hugging the roadside, now going the fastest I had gone in Canada. Despite there being a corner ahead, the truck started pulling level, until I was just behind the cab. I had no option but to keep my line, as there was no way I could leave the road going at 40mph. He was going far too fast and stamped on the brakes to try and slow his incredible weight. He dropped behind again, but I could hear the wheels protesting on the corner. Coming out of the long left-hander was a longer straight, and he pulled level again. This time the window was down and he let fly a volley of abuse that I couldn't even begin to publish. To summarize, he wanted me off the road and I was a great danger to all road users. His rage was uncontrolled and I had no response, trying to hold my line. He accelerated so the cab was just past me again then swung in, caus-ing the trailer to follow sharply. I saw it coming and pulled hard on my brakes, instinctively leaning to the right to do everything to avoid the ends of the logs. I have no idea how close it actually was, but it was close enough. I stopped, shaking, and stayed like that for a few minutes to allow the road to clear in case he was waiting for me up ahead.

That day had started by packing a soaking tent after a thunderstorm in the night. It ended in the absolute luxury of a hotel in the town of Fort Nelson. I had planned to stop here to pick up some memory cards that had been couriered out from Scotland, so my team had suggested booking a room for me as well. I had really been looking forward to it. A proper wash and a bed was always very welcome. However, I didn't feel particularly welcome. The receptionist looked at me suspiciously as I walked in, my white lycra top mottled with dirt. I realized for sure that I had now left the Yukon.

My new plan, now that I didn't want to ride late because of bears and because of an ever greater need to pace myself to protect my knee, was to start very early, eat more and sleep more. The eating and sleeping part came from my general skinniness and frequent feeling of lethargy. Life in the north had been scarily expensive and I had often not eaten as much as I wanted, as I couldn't face spending over $30 each meal. However, in the hope that the budget would balance itself from Mexico onwards, I decided that I really needed to feed myself more, regardless of what it cost.

More sleep, more cycling, more filming and more eating all sounded like a feasible plan, but I couldn't think what to do less of.

That evening I had two three-course meals, enjoying both the loosened constraints on my budget and not having to cook on my camp stove. In a nearby pizza place I enjoyed a bowl of soup, seafood linguine and a chocolate brownie with ice-cream before walking back to the hotel restaurant for a pound of mussels and some pesto tagliatelle, polishing it all off with a good wedge of chocolate cake with both cream and ice-cream. It was bliss, but I did feel pretty full. I then wallowed in the luxury of a bath, sipping a cup of tea, before sleeping for eleven hours.

In the morning I was at the post office first thing. I needed to take more weight off the bike somehow. A thicker jacket, which I had needed in Alaska, could go, plus some more items that had seemed essential but I hadn't yet used. It didn't seem like much but it added up to nearly 2kg.

The AlCan had been incredibly tough on my tyres. Never before had I experienced such quick wearing, but then again I had never cycled with so much weight on the bike. Having already switched the front and back around – the back wears much faster – I was still concerned. The plan had been to change them nearer the US border, but I decided to check in the only sports shop in town on the off chance they had my size tyres. First impressions weren't good. The small store was piled high with everything from guns to guitars, and they seemed to have only kids' bikes. The assistant, who turned out to be the owner's son, quickly stopped speaking to his only other customers when I walked in and was very keen to help. Amazingly, he did have tyres that fitted. He also gave me a generous discount and helped me fit the new tyres at the back of the store before anyone else was helped. 'One day I would like to cycle to Argentina,' he remarked.

My resupplying in Fort Nelson had mainly been a success. However, one error was speed-shopping in the pharmacy which resulted in picking up 'coconut twist' sun cream by mistake. Not that I carried such things, but I had been advised to steer clear of deodorants and perfumes when wild-camping here. Now, not only did I smell like a girl, but the bears could smell me coming from a long way off. I'd seen nine bears in the last three days, which did nothing to dispel my concern.

I was now east of the Rockies, so back into endless rolling forests. It was a bit dull in comparison, but I felt well fuelled. More importantly, the knee was definitely stronger. The last full day on the AlCan I did three hours straight in the saddle to start the day, to the small town of Wonowon. Oddly, but maybe not by coincidence, Wonowon is at Mile 101 of the AlCan. Everything south of Mile 101 was on the grid, and the effect was immediate.

For the first time in Canada I passed normal homesteads surrounded by fields, and there was noticeably more traffic. I also picked up good phone coverage for the first time. I had returned to the developed world, but apart from the prices I would have been happier left in the wilds. It was, however, lovely to pick up nearly three weeks of encouraging messages on my phone from friends back home. They helped me through that afternoon and evening's constant rainstorm.

It was now a month since leaving Denali and I was just over a week from the US border, if all went well. The following day I spent entirely on Route 29, a much smaller and quieter road than the AlCan. It was peaceful riding, with some long climbs, which I felt strong for. All day I saw only two bears, but the second got my heart racing. I saw it grazing up ahead to the right, so on my side of the road. As I drew level it was about 15 metres off but it turned quickly around, rising on to its hind legs. It looked young but was fully grown and stood around six feet. I hammered my legs around, sprinting forward. When I glanced back, it was still standing, but thankfully hadn't moved. A car had passed at the same time and I saw it stop a safe distance ahead. A young Chinese-looking man was driving, his wife in the passenger's seat and two kids in the back, all wide-eyed.

'Hey, are you OK?' he asked.

'Yes,' I gasped, trying to get my breath back.

'We will drive with you,' he suggested kindly.

I declined with thanks. I would be in bear country for a long time yet. I had been told that bears often have poor eyesight so they stand on their back legs simply to get a better look, not to be aggressive. It was a reasonable theory, but it was still pretty intimidating.

Now back in the mountains, I settled into some impressive climbs, stopping the following night to camp at a place called Azouzetta, at about 3,000ft. My knee felt healed and I spun a good cadence for hour upon hour, climbing steadily. Sometimes I would get lost in the present, taking in my surroundings, thinking about the day's plan; at other times I would drift off to think about anything else. I followed the Pine River upstream as the road meandered under sheer cliffs. The wildflowers were brilliant and everywhere, and I got off my bike for a while to film them, before I remembered the day's targets and refocused on making miles.

The next few days were spent slowly descending to the town of Prince George, where I had to face a slightly embarrassing issue. For any cyclist, being able to change a puncture is lesson number one, and I had been caught out. I had run out of spares. For over a week I had been on a run of bad luck with five punctures. I had enough patches to fix fifty normal punctures, but these had all happened at the valve and so were unfixable. I had no more spare inner tubes. Later I found out that with so much weight on the bike I was tightening the little nut on the outside of the rim too much, and this was pulling the valve off the inner tube. As mentioned, an embarrassingly simple issue for any cyclist to admit to.

Ten kilometres out of Prince George, my back wheel blew out as I descended at speed. There are always a few wild seconds when this happens, braking quickly, hoping you don't bust your wheel as you bounce along the road at 30mph on your metal rims. I was so close, but had no option but to change out of my cycling shoes and start walking the last few miles, pushing the bike along the verge. I had obviously broken down – why else would I be pushing? – and stopped regularly to wave down trucks. No one stopped, and by the time I was within 5km of Prince George I stopped trying. It was strange to be walking again, but I justified it as good exercise to stay in shape for the Aconcagua climb.

Luckily there was an excellent bike store in town where I picked up some spares and talked through my punctures. It was quite humiliating to have to tell them that I was cycling to Argentina yet seemed unable to fix a puncture properly.

There was no camp spot so I checked into a cheap motel. While fixing the bike I watched stage 18 of the Tour de France. Alberto Contador nailed the 40km individual Time Trial in forty-eight minutes and thirty seconds. On a good day on my bike that would have taken me two hours.

The next day I was aiming for the town of Quesnel, determined to make up a bit of lost ground. Until the last 35km I was flying. Still in the middle of the endless wilds, with the odd farm carved into the landscape, I was surprised to pass a large sign on the roadside that announced FREE CAMPING. Despite the attractive offer I wouldn't have slowed if it hadn't been for the unlikely number of cars parked along the driveway and in a small field. As soon as I stopped I heard a country song being strummed, and laughter. I had to explore.

There was an old wooden house with lots of tables outside, like in a beer garden, and what looked like a shop inside, but it seemed to be a private house. In the field to the right were maybe thirty campervans, trucks and caravans, but it was hard to count as they were all parked like a log jam in a river. Other cars were scattered about, and lots of people were wandering around. I stopped someone, who explained it was an annual local music festival.

Leaving my bike, I wandered over towards the sound of music, which was coming from the middle of the vehicle jam. Behind a very old cream-and-rust-coloured Dodge campervan was a home-made awning, under which sat eight people. I must have looked odd, dressed in lycra, snooping around with a camera in one hand, but as soon as I was spotted a lady hollered me over. Without a word of introduction she pulled me in, sat me down and handed me a plate of meat and potatoes and a can of beer. I couldn't say much, except thanks, as the rest of the circle of people were absorbed in a loud singsong. It looked like I was staying put.

The van was owned by John from Quebec, a big, smiling, gently spoken man, probably in his late fifties. He played the accordion and guitar with great gumption but sang very quietly. Another equally jovial big-bellied man with wild curly hair and white beard played the harmonica, his eyes closed. A second guitarist, Denis, sat on my left. He was bald but wore a brimmed hat, and had a boxer's nose, which gave his face a lopsided look. He would join in after a few bars of each new song, once he had figured out which chords to strum. A couple sitting on the far side were very drunk, and the kind lady who had invited me in eventually introduced herself as a local cashier at the supermarket in Quesnel. Then there was big Dave, who didn't seem quite as hillbilly as the rest, and who proudly explained that he was the American who had come to Canada to avoid the draft, and never gone home.

Lastly there was Jason. I later found out that Jason, like me, had just met everyone, but you wouldn't have known it by the way he held court. He seemed to know and play every song on the guitar, whoever started it. He also played with such ease, throwing in all kinds of twiddles and sparkle. Everyone was impressed.

Jason could have been anything between late twenties and mid-forties, with the manners and appearance of a hard-living man. A vest hung off very thin arms, while a couple of big tattoos spread up his neck. He wore a wide cowboy's hat, which accentuated his bony face and beady eyes. He was known simply as 'the Newfie', in reference to his being from Newfoundland in eastern Canada. Incredibly, he had walked to British Columbia; in fact he had spent ten years walking fairly aimlessly around Canada. He drank beer out of a huge tankard, chain-smoked, and swore profusely. All was excused, as his singing and storytelling were brilliant.

It was an unforgettable few hours of music, and I gave up on making it to Quesnel that night. I would make up the miles somehow.

Later, a stage was set up and some more bands played, this time with full electrics and a bigger crowd. They were all good, but it lacked the spontaneous charm of the afternoon's jamming.

I had been adopted as one of the motley crew. The fact I didn't play folk music was excused by the fact that I seemed odd enough to fit in. As it grew late a plan was hatched for the following day, and whether I liked it or not I was involved. By midnight I crawled into my tent, resigned to the fact I was losing further miles, but excited by the prospect of a day on the Cottonwood River.

The narrow sandy banks of the Cottonwood were doing their best the next morning to match the French Riviera, as sunbathers jostled for towel space. One bank had a rough access track so a number of pick-up trucks had been driven on to the wide gravel banks and provided the centrepiece for big barbecues. On the other bank was a sea of bikinis and children. It was certainly not what I had expected in the forests of northern British Columbia.

Legs and Wheels was one of the local bands I had met, so-named because their drummer was in a wheelchair. I was here to join them in a course of river tubing. I didn't really know what to expect and didn't have any swim shorts, but I waded in, holding an inflated tractor tyre tube in one hand while clutching a waterproof bag in the other. There was a good chance my cameras would get wet.

I managed to clamber onboard, sitting in the hole of the tyre. We were off. It had been built up as a mini expedition downstream, not for children or the faint-hearted, so there was applause and cheers as we drifted off. It was in fact wonderfully pedestrian and the only skill required was to be able to spin around and paddle your feet frantically to give the tyre vague direction. Not everyone got it, and a few kilometres downstream one of the flotilla, Steve, got caught in a small rapid and was skewered in some low-hanging branches. The tyre burst with a loud bang, and he was left swimming for the bank and with a long walk back upstream. It took nearly two hours to float about 4km. It was blissfully relaxing, save for a few hairy rapids, and whenever I floated near to one of the other four remaining tubers I managed to chat.

It seemed that everyone in the community was part of the lumber industry. The lead singer was a foreman in a major timber yard by day. Everyone's father, and grandfather before them, seemed to have been loggers too, and they were all raising families to continue the tradition. Everyone seemed pretty contented and proud of this way of life, and I could see why.

We pulled the tubes ashore and went to find a 10-metre river cliff to dive off, or in my case jump off, before bundling back into pickups and heading back for more music.

I felt fine at the river, but by the evening my left ear was very painful. A few years earlier I had burst my ear canal landing badly from a jump off a waterfall. It didn't feel that painful, but I had obviously aggravated it again. Despite the painkillers I couldn't sleep for many hours with the persistent ringing noise and earache.

Over the next five days I worked towards the US border, crossing by Oroville in Washington State. That was no longer in the high Rockies, but I didn't mind veering slightly west of the mountains for a few days in search of some faster miles. There was plenty more mountain riding to look forward to. However, as I had been warned, British Columbia was in the middle of its biggest heatwave since 1941. The faster I tried to go and the more I descended out of the Rockies, the hotter it was getting. Each day peaked at over 40 degrees and it stayed on the high side most days until gone four p.m. I'd never expected some of the hottest riding I had ever done to be in Canada. Getting in early miles was now even more essential.

The communities like Quesnel and McLeese Lake that I passed reminded me more of Californian living than the wilds I had learned to love further north. Charming as they were, the Canadian borderlands were undoubtedly more akin to their American neighbours than their northern relatives.

Three days after leaving the folk festival I did a stunning 40km descent from Begbie Pass at 1,232m (4,042ft) near the old-fashioned-looking town of Clinton to Cache Creek. In this time I dropped from the green mountain heights to an arid and parched valley bottom. The transition was amazing.

The forest fires that were sweeping the region dominated the news so I was surprised not even to have smelled smoke yet. However, I did share my next camp spot with a group of twenty volunteer fire-fighters who were working in fourteen-hour shifts to control the blazes. Now cycling through a tinder-dry landscape, I could see the scale of the problem. One spark and whole valleys could be torched.

The next morning I went to put my shoes on as usual. Picking them up, bleary-eyed, I heard a faint noise, almost like something being poured. My bare foot then crunched on what felt like a pile of rice. I jumped back in fright. A colony of ants had moved into my shoe. A few ants or spiders I am quite used to, but as I tipped my shoes back, hundreds of ants fell out, accompanied by a considerable pile of ants' eggs. I promised myself to check my shoes more carefully from now on.

On my second last day in Canada, I was late leaving. I was very tired after stopping to play and film some street hockey the night before and I had then lost time chatting to another eccentric 'Newfie'. I had passed him on his rusty bike, dressed in jeans and a shirt, before he hailed me to stop. He started talking fast, never meeting my eye. I could have just left, I was hardly involved in the conversation, but he was strangely fascinating. He bemoaned the fact that Canada was lost, having sold all its valuable assets to the Chinese, and how he had lost hope in everyone and their capitalist greed. Ironically, the one thing he was passionate about was his own plan to save $20,000 by doing odd jobs, and then to invest that and live off the interest for ever. He spent nearly an hour talking at me. After a while I could find no way to leave politely, so I simply wished him well and started cycling away faster than him.

I had lost the Newfie and left the town of Merritt when a council van pulled alongside and a lady shouted, 'Eight kilometres ahead there's rain so hard that wipers can't keep up.' Sure enough I could see the dark clouds rolling in. It was a long, tough climb to the hamlet of Aspen Grove. After about half an hour's climbing, the heavens opened. I couldn't get off the road fast enough; there was no way I could cycle in the downpour. Diving into the forest, I found a couple of huge softwoods with wide umbrella-like lower branches and snuggled down against one of the trunks. The sound of rain battering through the branches was wonderful, matched with the smell of the wet undergrowth and fresh tree sap. I sat there chuckling at some news I had heard back in Merritt. These lightning storms, which had been sweeping across the Rockies, had hit a number of RVs. Luckily no one was seriously hurt, so I found the idea of some unsuspecting 'road terrorists' getting mildly electrocuted in their mobile tin cans quite amusing.

I woke an hour later with a start, still crouching on my heels, leaning on the tree. My calves burst painfully into pins and needles as I went to move. Laughing again at my impromptu siesta, I pushed my bike back on to the road.

I finished the climb on zinging wet roads, then moved on to a beautiful dipping road that descended past a number of picture-postcard lakes. Small holiday cottage communities hugged the shores. By late afternoon I was just short of Princeton when the heavens opened again and I got pelted with hail. I stomped a bit harder on the pedals, going too fast, but I was too close to town to want to stop in the forests again.

To mark about 2,500 miles on the road and my leaving Canada, the production team had arranged a live broadcast with BBC Breakfast News. It was a simple Skype call, with the added pressure of speaking to about five million people. The BBC had already booked me into the Old Hedley Road Inn to do my live feed. Hedley was another 40km away. Because of the time difference with the UK I would be broadcasting at one a.m. Camping was therefore completely out of the question, unless they wanted a torchlight broadcast that would have looked like something out of *The Blair Witch Project*.

Thankfully Hedley was downstream so I made fast time to start with, but then I punctured. By the time I had fixed that it was almost dark and I continued with lights on. My back wheel then started rubbing against the guard. I quickly checked for a broken spoke. Everything looked fine. The bike was an unusual set-up, with internal gears and disc brakes, so I didn't fully understand what every bolt did. It took a few minutes for me to realize that one was missing. Pulling the wheel straight again and over-tensioning the remaining bolts, I hobbled on, hoping the minor wobble wouldn't worsen before I found a replacement.

By the time I reached Hedley it was almost completely dark and I pedalled straight out the far side without finding the inn. Backtracking, I stopped at another guesthouse. Jackpot: the man at the door was wearing a Shimano T-shirt, which assured me he was cycling friendly, but he had never heard of the Old Hedley Road Inn. He did, however, let me use his phone, as I had no mobile reception and the sat phone battery was dead. I had no option but to call my mum Una in Scotland, where it was 4.30 a.m. It took a few further phone calls to figure out that the Old Hedley Road Inn was actually nowhere near Hedley but back up the road I had just come down. There was no way I was backtracking 10 miles uphill in the dark. I tried to explain to the bemused owners of this guesthouse that I needed a perfect internet connection and a very bright spot to do a live broadcast in the middle of the night. It was obviously an odd request in these parts from a lost and pretty smelly cyclist.

I was glad when they went to bed early as it took nearly three hours to set up my makeshift studio. The whole house was filled with pale pink lights, giving a wonderfully homely soft light, but utterly hopeless for my purposes. The only white lights I could find were in the two bathrooms. Thankfully there were no other guests and the owners' bedroom was downstairs so I tiptoed around unscrewing all these lights, collecting bulbs from bedside lamps and swapping them. I then fixed a small camera to one of the lamps with a zip tie and placed this on an upturned drawer to get the right height. To bounce the light the right way I then took the sheet off the bed and draped it over the back of some chairs. More light was still needed so I shone a couple of head torches through my rain jacket, which was slightly opaque. I then sat on the floor against a white wall, using the back wheel of the bike and my helmet as props in the shot.

I connected with the BBC in Glasgow and spoke to the techies who agreed that it looked great, but could I find more light? No, I assured them, it had taken three hours and turning the house inside out to get what I had. I was patched through to London and listened to the live show through one headphone for over half an hour before going live myself. By that time I was incredibly uncomfortable and very hot, with sweat across my face. I hadn't moved for fear they would come to me live at any moment. Oddly, they could see me but I couldn't see them. I was simply staring into a lamp. One of the presenters, Bill Turnbull, eventually introduced me and I chatted for about five minutes about the journey to date, and what lay ahead. All the while a fly kept landing on my face, but there was no way I could react to it.

At 1.15 a.m. it was over and I had a quick call from my production team to let me know how well it had all worked. I hadn't even had time for dinner and was shattered. It took me the best part of another hour to convincingly put the house back to how it had been, and then I fell asleep, still in my cycling clothes, with my alarm set for seven a.m.

I needn't have got up so early. Breakfast was worth the effort and I ate enough to make up for my fifteen-hour fast, but soon after I left I found my road blocked. Ahead I could see thick smoke drifting over the trees. Unsure what to do, I took my camera out and started filming. Oddly, no cars passed for about ten minutes. Then a police car appeared behind me and drew level. The grass fire had only just started, the trooper said, probably from a cigarette butt, but was spreading quickly. A helicopter flew low overhead, back and forth from the river I had been following, dropping bucket after bucket of water on the blaze. The reason there was no traffic was that a roadblock had been set up a little way back and I was in the evacuation area.

An hour later, it was all over. The valley was still filled with smoke, but the flames were out. After the traffic had cleared I pedalled on and was soon cycling past an area of about 10 acres that had moments before been on fire.

The Keremeos Valley is the fruit basket of Canada, and once again it was baking hot. Mile upon mile of valley-bottom orchards and fruit stalls made a refreshing change after the mountains. In the town of Keremeos I found I was the only guy on a bike without an engine. The main street was lined with hundreds of low riders, Harleys, street bikes and cruisers, none of the enduros and mega BMWs which had plagued the far north. This was a mecca of speed, and every café and bar seemed to cater mainly for the leather-clad, tattooed and hairy fraternity. I felt the odd one out reversing my bicycle on to its stand amid a long line of chromed and custom-painted machines. It then took me considerably longer to get served than anyone else I could see. But I didn't dare grumble.

From there it was a long but gradual climb to the town of Osoyoos, whose sign proudly boasted CANADA'S WARMEST WELCOME. Surrounded by sage bush and arid brown hills, it looked more like northern Africa than southern Canada. The border controls were many times bigger than the ones I had cycled through from Alaska but the officers were equally clueless about my kit carnets. After I had talked them through what I needed, including some official stamps and signatures, I was in. Normally it's the border guards who do the questioning and you're doing the explaining so you can gain entry, but here I was delaying my own entry, while they were obviously keen to wave me through. I had certainly made it harder than was necessary to get across the border. Thankfully, once I was across and into the USA I knew that I shouldn't need the carnets any more. It seemed that Mexico and Central America weren't so worried about you bringing in expensive film gear that could get left behind.

From the border it was a suitably exhilarating descent for the first few miles into the United States. It was a return to the US, but this felt different. Alaska had felt like Alaska, not like any part of the US I knew. I crowned my return to the lower 48 with a 14-inch pizza and supersized drink at an Italian-American diner before checking into a cheap motel.

7

The US was the only country on this journey that I had cycled across before. My world route had taken me the 3,589 miles (5,775km) from San Francisco down the Californian coast and across the far southern states to Florida. It had been a winter ride, pretty cold and not without its incidents. In Louisiana I went over the bonnet of a car that had jumped a stop sign, and then later the same day I was mugged by a group of youths. However, they were incidents that could have happened anywhere and I was now looking forward to exploring the country some more, this time on a north-to-south route that would cross my previous path in about a month's time, near the Mexican border.

I had something else to look forward to. Three great friends had arranged to road-trip with me for a few days: my girlfriend Nicci, whom I had waved goodbye to in Scotland not knowing if I would see her at all during the nine-month expedition, and old university flatmates Laura and Brendan were currently en route west.

Day one in Washington State was a tough 100 miles to Grand Coulee Dam. It was scorching hot again. In one little town I passed a chemist's neon sign which flashed 108 degrees Fahrenheit (42°C). The first stretch followed a railway line down the Okanogan Valley into a hot headwind before turning off on to Route 155 for a two-hour climb up to Disautel Pass at 3,252ft (991m). On the valley bottom I had felt as parched as the fields around me and agitated on the bike. As I climbed, I eventually found my tempo and was rewarded with green grasses and then a full forest at higher altitude. I was now in the Colville Indian Reservation and I stopped for much-needed water before the final push. This turned out to be a spectacular road, which in parts had been cut through the rock producing huge pillars and sheer walls to cycle through and past. The evening light was golden across the wide river valley to my right and the small homesteads dotted throughout looked every bit the American dream.

Grand Coulee Dam was, in comparison, a tacky tourist spot, and very overpriced at that. As night fell, a laser light display started on the huge dam wall. It was a psychedelic cartoon of colour which brought many oohs and aahs from the watching crowd, but I felt it was completely out of place in a spot of such natural beauty. It catered to people who wanted to go on holiday 'in the wilds' but who couldn't leave home without TV and communications to distract from the boredom of not being constantly entertained. I sat on a wide grassy bank eating pizza. The leftovers would be good for breakfast.

From the dam it was another long climb before an almost continuous 20 miles of descent to the small town of Wilbur. I was now heading in a more easterly direction again. For the first time I dropped into a wide arable valley, in fact so wide I couldn't really see the surrounding hills once I was in it. It felt more like the Midwest prairies than anywhere near the Rockies. I came over the crest of one hill and stopped. In front of me the road ran completely straight for as far as the eye could see, slowly descending in waves that crested at regular intervals. To both sides, mile upon mile of corn swayed slowly in the breeze. The heat haze shimmered off the tar, confusing the horizon.

I set the camera up on the roadside and pedalled off down the hill. The temptation was to go and go in this immense landscape, but after half a kilometre I squeezed on the brakes, turned around and cycled back to pick up the camera. These shots were so important to give context to my journey, but they were the hardest shots to remember to do. Cycling back any distance, especially up a big hill, always felt frustrating. The more stunning a landscape, and therefore the more I wanted just to keep riding in it, the more important it was to take the time to stop and film myself in it. This was something I had never done when racing around the world and it required a very different mindset.

I passed through the next village without stopping until I spotted a couple of touring cyclists sheltering in a small park at the roadside. I hadn't seen any touring bikes in the north and I asked if they knew the road ahead. You only ever ask other cyclists for information on the road; car users tend to have no real concept of distance or terrain.

The couple were probably in their late forties and rode identical bikes, both heavily laden. They met me with big smiles, explaining that they were hiding from the heat of the day. Originally from New Jersey, William and Alexandra had been on the road for twelve years together, cycled in forty-four countries and clocked up about thirty thousand miles. They were obviously and rightly proud of their huge pilgrimage. Both of their bikes had a white cross neatly painted on the front to remind them of their guide. Maybe because of my inability to aptly answer the same question, I am always intrigued to learn what motivates people to take on such journeys. They also didn't seem too interested in knowing about my journey, so I felt free to ask away.

'So what's your idea when you travel, what's your main reason?' I said.

'To enjoy people through music.' William had answered that before.

'OK, so it's the bike and the music . . . where do you normally end up playing?'

'We will go to old age homes, hospitals, jails, schools, orphanages, homeless shelters. We have played for the dying, at funerals, for people just born and their families, and absolutely everything in between.'

They beamed at me. I kept on with the questions until I realized that any more would imply that I thought they were odd.

William was wearing a bright yellow T-shirt and round spectacles. Alexandra, who had a floral dress on, explained that they lived off donations and had just finished a long spell in Europe. They had no plans to go home. We chatted for a while before they insisted on taking out their guitars for a sing-song:

> Who am I, what do I know?
> Without love, where shall I go?
> . . . and you will walk a better way,
> See a brighter day,
> Build a better world for tomorrow and today.
> We can walk a better way . . .

For the rest of the day I cycled along with this simple melody going round and round my head. In twelve years of singing they still hadn't found their harmony. The result was slightly grating, but what they lacked in tuning they certainly made up for in gusto.

I was now following Interstate 90, by far the biggest road I had seen on the journey. Like I10 in the south, which I had done thousands of miles of, it was a fast dual carriageway. However, despite a wide hard shoulder, road signs soon made it unavoidably clear that I wasn't allowed to continue. This diversion added to the delay caused by my back wheel: since losing the bolt in southern Canada I had needed to stop every 20 miles to tighten the other bolts. I kicked myself for not carrying spares for these.

Cutting on to smaller frontier roads, I climbed and dropped over every hillock, looking enviously at the landscaped interstate that ran smoothly nearby. The city of Spokane was my biggest urban obstacle yet, but a large bike path information board was an encouraging sign. Alas, I had to keep cutting back on to main roads to stick close to I90. Once I did eventually commit to a cycle path that seemed to go in the right direction, it led me a quite a few miles into a residential neighbourhood and then stopped. It took over an hour to find my way back, following some amusing directions.

'Which way is I90, please?'

'You can't cycle on I90.'

'I know, thanks, but I need to go in the same direction, so if I can find it then I will follow on a smaller road.'

'That's not advisable, sir. If I were you I'd take signage to the city and get a bus.'

'I'm sure I can cycle. Please, can you point me in the right direction?'

I eventually did a 10-mile loop to go a few miles forward. By that time my wheel was rubbing again and I could no longer find a way to keep it temporarily in place. I couldn't face backtracking into Spokane to find a bike shop and wanted to get to the next town, Coeur d'Alene, across the state border in Idaho, where my friends were meeting me.

After a few more miles I decided to rejoin I90 as it would save so much time and the wide hard shoulder was enough for three bikes to ride safely. But as I cut on to the slip road a patrol car appeared from I have no idea where. My guilty conscience was obvious: I jumped with fright as the sirens and lights were turned on. I feigned ignorance and was sent back on to the frontage road.

It was only a 70-mile day to Coeur d'Alene, but with the delays I reached the bike shop Mum had been in touch with just as it was closing. Over the last 10 miles the wheel had repeatedly jammed in the guards; finally I gave up and walked the last six blocks. The shop mechanic turned out to be a keen endurance rider, and he stayed open to fix my bike for free. He had never worked on such an unusual mechanism, where an internal gearing system was mounted on to a vertical drop-out on the frame, with disc brakes built around this. He didn't have the right part but rummaged around for a while to find a replacement bolt that would do the job. I wheeled out amazed at how smooth the bike was again.

Brendan, Laura and Nicci were flying in from Boston and hiring a car for the road trip. It would be amazing to see them, but I already felt pressure to stay on target and was nervous about coming out of my solo focus. With even the best understanding, they would be in a holiday frame of mind. It was just three or four days out of nine months on the road, but I felt a bit self-conscious sharing the experience with anyone. It had been different with Heather in Alaska. We had started the cycle together.

En route to the edge of town where we had arranged to meet, I was flying along a cycle path when a wasp flew into my face and stung my lower lip. Through the heatwave my face had picked up a lot of sun, despite my diligence with the sun cream. My lips were slightly raw and tender as a result, so a wasp sting was far sharper than usual. I stopped the bike and spent the next few minutes pacing quickly around, swearing, unable to dissipate the pain. Anyone watching would have been highly entertained.

Though there were fewer mosquitoes so far in the US than in Canada, there was a new flying menace (besides irate wasps): large horseflies, or clegs as they are called in Scotland. These cumbersome little vampires hurt when they bite and seem attracted to black. My shorts were therefore a waiting pin cushion and I was genuinely terrorized when more than a couple buzzed around at the same time.

It was great to see my friends, but sure enough, as the evening progressed they did note how ill adjusted I was to normal company. They found it quite funny just how wild I looked, and how I seemed slightly lost in another world, but I felt a bit agitated, like being woken from a dream I really wanted to finish. There had been times in Canada when I had craved some company. Now that I had it, I partly wished I was alone again.

The following day I was legally allowed back on I90 and made much faster miles. On average I was climbing, although it was very undulating. It was stunning riding, back into the alpine forests in which I felt far more at home than the arid lowlands. I needn't have worried how the road trip would work out as I was pretty much left alone all day. The plan was to meet late on.

Finding a camp spot wasn't easy. The land and trespassing laws, combined with the aggressively defensive attitude held by many, makes the USA one of the hardest countries to wild-camp in – which is ironic when you consider the scale of wilderness compared to Europe. I eventually found a large picnic area in the forests a mile off the interstate. It had many empty fire pits and there were even a few long-drop toilet huts nearby, so it was the perfect public land to camp on. Large NO OVERNIGHT PARKING OR CAMPING notices stated otherwise, but I was out of options. Hiding a tent and bike was easy enough, but hiding a couple of tents, a bike and a car was trickier. We made some dinner on the camp stove and did everything else that needed to be done before putting up the tents in the last light, well away from the car. At least there were fewer bears to be concerned about here. I had seen sixteen in Canada but none at all since the border. While I was used to the idea of camping in bear country, a sighting might have been too much for the others. We were not disturbed that night, either by man or bear.

The wide interstate did a lot to disguise the climbs by averaging them out into long drags up and down, rather than following every natural contour. Though never steep, this did make for a lot of leg-sapping grinds uphill. With so much weight on the bike, and on such long climbs, it wasn't an option to get out of the saddle much. Instead I would choose a low gear, sit back, spin fast, drop my elbows and pull back on the middle of the bars. After a while it became trance-like, and I would only glance up every so often to spot a new target – maybe the next corner, or a particular tree, or a road sign. With that in mind I would look down again, seeing no more than a few metres ahead, sweat stinging my eyes and dripping off my chin. The tight ache in my thighs and calves would be worth focusing on, a distraction from time. Every twenty minutes or so my lower back would get too tight to bear and I would stand up for just a few pedals, immediately releasing the build-up of tension, before settling back down. I couldn't let myself stop before the top. If you gave in to the desire on such long climbs you would be stopping many times. Then all you would have to think about was how far you still had to climb, and that at that moment you weren't going anywhere. Momentum, no matter how slow, is your greatest friend.

It was a 6-mile climb that took me to the Montana border at Lookout Pass (1,440m/4,725ft). 'Big Sky Country' was the state I was looking forward to the most out of the eight I would see en route to Mexico. It also had an apt nickname. New York is famously 'The Empire State' and Alaska 'The Last Frontier'. But I had found Washington's 'The Evergreen State' not completely accurate, and Idaho's 'Famous Potatoes' was just odd. I did see a lot of potatoes, but it appeared a weak claim to fame. Those first miles through a hilly landscape of white pine trees I certainly hadn't seen anywhere you could hope to grow potatoes.

I celebrated getting to the top with a bag of chips and a photo before starting the longer descent. The valley was wide, green and mainly forested and the initial drop was very fast so that the yellow paint strips almost merged into a seamless line. Trucks still overtook me, but not by much, and even with sunglasses I blinked tears from my vision. My face was set with both exhilaration and pained concentration. Only once the bike started to slow naturally did a proper grin and whoop of joy escape.

The road continued to follow Clark Fork River downstream all day. It was utterly beautiful riding, except for heavy interstate traffic. In mid-afternoon I saw my friends' car parked off to the side and Brendan standing on a fallen log, waving madly. I learned later that they had spent a long time leaving a number of elaborate signs on the road made out of sticks and rocks, telling me where to stop and meet them. Thinking back, I had cycled over these, wondering how such debris had got there but not thinking it was a message for me. It was good to catch up with them as it was very hot and I had made good miles. After a picnic on the stony banks, with chilled meats and cold drinks, we all jumped into the river. It was shockingly cold. I yelped when I came to the surface. Much refreshed and well fed, I flew the remaining miles down the valley to the small town of Superior.

The plan was to camp again. As I clocked down the final mile markers I was also watching the clouds building overhead. When I had the turn-off marker in sight, a few bits of hail fell lazily around me. Over the next kilometre, as I followed the exit lane, the hail gradually increased in intensity, as if a big sack of it was slowly being ripped open. As I turned to dash under a bridge formed by the I90 going overhead, the heavens properly opened. The deluge was like nothing I had ever seen. Car alarms went off in unison at the petrol station across the street and the road was immediately thick with ice. I stared out in awe from the safety of the overpass, filming. A few cars and a motorbike pulled up under the pass as well, unable to drive on. By complete coincidence, one of them contained Brendan and the girls. No one was all that excited by the prospect of being in a tent that night so after a while they went on to recce the town. Over the next few hours, from the balcony of our cheap motel we watched helicopters trying to put out a forest fire which had been started by a lightning strike during the storm.

From there it was a flatter 60 miles to Missoula, a larger and very welcoming town that is home to the Adventure Cycling Association. The association had been of great help during the world cycle and for my current journey, with lots of good advice on how to cycle safely through the land of the internal combustion engine. Inevitably, Missoula itself was also well geared towards cycling and I could have spent a lot longer exploring its tree-lined boulevards, with street after street of wooden houses, many with their own little porch and veranda, the Stars and Stripes flying, just like in the movies.

As I headed directly south and off the interstate, the landscape changed. The first day south of Missoula I was following a wide arable valley. I was so used to the wilderness that it felt strange to look around and not be able to see anywhere that wasn't designed and controlled by man. Vast irrigation systems covered mile upon mile of crops. I flew along a cycle path, completely separate from the main road, until the town of Hamilton. From there the road started to climb again, and by the end of the day I had left the farm-land and was back in the trees. However, this was no forest. For the last few hours the hills were barren, except for the skeletons of thousands of trees. Tree beetles and fires had decimated a vast area so it felt like I was cycling through an apocalyptic scene.

Back in the Okanogan Valley I had dropped one of my cameras, which put a tiny scratch on the wide-angle lens. It was barely visible on the lens, but I could see it clearly on the playback. I had given this to Brendan, Nicci and Laura as their mission to fix, but neither Missoula nor Hamilton had had a camera shop with such specialist gear. Still slowly climbing, I now came to the tiny community of Conner and saw their car parked outside an old log-cabin bar and diner. Inside, I found they had made some friends.

The group of colourful characters turned out to be the film crew for a new series for the History Channel of *Axemen*, a documentary charting the 'extreme' world of clearing trees by helicopter. They were all excited by high-octane days filming with their 'hero' pilot who was also there to share the stories. In comparison my efforts seemed very low budget and ordinary. I marvelled at them talking about mounting mini cameras here and there, setting up all kinds of aerial shots, plus loads of other wizardry; they, in turn, couldn't get their heads around how I was filming a documentary series alone, diary style, with just a few handheld cameras. In a dimly lit 'locals' bar in the middle of this decimated landscape, they seemed as surprised to meet us as we were to meet them.

It was a point of pride that they could fix my lens. Tools were fetched and they strained to release the scratched UV lens, but it had absolutely welded on. Luckily, they were using some of the same kit and offered to swap my damaged one for a new one. One of the cameramen pointed out that with the amount of kit they broke, another lens wouldn't matter. We took them up on their kind offer, then all of us bundled into the car and drove back to

Hamilton, where they were staying, to pick up a $600 lens for free.

By the time we got back it was almost dark and I rushed to get some dinner cooked. I set the camp stove up on a picnic table, quickly primed it, and lit a drizzle of petrol to heat the unit so that when I relit it the petrol would vaporize. In the growing darkness I hadn't seen the leak, and with a flash, flames shot across the table. Everyone jumped back as I tried to drown the flames. The rapidly heating petrol bottle could explode. Apart from the fright, and the delay to dinner, no real harm was done. In the hundreds of times I had used a stove this was only the second unfortunate incident. The first had been in a hotel room in India, where I had burned a large table and narrowly avoided setting fire to the place.

The next morning I kept climbing, following the Bitterroot River all the way to the state border. It was my highest pass yet, at 7,264ft (2,214m), close to Lost Trail Ski Area. At the border sign, instead of heading back into Idaho I cut left on to a small connector road and headed east, over the Continental Divide, leaving the forests and moving back into a wide, flat valley.

By evening I had made the small village of Jackson, which boasted another hot spring at the only hotel. This one, however, was a long way from what I imagined a natural bubbling pool should be. They had made it into a large outdoor swimming pool so it lacked all the charm of a hot spring while also being far too hot to swim in.

We took rooms in the hotel, but to get from the rooms to the hot pool meant walking through a public bar, and I don't think the locals were used to seeing attractive women in swimsuits wandering through. On the way back one of the men caught Nicci's attention and struck up a conversation. He was wearing jeans, a checked shirt, a red neckerchief and a dark brown cowboy's hat, and sported a big moustache; along the bar, the next drinker turned out to be the local minister, who looked haggard with drink. By the time I joined the conversation Nicci had established that her newfound cowboy friend had his horses tied up outside and had arranged to go for a ride. It seemed our new friend was a prize-winning cowboy who had made a fortune from his herds. He spoke at length about how far his horses could ride and how much his cattle could fetch at market.

'But I don't like bicycles much,' he conceded. 'I borrowed a friend's and took it down the trail, but didn't know how to stop it.' He gestured as if he was pulling on the reins of a horse. 'It just went faster and faster, until my hat flew off, and the string was choking me,' he continued, talking loudly, describing the bike as if it was an untamed stallion. 'I pedalled backwards fast but nothing happened.'

By this time Brendan and I were laughing pretty hard at this detailed account of his kamikaze freewheel.

'I missed the turn-off to my ranch and went another two miles before falling off,' he exclaimed with great pride. 'I had to walk back and have never used the bike again. Horrible thing.'

How this man had got to midlife driving trucks and riding horses without the faintest idea of how bike brakes worked was unfathomable. He laughed with us. He gave me his number, inviting me to his ranch to learn to ride in exchange for teaching him to ride a bicycle.

Outside, we found not just his horses, which were less than enthusiastic, but also his wife, who had been left to look after them while he had a drink. She was even grumpier than the horses. The others went for a short ride; I stayed behind. There was plenty of real cowboy riding for me to look forward to.

I had made good miles and didn't feel I had seen that much of my friends, but I'd always looked forward to meeting up with them at the end of each day. So I had mixed emotions the next morning as I pedalled off alone again.

There wasn't much time to wallow in these thoughts, thankfully, as by lunchtime I had to reach the town of Dillon where I'd arranged to meet a lady called Mona. It was about 50 miles over a

7,630ft (2,326m) pass and I stayed on the bike all morning without a break. The message from my production team was that once I got a phone signal, and before my last descent, I should give Mona a call. Simple enough, but it was unclear how I should know which was the last descent in a constantly undulating road. Inevitably I had cycled down it before I realized.

Montana is true cowboy country and I wasn't going to pedal through it without seeing a working ranch. Mona owns one in the highlands (above 7,000ft). From the junction where she met me in her pick-up it was an hour's drive, following a wide gravel road before turning on to a single-lane dirt road for the last 7 miles. By that point we were a long way from any main roads. What's more, there wasn't a single house, phone or power line for as far as the eye could see. It's amazing how rarely this happens anywhere. The grassy and scrubby hills rolled away to vast horizons. This truly was Big Sky Country.

The ranch was on Muddy Creek, which I thought was an odd name as everything seemed parched dry. The grasses were greener than Mona had seen them in years, she said, but the road was dusty dry. We passed a cattle fank, used to pen and sort the animals going to market, and then I saw the tiny log cabin, nestled under the lee of a hill. A little stream had sunk its course a short distance from the front. This provided a mini oasis for a few small trees to grow, but the rest of the landscape for as far as I could see looked too windswept and rugged.

The cabin was a single room, maybe 15 metres by 5 metres across, and pushing open the door meant also pushing aside the horses that had climbed the steep banks from the stream to meet the new arrivals. Inside it was stocked with enough food and clean water to last for long periods. In the middle was a rough table, the top about a foot thick and cut from a single piece of wood, bark still attached. A beam in the middle of the room had a pair of antlers mounted on it and a gas lantern hanging from it. Along the far wall were three very basic beds, a wooden one on the left and an army-style metal one in the middle; both had big Western saddles draped over their foot rails. The cabin smelled of leather and horses. The inside walls were as basic as the exterior, bare logs stacked on top of one another.

I set about starting a campfire outside while Mona prepared some steaks. All the while the three horses and three dogs, two Jack Russells and an Australian shepherd, wandered around keeping us company. I grew up on a farm and rode a lot until the age of fifteen – about the time when I cycled from John O'Groats to Land's End – when I got a motorbike to ride instead. However, I was always used to horses being in stables or fields, separate from humans. Here they stood at the cabin door looking in. We were staying in their field.

As it got dark, we sat around the fire, the horses nuzzling us for attention. Eventually the only other light was a faint blue on the far horizon. The firelight danced in the horses' watery eyes. Sitting at ground level, they were gentle giants above us. Mona was great company, but we didn't say much. It was perfect.

I slept even better than normal.

The plan was to spend the day moving some cattle, but it was nearly midday by the time we were saddled up. Another rancher drove by and stopped for a chat over the gate. There was no rush. In fact, it was one of the slowest conversations I have ever heard. I thought we had a lot to do so I felt myself getting agitated. Nothing rushed Mona, and when she noticed me trying to speed things up she reminded me, 'This is Montana time. This . . . is . . . Montana . . . time.' There were no clocks here.

My horse was called Treasure, a painted Quarter Horse, meaning chestnut and grey (white) patches. He was finely built but muscular. It was ten years since I had ridden but I didn't make a point of this with Mona. I had also never ridden Western style. A standard British saddle is a completely different shape. My Western had a high back as well as front to it, and a 'horn' at the front that I could tie a rope to if I felt the need to lasso a cow. Furthermore, I had

Starting out: the mist hangs low over the mountains as I cycle away from the Pacific, near Anchorage.

Sharing another adventure: David Peat joining me to film the first days of the expedition.

The walk-in *(right)*: moving up the Kahiltna glacier, pulling and carrying 80lb of gear.

Denali, which means The Great One, as seen from the air.

Walled in *(below)*: snow walls protect my tent at 11,000ft camp, with a view over Kahiltna Dome.

Climbing out of the shadows *(above)*: a view over our first week's climbing, with the Kahiltna glacier already in the sunlight.

A loo with a view *(left)*: at advanced base camp 14,400ft, I was surprised to find this long-drop, which boasts an unbroken view of the neighbouring peaks.

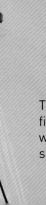

The headwall: scaling the 800m fixed line up to 16,000 ridge with advanced base camp just a speckle of tents far below.

Denali's summit *(left):* in a complete white-out at 6,198m (20,335ft), North America's highest peak.

Blizzard *(below):* descending the steepest part of the mountain in very limited visibility.

The air taxi back to Talkeetna *(above):* exhausted, we load up the small plane to fly off the mountain.

Heather comes to help *(left)*: wonderful to see my big sister after the climb and to share the first week on the road with her.

Gravel roads *(above)*: long stretches of untarred road in the Yukon Territory make cycling slow and dusty work.

That's not meant to happen! *(below)*: breaking the pedal clean off means I have to turn back.

Punctures galore *(below)*: a bad run of luck and very few bike shops through northern Canada.

Big bear country *(left)*: I soon became used to the sight of black bears throughout Canada.

More wildlife *(below)*: wood bison, moose, bears, stone sheep and other animals seemed far more abundant than people throughout the north.

Head-cam view *(right)*: getting the hang of the new camera equipment.

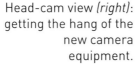

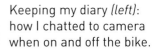

Keeping my diary *(left)*: how I chatted to camera when on and off the bike.

Beautiful British Columbia *(above)*: after weeks of trees, I reach the lakes and mountains.

Tailgating *(above)*: John and Jason singing and playing folk songs near Quesnel.

America in a heatwave *(above)*: crossing into Washington State for some hot and hilly riding.

First day cowboy *(right)*: Treasure (my horse) and me pushing the cattle on to higher pastures, away from the creek.

Going the distance *(left)*: Mike and Alanna Clear meet me in Utah for the first time on their documented honeymoon.

Canyonlands
(above): filming
on the high
plateau in the
desert.

Red rocks at sunrise (above): Arches National Park, Utah.

An unappetizing proposition
(right): struggling to find the
right quality of food.

Mountain biking on the edge
(below): looking over a vast
drop near Deadhorse Trail,
by Moab.

saddlebags on each side. There was space within the saddle's ornate design to take my GPS tracker, some water, a couple of cameras and even a tripod.

We headed back down the road we had driven up the day before, following Muddy Creek upstream. Treasure had an easy stride, and riding quickly came back to me. However, at the first water crossing I had my first refusal. Sitting deep and gathering some rein, I kept Treasure facing the water, encouraging him and expecting him to leap across. Eventually, with Mona's horse to follow, he wandered reluctantly across.

I was a bit nervous to be riding without a helmet. It was the cowboy way, but I had never ridden a horse without one, and I felt very high off the ground. Considering I often cycle without a helmet it shouldn't have been so odd, but I felt far more vulnerable.

There were over a hundred head of cattle spread across the valley bottom and Mona instructed me to split from her and with the help of the dogs move them to higher pastures. The cattle, however, seemed keen to stay near the water, so rather than move together they split and bolted in different directions as we moved in. I was on my own now with Mona taking the far side of the valley. We reached another water crossing and Treasure stopped stubbornly again. After a minute's failed negotiation, I leapt off and jumped in myself to lead him through, then jumped back on and tried to catch up with the herd. It was hot work, racing back and forth, up and down steep hills, going from a walk to a canter then stopping to turn fast and race after other scattering cows. It took a few hours to move them where we wanted, by which time I was feeling hoarse from shouting.

On the higher pastures the view across the gently rolling hills was framed dramatically by heavy dark clouds rolling in. I stopped to take it in. I could see the rain falling on the horizon and the cows starting to spread out in their new pastures. A cool breeze was ruffling Treasure's mane. On horseback was the only way to see this rugged and barren world. Even mountain biking or a quad bike up here would have been slow and exhausting, but the horses were sure-footed and so strong. I had never ridden such tough terrain, but quickly learned to trust Treasure. Wherever I wanted to go, he would find a way there – as long as it wasn't across water.

On the long ride home we crossed a number of streams, one of which had steep banks so there was no way I could walk Treasure through. I gave him some encouragement and he broke into a trot; he hesitated momentarily before taking a huge leap. If I hadn't been on a wide Western saddle which I could grab hold of I would prob-ably have been off the back. It had been a wonderful first day ranching, and not without its hairy moments, especially trying to film from horseback while riding over such uneven ground. Afterwards I was more saddle-sore than I'd been at any time on the bike since Alaska, and felt weather-beaten and exhausted. But I wanted to stay. I liked Montana time. With more practice, Mona thought I could make a good cowboy.

I had to keep going, though, so after attending to the horses we loaded the pick-up. I then discovered why it was called Muddy Creek. The rain had never reached the cabin, but to within a few miles it had, and the fine dust had created a layer of mud. It was a very thin layer and nothing I was worried about, but when the pick-up started to slew sideways I realized this silky mud was like oil on the road. We skidded constantly for the next 4 miles, never once going completely straight. I sat absolutely still, quietly impressed as Mona yanked the steering from right to left and back again, catch-ing each skid before we went off the road. Mud flew everywhere, caking the truck. We crawled our way out, eventually turning on to the gravel. Mona seemed to have enjoyed the drive. She pointed out that that was what it was like after a light shower; if it had rained properly we would have been stuck until the road had dried out. This had evidently happened many times, but wasn't a big issue. Why should a few days matter when working by Montana time? I could see that it was a tough existence in terms of money to survive, but it was a lifestyle I loved the idea of.

Back on the bike, I spent long hours wishing I was back on a horse. A bike is an inanimate machine, wonderfully efficient but, no matter how good, lacking real spirit. I tried to think of an expedition with dogs or horses that I could do.

Perhaps my mind was wandering because I was following Interstate 15 – less interesting riding, and into the wind for a few days. The first day took me 90 miles and back into Idaho. A huge meteor storm was forecast, so in the late evening I laid out my sleeping-roll in a field to watch the spectacle for a while. A few shooting stars streaked across the sky, but the next thing I knew I was waking up at two a.m., freezing. I quickly found my tent and crawled into my sleeping-bag.

8

I had less than three weeks left in the English-speaking world and my Spanish certainly wasn't ready. Since Canada I had been trying to discipline myself to a few hours a day listening to lessons on my iPod. At times this had worked, but trying to get in the right zone to pedal big hills and big miles while listening to Spanish for beginners just didn't inspire me. I felt slightly ridiculous pedalling along, reciting phrases aloud. In total I reckoned I probably knew a few hundred words.

I stopped in one little village called Hamer to find the only place open to eat was a taco van. Out of options, I grudgingly went over to order. It didn't look very clean and welcoming. A lady appeared at the window and I asked for a bottle of water and a few tacos. She replied in Spanish. I stood there dumbly, with no idea what she had said. Not a word. I then realized that for all the useless phrases I now knew, I didn't know the word for 'water'. The charade that followed was ridiculous. As I left with my lunch I wondered which was more worrying, that I was soon to pedal into Mexico not knowing how to say 'water' or that this lady was working in Idaho, in the north of the United States, and didn't know the English for 'water'.

My route had already climbed over a couple of high passes to the small community of Spencer, which is nicknamed the Opal Mining Capital of the World. I then passed the intriguingly named US Sheep Experiment Station before reaching the large town of Idaho

Falls. It's a shame that the true characters of US towns are normally hidden behind outskirts filled with generic drive-thru fast food diners, chain motels and out-of-town showrooms. Idaho Falls was no different.

There was nowhere obvious to camp so I walked into one of these motels and greeted the receptionist with a cheery 'Howdy!' He didn't seem to find it odd, but I was so startled by myself that I handed over my credit card without even asking the price. That evening, as well as staying up late to do my weekly live call to Greg James on Radio 1, I received a number of messages from a young English cyclist called Jon Lee who was currently cycling across America.

Early the next morning Jon turned up at my motel to join me for the first 40 miles, almost until the Wyoming border. I had forgotten there was a bit of Wyoming before Utah on my route. It was a slow climb, with only one odd highlight: a big yellow billboard exclaiming TOURISTS. PLEASE DON'T LAUGH AT THE NATIVES.

It was great to have some company on the road, and Jon explained how he had decided to cycle across America after watching the documentary *The Man Who Cycled the World*. He had been following my Twitter feed and had realized we were within a state of each other, so he hitched a lift to Idaho Falls. He was only eighteen and loving the adventure. He was already brainstorming what to do next, despite the worry he explained his mother was going through. I wasn't used to keeping pace with anyone and was amazed to find how much faster we were cycling together. While great for me, it wasn't helping Jon, who had to now cycle back east. We stopped for a big burger and ice-cream lunch before going our separate ways.

It was a tough, hilly and beautiful section through Caribou-Targhee National Forest, just south of Yellowstone National Park. But my one night in Wyoming wasn't so great. There wasn't a single camp spot or room as a big quad bike meeting had taken over the area, and I ended up hiding my tent at the back of a lay-by.

Hundreds of race machines buzzed about, turning the quiet town of Alpine into a high-octane circus. Back in the mountains and out of the heatwave the temperature dropped to -1°C that night. It was the first time I'd been cold in the tent.

The next day my route took me back into Idaho and through Geneva, Montpellier and Paris before crossing into Utah and starting an 11-mile climb towards Salt Lake City. Unfortunately these faux French communities didn't have any of the charm and good food that their names suggested.

The descent was my favourite yet, an almost continuous 25 miles including Logan Canyon. The road weaved a tight path downstream, overshadowed by walls of rock hundreds of metres high on both sides. Aside from being scared by some drivers obviously not used to such technical roads, it was a breathtaking ride.

In comparison, the whole Salt Lake City valley was an urban jungle. As I cycled down by far the busiest roads yet, the suburbs merged one into another without distinction. I had forgotten how intimidating US city riding could be. Vast and fast was the name of the game. For over a day I barely saw a field. It wasn't what I had expected at all.

The city was founded by the Mormon Church, or Church of the Latter Day Saints as they prefer to be called. I had noticed their increasing influence as I had pedalled south. Each Mormon church seemed to have been cast from the same mould, and they were the grandest and best-kept buildings in many of the communities I had cycled through. I spent a few hours looking around Temple Square, their heartland, which was undeniably impressive. The Church also owns 35 acres of downtown Salt Lake, and the entire area surrounding Temple Square seemed to be under construction, mainly new malls and businesses. The Church was obviously a major business as well as a religious organization. This fascinated me, as outside the Vatican I couldn't think of any place where religion, business and politics were so connected. I tried to speak to one of the Church leaders but it didn't go well. As soon as I veered towards any vaguely interesting questions, defensive answers warned me that they were too used to being victimized by the media. I wasn't there to do that, but I came away none the wiser about what the Church was really about. That said, I had a lot to learn about how to hold such interviews. I'd certainly felt out of my depth trying to film it.

It was a relief to leave the valley some way south and climb into the wilderness again. The road rose steadily for 25 miles to a barren spot called Soldier Summit at 7,400ft (2,256m). Some way up the climb I was shirtless, sweating away, lost in my own world when a weird sight passed me and stopped. I'd had some forewarning about this vision, but it still surprised me: a black vintage-looking motorbike and sidecar being ridden by a couple in all-white overalls and huge Thunderbird helmets.

Mike and Alanna Clear seemed as mad as their set-up suggested, or at least Alanna was. Mike was, if anything, slightly apologetic about her exuberance. Wielding a film camera many times the size of mine, they introduced themselves.

They had left Alaska about the same time as me and were also on a journey to Ushuaia in Tierra del Fuego. As newlyweds, and with a background in production, their dream was to make and sell a documentary about love. The story would follow their long honeymoon, driving their Ural motorbike and sidecar from north to south, interviewing everyone from pastors to polygamists and porn stars, asking them all what was their secret to lasting love. It was a charming idea; but they had recently had a run of bad luck, and I was partly to blame. Their proposed documentary was called *Going the Distance*, but just a few weeks earlier they had discovered that Hollywood was about to bring out a blockbuster by the same name; then, days later, they had learned that someone was making a BBC documentary about the same journey, albeit with a different focus. And here I was.

Despite having never met them before, Alanna threw abuse at me like I was an old friend. Boom, boom, boom! I was shaken out of my world by her loud London banter. It was all done in good humour, but I was slow to react. I'm sure I seemed very reserved and slightly odd to them. As I was blatantly alone, their standard interview about love was instead turned into questions about my love for adventure. On the back foot and unprepared, I talked quickly about the joy of getting through tough moments; this boiled down to a strange concluding statement about love being pain. It wasn't what I had meant to say at all – I just couldn't think of the correct way to describe my love for what I do – but Mike and Alanna were delighted. After this impromptu interview and a long chat, she got back in her sidecar, he in the saddle, and they left. As their plan was also to be in Ushuaia around mid-February, there was a very high chance our paths would cross again.

My wild camp at Soldier Summit was very exposed, in the narrow strip of land between the railway and the road. I relied on the cover of night to keep me hidden. The long climb was rewarded the next day with a cruisy 27 miles downhill. Great sandstone cliffs started appearing along the road, and the earth was turning from soil to windblown sand. In the north I had been caught in the heat-wave that had parched the normally green land, but here I could see that the earth was usually parched. Sage brush, coarse grass and tumbleweed were the only plants that survived. The Grand Canyon was a few hundred miles to the south, but I was now cycling in the network of plateaus and canyons that make up much of southern Utah and northern Arizona.

It was another 100-mile push to reach the town of Green River, where I welcomed my first shower in half a week and a campground with laundry. Long periods without washing have to be expected when you're living wild and filling every hour of the day. My unwashed record stands at about 2,000 miles (3,200km), from Trondheim in Norway to Warsaw in Poland. However, while in some climates I can quite happily go for weeks unwashed, in very hot and dry parts the sweat and dirt stick to me, making me far more self-conscious when I stop and meet people.

By mid-afternoon the next day I had reached the mountain biking mecca of Moab. The sandy earth gradually deepened in colour as I rode south, until the rock walls and outcrops on the long descent into town were a striking red ochre. Since Salt Lake I had met a few cyclists. The first guy had stopped when I was sitting in the dirt at the roadside, sheltered in the shadow of my bike, having a drink and some food. He had just a small bag on the back of his bike and was going fast despite a nasty headwind. I had been flying in the opposite direction with the tailwind. It was great to share such a wild spot with another person who had also pedalled his way there. The many tourists who passed in their cars and RVs would never get the same sense of wonder at this barren landscape.

The second man was much older and sitting on the roadside with a cardboard sign asking for money. I sat with him for a long while, sharing stories. He had a very old steel mountain bike that would have been next to worthless, except that it was his reliable transport. He was begging in a place where it was very unlikely cars would stop, even if they did feel sympathetic when they saw him. I soon realized that he knew this and didn't care. He enjoyed being there, watching the world go by. Inevitably he had a rough life story to tell – a teenage child he never saw and no place he could call home. He did, however, talk about his love of travelling by bike and exploring. My bike and kit was worth many thousand times his yet he asked for nothing. I shared some of my lunch, gave him enough for a few days, and carried on.

In Moab I met Allan and Pat Poertner, who despite being in their mid-sixties were passionate mountain bikers. The town itself felt like Aviemore in Scotland, or Chamonix in France, with a high street of outdoor and rental shops interspersed with cafés and the odd non-tourism business. I couldn't have pedalled through here without a closer look.

At five a.m. the next morning my alarm sounded after five hours' sleep and we drove out to Arches National Park, just north of the town. As the sun crept over the horizon I was in place to film the world turning from a shadowy grey to a fiery red. All around fins, cliffs and stacks of rock were ablaze with the day's first rays. The contrast between the light-show and the deep shadows as the sunrise raced across the valley was brilliant. We were the only people around. I barely needed a time-lapse to capture the speed of the change around me. Allan, despite having lived in Moab for many years, had also never seen the sun rise over the red sandstone and ran around exclaiming about its beauty, excitedly taking many photos.

By seven the light was subtler and the first of the day's tourists were arriving as we left the park to get some breakfast. By 9.30 we had made it to Canyonlands National Park, south of Moab, to cycle some of the famous Slickrock Trails. The Intrepid is a single-track loop in an area called Deadhorse. Our route followed the rim of the Colorado River Canyon. The trail was fairly safe, but not far off to the side was a few-thousand-foot vertical drop, which I stopped to appreciate a few times. I was borrowing one of Allan's bikes and armed with leg and arm guards. To start with I couldn't get used to the bike. It felt twitchy and bouncy compared to my heavily laden expedition bike. Allan might have been sixty-seven but he could ride this sandy, rocky terrain like a pro and I was left working far harder to keep up. Riding this fast-turning single track with a camera in one hand made for an even more exciting ride, including a few excursions into the bushes, much to Allan's amusement. By the afternoon I was shattered, and I was reassured to see that Allan was as well.

As always there was a lot to be done in any spare time: blogs to be written, photos to be uploaded and captioned, film to be backed up and couriered off, radio sections to be recorded, diaries to be written up, and social media and filming to be done, not to mention forward planning with the team. There was now more opportunity for communication on this journey than at any time before, and I no longer had the chance to wander off into my own world for long.

Looking at the big picture, I was slightly behind my original target. The production team didn't seem concerned, but it kept niggling me that from Mexico onwards the roads, food and almost every logistical concern were going to get harder. Logically, I should have been putting spare miles in the bank in North America, not assuming I could speed up when things got tougher. Now, in late August, getting to Aconcagua in the Argentine Andes by late December still seemed a very distant concern, but there was a long way and a lot of uncertainty ahead.

On a day-by-day basis I was loving the journey, but I had to admit to underestimating the scale of the task outside the cycling itself. Every time I thought ahead too far I got worried. Even if I got to Aconcagua in time there was no guarantee I would be in good enough shape to climb. Quite simply, I felt I was struggling to balance my day-to-day mileage targets with the exploring and documenting. I found I was constantly justifying to myself the stops and the filming in terms of lost miles. I was loving this opportunity to explore more of the world, but there were times, even when I was shattered, when I missed the world cycle and its simple target of 100 miles a day.

The next day I started out in a tough headwind on a road that would take me from 4,700 feet to over 7,000 feet, with many ups and downs in between, and, reduced to an average of 7mph, I soon realized that I had completely underestimated something else in these conditions: my water supply. The wind blasted my already cracking lips and dried my mouth out. I started to ration my water, rewarding myself with a sip every mile or so. With about 25 miles still to go to the next village I 'hit the wall'; my vision went blurry and my legs felt leaden. It was the first time on the journey that my body had crashed. I stopped, ate some energy bars and waited a few minutes.

I felt very vulnerable after that, and the last hour to the village of Monticello was horrid. I stopped at the only house I saw to ask for water, but it seemed deserted. Staring at my front wheel, I counted down the final 10 miles. I had less than 20ml of water left. I saved it, just in case and held a thought about the first sip of water. I was annoyed at myself for being caught short. It had taken nearly twice the time I thought it would from Moab.

Eventually, I wheeled into a garage. The first bottle lasted just a few seconds. The experts always say drink slowly when you're dehydrated, but I would like to see them actually try to do that. I had only ever been that dehydrated a couple of times and, combined with a lack of sleep, I felt completely washed out.

After a couple of big meals and drinking a lot of electrolytes I felt better the next day, but still decided to take a proper day off. That plan lasted till lunchtime, when the chance arose to go and film more of the desert landscape with a French lady I'd met in the diner. So I spent the afternoon walking, filming and taking photographs instead.

The day out of the saddle worked and I felt much stronger the next few days as I cycled into Arizona. Looking back, I realized that Salt Lake had marked a distinct north–south divide in the US. For a few months the forests had trapped me, but now I missed them. Looking ahead, I wouldn't escape these arid latitudes until mid-Mexico, when I'd reach the humid and greener tropics. At bike speed it was wild to reflect on the gradual changes from the Alaskan sub-arctic to Arizona's red deserts.

All of north-east Arizona is Navajo and Hopi Indian Reserves and I was looking forward to seeing what that actually meant. I was hoping it would be a break from small-town America, which was starting to lose its charm. I had met welcoming and kind people almost throughout this leg of the journey, but many places were predictable. Having said that, such a statement does sore injustice to some wonderfully original people and fascinating conversations. The US is beaten on too often by foreigners, because it's fashionable to do so. It is partly self-inflicted, though, because a visitor rarely sees under the hard sell to the country's real character. Most Europeans find the idea of Churches competing with each other through billboard campaigns and slogans as if they were second-hand garages, having two Starbucks per block, and being obliged to tip all a bit intimidating. But it's also a country with one of the greatest ranges of geography and culture in the world. The great irony I find in the US is that while a lot is made of freedoms and identities, you actually need to go quite far or explore quite deep to find real variety, not because it's not there, but because it's hidden under mass media and crass marketing.

On the map it said 'Indian Reserve'. However, when blogging about this, I got an offended reply for not using the term 'First Nation'. Indians are from India, I was lectured. I respect such correctness, but this was a telltale sign of a deeper fall-out. In parts of Canada I had encountered resentment between the First Nations and some white Canadians. The First Nations felt their homelands had been taken, while other Canadians felt that many of them lived off unfair benefits, which, despite being intended to accelerate education and the acquisition of skills and to allow equal opportunities, had perversely led to high unemployment and drug and alcohol abuse as there were few real jobs available and little incentive to work. However, the Navajo nation had a better chance of success. The territory is 26,000 acres, a vast homeland that is run semi-autonomously from the state. Admittedly it is also one of the least fertile, inhospitable corners of the mainland US. I wondered how it was possible to create a living in this great desert.

My first night in the reservation I camped at the back of a garage in the crossroads community of Mexican Water. The following night I made it to the touristy town of Chinle, which was overrun with Harley Davidson bikers. A market lined the main street selling all kinds of fare from Navajo wicker baskets to rip-off DVDs. The towns were friendly places, but much of the housing was very poor. Dusty yards with metal fences, old abandoned trucks and stray dogs lying around, and a white caravan or simple wooden house fitted the Midwest stereotype of tumbleweed towns. Some were undoubtedly much-loved homes, but the change in the standard of living from southern Utah was noticeable.

The cycling was magical, especially early in the morning and late on with the golden light across the ochre sands. Cactus and brush dotted the landscape, casting long shadows. If you painted it you wouldn't believe it. Late in the day my shadow pedalled along the road beside me, my only company on some very empty stretches. The communities were still far apart and I was taking extra care to carry more water and supplies. Having 6 litres strapped on to my front panniers made a noticeable difference to the bike.

Midway through Arizona I stopped for a school visit at a small town called Sanders. I was looking forward to talking to the Navajo school kids about my expedition and hoped to ask them about the reservations. I thought that the plan was to arrive in the late after-noon, be met by a lady called Mindy Porter, and stay the night with one of the school families before going into class for a few hours in the morning.

It had been a fairly tough day's riding and I was pushing hard to make the distance. With 10 miles to go I moved into an area with a phone signal and immediately got a call asking where I was and how long I would be. Unsure as to why there was such urgency, I upped the pace. When I pulled up at Sanders School, I found about thirty people gathered there, applauding and cheering loudly. The headmaster and leaders of the community came forward to introduce themselves, dressed for an occasion. I felt very self-conscious, smelly and dirty. I am guessing that I didn't match their expectations of 'Mr BBC', but they did a very good job of welcoming me. The local press had turned out too and they made a great celebrity of me, despite having never heard of me.

I was well aware of the power of the BBC name. Being part of such a known brand brings certain benefits, and it can be useful for introductions. However, having Mark Beaumont cycle into town didn't often meet people's expectations. My bearded, dirty appearance and the fact that I travelled alone and filmed on handheld cameras just did not tally with the way people around the world see Aunty Beeb. Maybe if I had been on a penny-farthing wearing a pinstripe suit and bowler hat it would have been closer to the British stereotype. In British Columbia I'd introduced myself to a lumber worker saying I was filming for a BBC documentary. The man had paused before retorting, 'Yeah right,' and walking off. I had been too amused to be offended.

I had no time to change and was led through to a back playground where a lot more people were waiting and a feast had been prepared. After a couple of short speeches of introduction, including one by the youngest children in traditional dress for a traditional Navajo welcome, everyone turned to me, expectantly. There were a lot of parents present, all of them looking at me, undoubtedly wondering why they were there. My impromptu five-minute speech was met with a flurry of polite applause.

Open fires had been set to show me how traditional Navajo bread was made. Like pizza makers, the mums gathered round, patting and flipping the dough into wide rounds before dropping them into hot oil. Some of the children were also ready to sing a few songs. It was wonderful, and I wanted to step back and capture the scene, but everyone wanted a turn speaking to me. I tried to remain as polite as possible, as I rushed around. When I turned the camera around to film a few pieces, everyone stopped and stared. Telling everyone to please act normally did little to help. I also spent my time doing a dance with the local press. To get a photo of me they inevitably ended up in my shots. As a documentary sequence it all looked very traditional and interesting until a photographer moved into frame, flashing away.

The food was delicious, and by the time it was too dark to film I was quite relieved to put the camera away and just chat. My hosts were the Goodluck family, whose girls were at the school and whose parents were traditional jewellery makers. Their great-grandfather, who had spoken little English, picked up his unusual name when people kept wishing him good luck selling his wares at the market.

He thought that 'Goodluck' was what people were calling him.

Their home was very simple but wonderfully welcoming and we sat late into the evening chatting about life on the reserve. I learned about 'the Long Walk', the period when the Navajo were expelled from their homeland only to return to find their farms and livelihoods destroyed. Their history seemed like one long battle for recognition. There was unquestionable pride in their culture but also real fears about the future as their children grew up and left the reserve in search of a different way of life.

The next morning I visited the primary and secondary school to give talks, and it was late when I got on the road. I didn't mind, it had been an amazing place to see. Sanders felt like an island in the middle of a desert. It was a part of the United States but really felt very apart. The headmaster's words stuck with me: 'Thank you for spending time here, no one ever stops in Sanders.'

The seemingly endless scrub and desert lands were becoming hard to focus on. I recorded these thoughts in my diary:

> These never-ending horizons in the US are starting to drive me nuts. It's quite impressive when you start riding these long straight roads that just dip and trough, for miles and miles. But day after day, week upon week, it's all I have had through Arizona, Utah and quite a lot for the north as well. The only place I have ever been like it is Australia – there is nobody out here. I am quite looking forward to a change. I will be in Mexico in a week and maybe it will be the same down there, but the USA has gone on for a long time. I have really enjoyed it, especially some of the mountain riding, but it's been a real challenge. These horizons, they test your mettle for sure. It will take me half an hour to get where I can see, and I am sure when I get there it will be half an hour to the next viewpoint. It doesn't help that it's a heatwave in Arizona – it's about 42 degrees.

By the following afternoon I was back into small-town America. It was just starting to rain when I spotted a rodeo arena by the roadside and turned in to see what was being heralded over the tannoy. I watched in amazement as a young teenage boy rode a young bullock into the ring for just a few seconds until he was bucked off. Standing up slowly, crying, he limped off into the arms of his proud father. A lady who was watching from the shelter of her pick-up called me over. Maybe she had noticed my mystified stare. She explained that the kids started aged six or seven on sheep before moving on to young bullocks.

In the town of Springerville, I ordered a plate of chicken and gravy. What arrived also looked like it had something to do with bullocks. However, it was the best-tasting horrible-looking meal I could remember having. Who knows what was in there. Perhaps I should have gone with my first instinct and left it.

I soon started to feel very average, which was bad news as the road towards the Arizona–New Mexico border rose gradually but constantly towards the highest point on my route so far. After a few miles the rain picked up and I felt really awful. I stopped, left the bike at the roadside and raced under a nearby tree to be sick. After hiding out there for about twenty minutes I felt much better, and the rain was easing, so I started out again.

I was soon in the tree line and had 25 miles of constant uphill to Alpine Pass at 8,550ft (2,606m). As I'd done before, I watched the world around me change from arid valley floor to thick pinewoods at the summit. The air was cooler there, with the promise of more rain. By the time I reached the top I was in better form again, at home in the highlands and back in the zone.

The next morning I relished the sweeping roads of New Mexico, every twist and turn a joy to explore. Sunset over the town of Alpine (there seemed to be several) had been a brilliant orange, the whole sky on fire, an unreal glow. During the night the crashing thunder and lightning flashes had kept on waking me. I was back into the ranchlands for the first time since Wyoming, except this was rodeo country. Each gate sported some image of a silhouetted rodeo rider, a few boasting which year their ranch had won the state championship. For the first time I was now descending instead of climbing to a crossing of the Continental Divide. In the final miles the road kicked back up to reach 6,230ft (1,900m), my final watershed in the US, before a very fast descent to Silver City.

Silver City had for a long time signified the end of the US leg. There were in fact a few days in the saddle left before arriving at the border; however, the plan was to stop here for a day to get the bike serviced and to check all my kit before heading into Mexico. The city's outskirts were as uninspiring as most US suburbs, but its heart proved to be charming. While definitely faded since its heyday as a frontier and mining town, the grand buildings in its relatively narrow streets now housed a newer array of organic cafés, tea rooms and fine restaurants. It felt rather hippy and Californian compared to the Wild West I had just cycled out of.

I have never been much of a mechanic but I can bumble by on most roadside repairs. Gila Bike and Hike, however, was the sort of bike shop where I didn't dare say much about my bike. Jack, the owner, and his fellow mechanics had that wonderfully eager and all-knowing confidence that can only be found in proper bike geeks. The fact that they too had never before worked on a Rohloff internal gearing system didn't worry them.

Leaving them to it, I set off to the laundry with unreasonable levels of excitement, before checking into the luxury of a bed and breakfast. A bath and wifi internet were my only stipulations. Later that evening I treated myself to the best meal I had in the US. I hadn't meant to go so upmarket, but I was already seated in the charming Turkish-themed restaurant when I checked the menu. I had lived through enough fast food and camp cooking to permit this, I justified. It was a slightly lonely ritual – I was the only single table in a busy room – but the food was incredible. I finished with all three of the dessert options. This was enough to bring the head chef to my table at the end of service. He stayed and chatted for half an hour, delighted to have found a European to talk food with.

I left Silver City reluctantly. My bike, my clothes and I were as clean as we had been since Anchorage. I was also well rested and well fed. In a few days I would be in Mexico, and I'd remain in the Spanish-speaking world for half a year. Things would undoubtedly be more difficult until I learned to speak some Spanish, not to mention the dangers of the borderlands. While I was definitely looking forward to the change and to seeing Mexico, I had a strong urge to pause a while longer before heading into the unknown.

It took two more days to reach the border. At lunchtime on the first day I turned left on to Interstate 10 and thus rejoined the only section that was the same for the round-the-world expedition. It was the end of August, just nineteen months after I had last been there. The 70 miles from that point to El Paso were all familiar, albeit now with the heat and limited greenery of the New Mexican summer. I even recognized a lady working in one of the gas stations, and half-expected her to recognize me. Fittingly, my last night in the US was a wild camp a short distance off the inter-state, behind some bushes. I laid the bike flat and attached myself to it by a cord, in case anyone happened to stop by in the night.

I lay in my tent that night listening to the trucks thundering by and thinking about what tomorrow would hold. The Mexican border lay just 20 miles south as the crow flew. It felt like a new chapter.

9

I planned to cross into Mexico near El Paso, Texas. This border is a stark meeting of cultures and the greatest contrast in standards of living I have witnessed. On one side is a modern US city with one million people, and through the fence is what looks from the US side like a dilapidated shanty-town of two million people. Children swim in the narrow river and stray dogs wander on the dusty pot-holed streets that are populated by army jeeps with armed soldiers.

Ciudad Juarez is the Mexican sister city to El Paso. In January 2008 I pedalled this same road, following the mesh-wire border and the Rio Grande River. I had stopped to film, but within ten minutes two border patrol jeeps arrived at speed, pulling on to the verge behind me. They were adamant that I wasn't allowed to film here, despite it being a public area. Their suspicion increased when they found Iranian and Pakistani visas in my passport. I couldn't see a possible link with protecting the Mexican border but it still took some explaining. After twenty more minutes they had waved me on with a warning.

This time I actually wanted to meet the border guards. I thought they could show me the US side of the divide and explain what I was about to face in Mexico. Before that I went to explore down-town El Paso, where I picked up a copy of the *El Paso Times*. It led with the headline JUAREZ IN SHOCK. The article detailed how two days earlier eighteen people had been shot dead outside a drug rehabilitation centre. 'The massacre is believed to be the worst ever in Juarez,' the text stated, 'which is a battleground in a war between Juarez and Sinaloa drug cartels – a war that has left more than 3,000 dead since January 2008.'

My first stop was with the blue-dress US Customs and Border Protection (CBP) department whose job it is to man the border crossings. Then I would be meeting the green-dress Border Patrol Guards, a federal agency within the CBP whose job it is to patrol anywhere on the 1,969-mile US–Mexico border that isn't a border crossing. Over the previous twelve months the CBP had checked over fifteen million vehicles and pedestrians at the border and seized about 170,000lb of illegal drugs. It was certainly interesting to watch the car searches and be allowed behind the scenes, but apart from appreciating the scale of their task, I didn't leave much the wiser about the situation I was about to face the next day in Mexico. They did, however, give me a 'US Customs and Border Protection' baseball cap – something I definitely wouldn't be wearing once across the border.

In a vehicle depot full of green-and-white-decaled Border Patrol jeeps I met a Mexican-looking lady. She looked vaguely familiar. It took me a few minutes to work it out: she was one of the guards who had reprimanded me on my last visit. I stayed quiet, but she wasn't far behind me, and within a few minutes had mentioned that I looked familiar.

We drove out together along the no-man's land on the US bank of the river. Maria had grown up in Juarez but now lived with her family in El Paso. This gave her an in-depth understanding of the issues, and as I spoke with her I was struck by her lack of ego, or all-American bias. Many of the people I had met that morning seemed to lack any affinity with the Mexicans. It was refreshing to hear an informed female point of view in such a male-dominated world.

I learned that the drug cartels and human trafficking had long been behind Juarez's violent history. The city is home to over two hundred thousand drug addicts. However, the stakes had changed recently. When the National Action Party came into power in 2000, the first change in the governing party in Mexico for seventy years, they had tried to act swiftly to break up the numerous mafias' stranglehold on the city. But the government hadn't trusted the local police not to get embroiled in the conflict and had sent in the Mexican Army, which brought scenes of civil war to the streets. Breaking up the established drug scene and human trafficking routes then caused what had been mainly infighting to spread into the wider community. The situation was now more dangerous instead of less, and most residents trusted neither the criminals nor the police and army. Another consequence of disrupting the criminal income in the region was an increase in kidnapping.

It wasn't uncommon for solo Border Patrol guards to come across big groups of illegal immigrants. Situations could get dangerous, but others were more like humanitarian missions, helping woefully supplied people with food and water so they wouldn't perish in the arid wilderness along the border, before returning them to Mexico. Some of the stories were desperate. For the human traffickers, life seemed to be no more valuable than the cost of each person's transfer to US soil.

There was a lot of radio chat in the hours during which Maria and I drove around, but no captures or border breaks happened close enough to witness. It wasn't something I felt I needed to see.

Back downtown I met a man called Julian, a Reuters journalist from Juarez, whose task it was to make sure I got past Juarez safely. In fact, the plan was for him to shadow me through the whole Chihuahua region – about 700km (435 miles) from north to south. Despite its innocent name – for most people a cute lap dog would spring to mind – Chihuahua was high on the BBC High Risk Team's 'concern' list. There was no way I would be allowed to carry on alone.

It was an interesting testing point with the production team. I almost always wanted to carry on alone, therefore keeping my profile and costs lower. But this was an in-house BBC project and I no longer controlled such decisions. During the world cycle I had pedalled into southern Pakistan for the best part of a thousand miles against the advice of the BBC, because it had been my decision to make. An organization can't take the same risks as an individual, but it was still a dynamic I was getting used to. It's always nice to feel looked after, but that comes at the cost of a degree of freedom.

I chose to cross the border at a quieter point, just west of Juarez, which was more bike-friendly. Leaving the US was incredibly easy; the border guards hardly seemed to care. Then, when I was already in Mexico, I realized that my equipment carnet hadn't been signed out. Going back north wasn't so easy. I managed to get back to the office, but the officers wouldn't sign or stamp what I needed. Out of options, I left, knowing it would almost certainly cause a problem for me later.

Despite now being on a road that skirted the city, I wasn't going to come this far without seeing downtown Juarez, especially now that I had Julian's help. Leaving my bike and his van locked up, we walked the final bit, until we were standing at the opposite side of the bridge I had stood on with the CBP officers the day before. It was only a few hundred metres, but it felt like another world. The tension was palpable, or maybe that was just my impression because I was feeling jumpy. I stuck close to Julian, nervously looking around. He was wonderfully laid back. In his forties, medium-framed but slim with a trim moustache, he was dressed a shade smarter than most others around us.

Filming was definitely attracting more attention than normal, and Julian was keen to keep moving. I had never before seriously checked for anyone following me while I was filming. We were both careful not to meet anyone's eye. There were very few white people around and I felt I really stood out, far taller than most. He had his Reuters journalist identity with him, and I had my BBC business card. We had every right to film in public places, but Julian predicted that we would be stopped.

The bridge was a confusion of civilians, police and army. With so many people around I hoped to go unnoticed for a few minutes. To start with I kept the camera at waist height, as if I wasn't filming, panning slowly around then walking across the road. Then I noticed a soldier standing on guard. Despite looking away quickly, I knew he was watching me. We were approached and waved over to a quieter space. Julian spent the next twenty minutes being questioned, and our identity cards were copied down. Three soldiers stood around us, playing idly with their rifles. I kept quiet, despite direct questions, as I had no idea what was being said and Julian made no effort to involve me by translating. None of them spoke any English either so copying down the details on my BBC card was a very laborious process, and ultimately useless. Julian acted unconcerned, which was reassuring, but I was worried. The worst part was that there didn't seem to be anything formal or systematic about their actions. The fact that they didn't seem sure what to do made me very nervous about what they might decide to do next.

I could tell that they were asking to see what was on my camera, and that Julian was doing his best to talk that down. We were eventually released and walked away. I tried to walk normally, but just wanted to keep looking behind me. Julian was more angry than worried, and kept repeating how stupid the soldiers were. The soldiers hadn't known who Reuters or the BBC were, or what rights journalists had. They were simply suspicious of everyone, and were therefore more a part of the problem than the solution. It was a fight that Julian was used to.

Downtown Juarez was not as dilapidated as the views from the US suggested. Old American school buses, colourfully repainted, filled the air with diesel fumes, and there was a confusion of commuters, street-sellers and youths. The imposing buildings had a tired majesty about them, reminders of brighter days when Juarez had been a vibrant border town. On most streets, signs jostled messily for space, while telephone lines stretched overhead like a frantic spider's web. The vehicles were all the same as in the US, but most were a generation older. Towards the south, the outskirts were once again familiarly filled with fast food diners, showrooms and US-style motels and hotels. There were no tourists to be seen now, but the influence of the north had undoubtedly stuck.

It was about one p.m. when I finally cleared the city and was cycling in scrubland. By sunset I had made 83 miles. On a fully laden bike it was a massive push, partly motivated by a wish to leave Juarez far behind, partly by a need to reach Villa Ahumada. There would be no wild-camping in the Chihuahua region. All afternoon Julian stayed within sight, which must have been a very dull drive in his noisy red pick-up. The roadside was empty. Only the toughest of grass would grow on this arid ranchland, and I couldn't see any livestock. However, the road was busy, with a considerable army and police presence. Julian pointed out how each police pick-up had at least one army soldier in it in an effort to break down corruption in the force. The army pick-ups looked particularly intimidating, often with a mini machine-gun attached to the cab roof, the officers with masked faces. It was not something I ever expected to see outside a war zone, and I had never considered Mexico to be a war zone. I certainly hadn't ever picked up from the press the seriousness of the situation.

Entering Villa Ahumada, I saw a long line of brightly lit stalls off to the right. Quite a few men were on the roadside, waving their arms or pieces of clothing, calling loudly, beckoning. I was unsure what was going on. Julian was delighted. After being ushered towards one of the many trolleys, owned by a man called Rica if the sign was anything to go by, he ordered a couple of *quesadillas* with *asaderos*. I was very hungry, but couldn't imagine anything worse than trying to satisfy that with a bundle of chilli-infused cheese wrapped in a tortilla. I have always been bad with spicy food, maybe because I wasn't brought up eating it. Pakistan, India and Thailand were my greatest culinary challenges on the round-the-world cycle, but I could see that Mexico would also be tricky. Still,

I was up for trying this, until I spotted Julian starting to sweat. He seemed to be taking great pleasure from the obvious pain his food was causing him. If it was at his threshold, it would have blown my head off, so I declined and went in search of some pizza. I would have to tiptoe around the hot stuff until my tolerance increased.

Being under escort took some getting used to, mainly because it was harder to pace myself. My only previous escort had been an armed one through southern Pakistan. In comparison, Julian spoke English and was great company. As I pushed more big days through northern Mexico, I started to really enjoy the change of scene with the fast rolling roads. Hills silhouetted the far horizon, sometimes rolling, at other times impressive table-tops and ledges, but there were no natural obstacles to the road. There were, however, numerous army checkpoints, and we nearly got turned back at the first hurdle. Julian didn't have the correct papers for his vehicle. Only after a long wait and a heated dispute on his part were we let through.

Power lines were the only constant at the roadside until the city of Chihuahua. It was relatively dull cycling, therefore easy to focus on fast miles. But near the city I passed a series of huge billboards that shocked me out of my own thoughts: SECUESTRADORES: HASTA $1 MILLION DE PESOS DE RECOMPENSA. Underneath were four large mugshots of three men and a woman, followed by a phone number to call. Different boards had different messages with different wanted persons and different rewards, including one that had five photos of the De La Cruz family. A family business, Julian pointed out. Like the old Wild West, here was a bounty on the head of kidnappers and other wanted criminals.

These billboards were one of the only reminders that this was the kidnap capital of the world. It was so barren and empty otherwise. It struck me that even if I was targeted, there was little defence either Julian or I had. Neither of us was armed. I would be relying only on his local knowledge, ability to communicate and his vehicle as a means of making a quick get-away. In my first few days in

Mexico I had barely used a word of Spanish. I knew many words and phrases by now, but when I listened to any Mexicans I couldn't understand a word. It worried me; soon I would be on my own again. So I asked Julian to teach me more Mexican Spanish.

On the outskirts of Chihuahua were huge developments of breezeblock bungalows nestled together in row after row, each as nondescript as the next, with no gardens or parks. Much of Mexico's industry comes from factories, mainly supplying to the North American markets. This was the hive where the workers lived. It was a better standard of living than in many places I had seen, but it was striking to see humans so massed together, reduced to numbers.

The city itself is key to Mexico's history. The Catholic priest Father Miguel Hidalgo was shot and killed here in 1811 for leading the revolution against the Spanish government which led to the independence of the Mexican people. The Government Palace was an interesting building, with elaborate wall paintings depicting scenes from battles in Mexico's history.

I found the city centre most telling. It seemed less run-down than Juarez and was brightly decorated for the forthcoming Independence Day celebrations. The military presence seemed even more out of place, maybe because of the grandeur and seeming order of the surroundings. Around the government buildings were heavily armed vehicles and soldiers whom I again tried to film, with greater success.

Across from the Government Palace, in a large public square, stood a wooden board that had been lined with hundreds of large nails. From many of these nails a nametag hung. Also attached to the board was a four-foot wooden cross that bore the text ¡NI UNA MAS! (No More!). It served as a permanent protest to the government against the violence, each nail signifying a girl or woman who had been killed in Juarez in the recent conflicts. Some of the victims' photos had been stuck on the back of the board. It was a ghostly and sad summary of the situation.

*

It was 101 days since leaving Anchorage when I pedalled out of Chihuahua. I was in contemplative mood, both reflecting on all the experiences so far and musing on what I was now seeing in Mexico. Parts of the country remain such popular holiday destinations that it is easy to get a false impression of the place. While I had acknowledged that parts of Mexico would be tricky, I now realized how ignorant I had been of the scale of the country's problems. It's a part of the world that gets relatively little press. If international news agendas were set proportionately to the number of kidnappings and murders, Mexico would be the biggest regular news story. There had been close to a thousand reported kidnappings in the Chihuahua region alone in the last year.

Apart from Julian, and partly because of Julian, I hadn't met many other Mexicans yet. Everyone I had come across, with the exception of the police and army, had seemed very friendly, immediately welcoming in nature. I had long wanted to experience the colours, music and warmth of the Latino countries. Even here, in the troubled north of Mexico, which in many ways fashions itself after the USA, I could see this tradition fighting through.

On my second last day with Julian three road cyclists had passed me, waited for me to catch up, then for the last 40km that day had stayed with me. Despite my saying they should go on at their own pace if they wanted to, they insisted on keeping me company. My bike probably weighed as much as all of theirs put together, but I pedalled harder to try to give them a fair run. It was my best Spanish lesson yet. The conversation was limited and confusing but very funny. It was certainly a kind gesture that I can't imagine happening that often back in Europe whenever a group of racers meet a tourer.

On my last day with Julian I had spotted some smoke rising from what looked like a building site at the side of the road. On the side of a brick wall was scrawled in red graffiti SE COMPRA CHILE ROJO. Even my poor Spanish could translate that they were in the business of buying red chillies. I stopped, waited for Julian to catch up and suggested we go and have a look.

As I cycled down the dry rutted driveway I could see two men in discussion standing at the back of a big blue pick-up truck. At the side was a hook and scales to weigh large bags. I had arrived just in time to see a farmer selling his fresh crop of jalapeño chillies. I let Julian do the initial talking. We were immediately welcomed with the offer of a full tour.

What had looked like the foundations of a building site were in fact six vast open-air ovens, each about 5 metres wide by 50 metres long, with slatted floors and low brick walls, and shallow trenches dug along the outside so logs could be fed underneath to keep fires burning. Leaving the bike, I walked over and was met by the sight of a bed of chillies being slowly smoked and toasted; each oven was a different shade of toasted. The idea of one chilli strikes fear into me, so the sight of millions, everywhere I looked, was my idea of hell. The man who had bought the fresh chillies explained that it took about five days of smoking and sun-drying to turn jalapeños, already one of the spiciest of chillies, into a chipotle, which is reserved only for the hottest sauces. It took 4.5kg of fresh chillies to make a kilo of chipotle, and these were all destined for a factory in Mexico City.

We wandered over to one of the ovens where a couple of younger workers were shovelling up the finished chipotles into bags. I was trying to film but my eyes started running and I kept sneezing. The air was thick with chilli vapours. I asked Julian to translate for me.

'In Mexico, is it a test of being a real man being able to eat the hot chilli?'

'Of course,' Julian laughed.

'No, please ask the worker,' I insisted, gesturing towards the young man with the shovel. He had a thin towel draped over his head to keep the beating sun off, was a bit overweight, and looked in his early twenties. I hoped he would take the bait.

He paused, obviously weighing up whether to demonstrate it or not.

'That thing is hot, it's good,' he said as he picked up a toasted dry chipotle. 'Often, when we have lunch we just grab one of these chillies and . . .' He bit it in half. 'Es pica,' he muttered after a few seconds – 'It's hot.' Within a few seconds he started pumping one arm up and down and turning around on the spot in the fashion of a man who had trapped a finger in a door. '¡Es picoso!' he shouted, jumping out of the bed of chillies – 'It's the hottest!' 'I need some water!' he bellowed over his shoulder as he ran off for the tap. The other workers, Julian and I were left in stitches. I have no doubt that if I had tried the same thing I would have woken up in hospital.

Crossing into the Durango region the next day felt like a major milestone. I was now heading off on my own having got used to Julian's amicable company, and I felt the trepidation. I felt tired, too, having pushed six big days since entering Mexico. With little ceremony we shook hands, and I waved goodbye. He did a U-turn and sped off. The road was straight for as far as I could see and I stood next to my bike for a while, watching his pick-up getting smaller, just as it started to rain.

Julian was a wonderfully overqualified escort. We had talked late into most evenings about all kinds of things, and it had been easy to relax into having company on the road. Having part-published a book called *Juarez: The Laboratory of Our Future*, he was certainly an expert on the area.

It had rained most nights in Mexico, but this was the first time during the day, when it was far too hot to wear a rain shell, which would become just as wet inside with sweat. Over the next ten days I planned to head over the Sierra Madre Occidental Mountains and down to the Pacific, a transition that would take me well into the tropics. I would need to get used to the rain, then. Looking around at the hardy bushes and grasses that clung to life in the dry soils of Durango it was bizarre to imagine such a complete change.

I planned to carry on finding a room for the night rather than wild-camp for now so I had to work out my distances to towns ahead carefully. But within a mile of the Chihuahua/Durango border I passed a sign with a red line drawn over a picture of a bicycle. For no obvious reason I was no longer allowed to ride here. There was certainly plenty of space down the generous hard shoulder, so this concerned me. Twenty kilometres further on I reached a petrol station which had the odd feature of open-plan toilets – no doors on the cubicles. Studying the map, I saw that a smaller road ran parallel to me about 10km to the west; being the older road, it also passed through more towns. If I stayed on this trunk road, there was no way I would reach a town that night.

I turned off and found myself on a single-lane connector track. Within a kilometre it ran out of tar. What should have taken less than thirty minutes on a tarred road surface took well over an hour as I crawled along on the worst road I had seen since Hatcher Pass in Alaska. The stony dry earth made for a jarring ride and I stopped after a few kilometres to give serious thought to turning back, saving time, saving my bike and taking a risk with wild-camping. Thankfully, just before reaching the old road, the tar restarted again. I had been worried that this was also going to be a dirt road, in which case I would have had no choice but to go back.

Finding a room in Ceballos was tricky because of my limited Spanish. I knew a good amount of basic phrases but needed to learn how to join them up in conversation. My ear for the language was improving and I could now understand far more than I could say, but in these rural parts people obviously weren't used to helping out beginners by speaking slowly and using simpler vocabulary. They tended just to look at me as if I was stupid. It was quite funny but frustrating. I was certainly going to learn. Eventually I was successful and was pleased to find a room for 200 pesos (about £10).

Across the street I found a small restaurant where I ordered my first meal in Spanish. The doors and windows were all open, and metal tables with plastic covers stood on the bare concrete floor, with plastic seats. A group of about a dozen middle-aged men had pushed together some tables into an island and were drinking Modelo beer out of cans, talking and joking loudly. I was the only other customer. There was no menu to try to decipher; the owner, who looked as much of a manual worker as the drinking men, recited the options quickly. Among many unknown words I heard 'burrito'.

'Sí, burrito, por favor,' I said. '¿Es carne o pollo?' I was trying to figure out if they were meat or chicken burritos.

Back in the US a burrito is normally a brick of food with beans, cheese, guacamole, some salsa, maybe meat and some other bits all wrapped in a large tortilla. It's a big meal. In Mexico, the home of the burrito, I was still hungry after six of them: each one was a modest tortilla with a little meat and beans inside. The man looked unsure when I ordered just two, then laughed when I ordered two more, and gave me a free Coke when I ordered the last two.

Halfway through my meal four more men came in, each carrying an instrument. Without any introduction, they started up. The noise was remarkable; no wonder the windows were left open. One man bellowed forth in song while his friends accompanied him on *guitarrón, vihuela* (another guitar-like instrument) and maracas. It seemed an unlikely cheap diner for such live music. The drinking men sat back, unable to converse over the din of the mariachis, clapping and cheering enthusiastically. Being the only other customer, it felt like a private concert and I did my best to join in. However, when one of the singers shouted over some banter, I obviously had no idea what he'd said, nor did I have the words to reply, so I just smiled as all the men in the place turned to look at me.

The clocks had gone back again at the border. Having started in Alaska eight hours behind the UK, I had now cycled across four time zones. Regardless of this I was very tired, and I soon made my way back to my very basic room for eleven hours' sleep.

The smaller road was far busier than the highway, which I

couldn't understand to start with. It was more dangerous cycling as I now had no hard shoulder and was constantly being passed by some big and very smoky trucks. When they passed each other in opposite directions at the same time as passing me they had no room at all to pull wide and I would be forced on to the verge for a few metres. I then got completely lost in the city of Torreón, which wasted a few hours, and was relieved to reach the outskirts again. It was then that I figured out the issue with the highways. The 'Libro 49' was the old road that I was allowed on, whereas the trunk road was now a toll road. It seemed that most Mexicans preferred the busy, potholed and longer old road than paying for the fast dual carriageway. On the way out of the city from my road, I looked down enviously at a tollbooth and the trickle of vehicles passing through.

Over the next 6 miles I was twice forced off the road completely. It was by far the most dangerous road I had been on since Alaska and I was making slow progress along the broken edge, rarely able to cycle wide where the road was smoother. The dual carriageway was still in the same valley, a few miles to the east, so at the first village of La Loma I decided to try to find it. I would be breaking the law, but I was willing to take that risk over the dangers of the small road. La Loma was tiny, and a donkey and cart was tied up outside the main village shop where I managed to find a couple of bananas and some sweet but stale pastries for lunch. It wasn't ideal but it was all they had.

On the far side of town the road ran out so I persevered on a dirt track along the edge of a field. A group of boys who were kicking a football about stopped and stared as I now pushed my bike past them. It was another few kilometres pushing uphill before I spotted the dual carriageway up a steep bank a few hundred metres ahead. The last embankment was a loose footpath and I had to take all the pannier bags off and carry them up to the roadside before putting the bike on my shoulder and clambering up the loose gravel. The road was empty – a vehicle passed once every few minutes – and I pedalled along in complete peace. Unfortunately the lunch had given me a sore stomach and I felt pretty down on the bike. I had to stop a couple of times to be sick. Steeper terrain was now far closer, with hills rising on both sides and the road rising and falling in long drags.

When I did reach the next tollbooth I carried on cycling, assuming I would just be waved through. A large office building was off to the side and a number of booths allowed the traffic, what there was of it, to fan out and get through faster. As I drew level I heard a stern shout. A man about my age walked out from his booth talking loudly as he approached me. It took a minute for me to realize that as well as telling me off for being there, he was also asking me to pay. He was now talking at me angrily; I hadn't said a word yet. If he had calmly asked me to pay the same as a motorbike I probably would have done so, but his aggression annoyed me.

In my broken Spanish I pointed out that there was no charge for bikes, and made to cycle on. He then lifted his baton out of his belt loop, saying something else I didn't understand. I realized that I had handled this badly. It was a tiny amount of money to quibble over, but I was doing it on principle. I tried to string together some explanation about being on this road as the other was too danger-ous. He didn't understand or care. This went on for quite a while, each of us at best half-understanding the other. The winning ticket was asking him to call his boss – a phrase I surprised myself by producing. He eventually did. Returning from his booth, he waved me on with his baton without another word. I pedalled off, feeling victorious but also a bit stupid for getting into such a situation.

Over the next few days the road gradually climbed on to the central Mexican plateau at nearly 8,000ft (2,440m). The next goal was to reach the sixteenth-century city of Zacatecas by 15 September to witness the Independence Day celebrations. It was hot climbing. I remained in a real mental trough and struggled to stay focused on the miles. The tollbooth fall-out was just one sign of a dark mood I had been struggling with for nearly a week now.

Every journey is a mental rollercoaster, and there had been many highs and lows already since the end of May. I am normally pretty good at blanking out the big picture and getting lost in the day-to-day focus, but now I felt exhausted. The sheer scale of the challenge ahead, on top of how isolated I now felt, was too daunting. I wasn't even at the halfway point, and the pressure to reach Aconcagua was greater than ever. Climbing an even higher peak than Denali wasn't an easy thing to motivate myself for when I felt burned out on the bike.

On a day-to-day basis I loved every challenge, but it felt endless; there were still five months to go. I needed a different focus, so I devised a plan to try to reach Aconcagua in time to take at least three days off before the climb. That gave me a three-month target to a short rest, which was easier to focus on and stay motivated for than a three-month target to start a climb. On the grand scale it would be a very short break, but I hoped it would prove enough of a change to dig myself out of the mental slump.

10

In the end, the afternoon rains were the only thing I had to outrun in northern Mexico. Some of the downpours were torrential. I sat out one storm in a village, looking out of a shop window at the street as it became a fast-flowing stream. It then stopped as quickly as it had started and I carried on, past a group of children swimming in the floodwaters at the roadside.

At another small town about 1,200km (750 miles) into Mexico I finally figured out how to ask where a laundry was and get my kit cleaned. The women there were all smiles, but I think the laugh was on me for my attempts at conversation, and no doubt my smell.

The road to Zacatecas meant days of climbing, but I arrived on schedule, at lunchtime on the 15th, to find the narrow roads jammed with traffic, the pavements busy and glittery decorations draped from every lamppost. The atmosphere was one of eager anticipation. After finding the hotel my team had booked me into, I changed out of my cycling clothes and went off to explore.

The army were out in force again, this time constructing barriers around the Plaza de Armas, the central square, with walk-through metal detectors. Each soldier wore knee-guards, a thick stab vest, and a black face-mask. Most wore sunglasses too. I would later be told that soldiers rarely work in the area they are from, thus reducing the possibility of family ties with criminals, and the chances of families of soldiers being held hostage. Even so, they obviously didn't want to be recognized. Along one of the main streets, which were paved with large cobbles, vendors were selling their wares, like flags and huge straw hats. Many of the men were dressed in what looked like old-fashioned soldiers' outfits, with bright red loose trousers and white shirts held tight with blue cloth belts. There were variations on this theme of the nineteenth-century Mexican independence fighter, but one feature in common was the carrying of a firearm. I leaned against the cathedral wall for a long while watching the real soldiers stopping the fancy-dress soldiers to check their rifles.

Zacatecas sits in a bowl, with the houses built on its steep sides. Many of its buildings were orange-tinged sandstone, with balcony windows and intricate ornamentation. A cable car runs across the whole city from one side to the other. I didn't have time to take this tourist trail but I did want to climb up one side to get the lie of the land. I started following steep steps cut between houses, then along narrow streets at different levels, before finding more steps upwards. Some were so narrow and broken that I wasn't sure if I was now on private property or still on the city streets. As I climbed, loud bangs started exploding above me. I paused, unsure what they were. Most likely fireworks, I reasoned. But it was still daylight, so I didn't see the point. Rifles may not have been allowed downtown, but as a re-enactment of the fight for independence they were firing rifles on the hill.

I carried on cautiously, and after about twenty minutes cleared the last houses. The irregular explosions were still going off above me, so I headed on up the steep dirt track very carefully. Standing on a small plateau, a group of about twenty dressed-up soldiers were firing muzzle-loading rifles into the air, among them a few teenage girls. I watched as they were handed loaded rifles that they then fired off at arm's length, hiding from the recoil. I skirted wide around until I was on a high rock behind them with a great view of Zacatecas at my feet. No one took any notice of me. I reasoned that they must be firing blanks, as real shots would have to rain down somewhere. However, it was very realistic, and each rifle went off with a puff of smoke. I sat there for over an hour taking it in. By then it was almost completely dark and the city lights were looking very welcoming: I'd started to feel a bit vulnerable up here with these exuberant youths.

Back in the city centre it was nine p.m. and parties were going on everywhere. I felt like a spectator with no idea about what I was watching. My confidence with the Spanish language was certainly growing, but conversation was still limited to finding food, accommodation and basic directions. Explanations of Mexico's history were beyond me. So I went to a youth hostel – always a safe bet for bilingual and welcoming people – which the research team had already contacted so that I could join someone local for the celebrations. I was met by Maria, who agreed to be my guide.

The hostel had an open rooftop which was crammed with people from all over the world. It was a good starting point, but I was keen to escape to see how the locals party. The hostel owner was an exuberant character and appeared clutching a bottle of Antiguo Origen, his favourite tequila. I wasn't keen, but I wasn't given much of an option. I hadn't had a drink for months, but his friends threw a huge sombrero on my head and he started pouring into my mouth. 'Uno, dos, tres . . .' – I'd assumed he would stop after 'three' – '. . . nueve, diez!' On the count of ten he moved on to his next victim. Not everyone managed to down this in one, and I soon wished I hadn't. My tolerance was shot and I still had filming to do.

Maria and I escaped and headed into the central square. It was now crammed with people, and we were checked for weapons.

At exactly eleven p.m. on 15 September, every town and city in Mexico marks the moment of independence from Spanish rule. The female mayor of Zacatecas appeared shortly before the hour on the town hall balcony. Huge national flags were draped across the front of the building and spotlights danced across the façade. A brass and drum band added a military beat to the din of thousands of people. The mayor's speech was beyond me, but its patriotic rallying was contagious and I joined the crowds in their whoops and cheers. The speech culminated in her shouts of '¡Viva Mexico!' ('Long live Mexico!') at which the crowd echoed '¡Viva!'

'¡Viva Mexico!'

'¡Viva!'

The crowd cheered again as fireworks broke out. They came from the rooftops of the surrounding buildings, far closer than I had ever seen them. It definitely made them more exciting, as each flash illuminated the faces of the watching multitude. The cable car wire that hung across the city had also been set with a firework that rained down like sparks off an arc welder. The atmosphere, trapped in a sea of bodies with fireworks going off so close, was electric. I doubt that 'safe' fireworks will ever have the same effect for me now.

The party went on till gone three a.m. I barely drank anything else because my body hadn't appreciated the shock of the tequila, and I went to bed feeling decidedly average. At nine I woke to the sound of a marching band. My window was wide open and all I wanted was the bed to swallow me up. After getting dressed I went to the balcony and saw that the streets were lined with people and a parade was passing. For over an hour the military, emergency services and even schools marched by in time to drums and brass bands. The sunlight hurt my eyes and the noise offended my head, but I filmed it all. It was a brilliant spectacle; I just wasn't ready for it.

I had planned to cycle on without a day off, but late the previous night a visit to the Zacatecas bullfight had been suggested. My natural response was no. As a tourist I would have no interest in seeing a bullfight, but the locals had spoken very passionately about it and I reasoned that if it were as important a cultural event as they were saying it was then it would be worth seeing. I might not like it, but it would help me understand Mexico better.

Going to see *los toros* is very much a family day out in parts of Mexico; in Zacatecas, around what looked like an ancient gladiators' arena was a kids' carnival. Maria had brought along another friend of hers. In his late fifties, Carlos had been born in Texas, but was half Mexican and now lived for most of the year in Japan. As a lifelong enthusiast of bullfighting, he was the reason we were both here. 'It's the only thing that ever starts on time in Mexico,' he joked as we joined the big queues.

Inside the arena we sat in steep tiers around a bullring lined with high barriers painted bright red. As the place filled, so the excitement grew. There were a lot of women in the crowd, and a lot of children.

'So, is this considered a sport?' I asked naively.

'First of all, it's not a sport.' Carlos had to speak up to be heard. 'It's a spectacle of death.' He didn't look the sort of man prone to exaggeration. 'Hopefully, you won't see death today,' he added, reassuringly.

'Oh, they don't always kill the animals?' I asked, relieved.

'No, they always kill the animals, but they don't always kill the bullfighters. If a bullfighter gets killed, the next one takes his bull and the two that belong to him. If two bullfighters get killed, one guy has to kill all six bulls.'

'The event doesn't get stopped if a bullfighter dies?'

'No. Death is just temporary – it goes away.'

Carlos's explanation surprised me. In Spanish there are two verbs for 'to be'. In English you would say both 'I am a man' and 'I am tired', whether the state is a permanent or a temporary one. In Spanish there are two verbs: *ser* describes a permanent state while *estar* describes any temporary state. The Spanish for 'he is dead' is 'está muerto'.

'We consider death to be temporary,' Carlos reiterated.

This sort of philosophy was too fanciful for me. There is nothing more permanent than death. I don't believe anything happens once you're dead – all the more motivation to do something worthwhile while you're alive.

My thoughts wandered outside those gladiatorial walls to many of the people I had already met in Mexico and how they remained upbeat and outgoing in the face of conflict and danger. Certainly what Carlos had said explained a lot about the attitudes of the Mexican people as a whole.

The first bullfighter was on horseback, and he rode around show-boating to the crowd dressed in a cream embroidered jacket and other finery, his horse's mane tied in big blue ribbons. A bull was released. The bullfighter made another half circuit of the arena before the bull cut him off, charging the horse. The fighter fell under his own horse as the bull circled off. The crowd leapt to their feet, gasping. A number of bullfighters ran into the arena to divert a second attack on the fallen rider who was lying still on the ground. Just moments before Carlos had been explaining how famous that rider was, how he was one of the best. To my novice eyes he hadn't been very observant or quick to react to the bull. His horse could easily have outrun it with a bit of direction. The rider had been focused on the crowd instead. A stretcher was brought into the arena and the man was carried off, now moving but in obvious pain with a broken leg. I think I was more relieved to see his horse on its feet, trotting out of the arena safely.

The next bullfighter entered the ring on foot to take on the loose bull, but only once they had drawn its blood from the safety of horseback. This second horse had been a very heavy breed, like a Shire, and wore thick armour over its legs so that when the bull charged it made no impression, which allowed the rider to spear its neck with impunity. The weakened bull now faced the bullfighter.

What I hadn't realized was that he had to follow a very strict process. First, sharp stakes needed to be stuck into the bull's shoulders. Bulls can't see straight in front of them, only out to the side, so the safest way to do this is straight over the horns. Then came the traditional dance with the red cape, where the fighter showed his daring. Then came the kill, with a sword between the shoulders. There is only a very small area that will allow a clean kill.

The bullfighter took many attempts to find this, the crowd booing its disapproval.

A couple of other heavy workhorses came into the ring and were harnessed to the fallen bull which was dragged out as the fighter turned to the crowd. The president of the bullfight, watching from his private box, was meant to listen to the crowd before rewarding the fighter. If the crowd decided it was a good fight he would be given an ear, or two ears; if it was deemed excellent, he could be awarded a hoof. Mixed booing and cheering echoed around the arena; flowers and hats were thrown into the ring.

This routine was repeated with five more bulls and two other fighters.

The next day I cycled out of Zacatecas still thinking about the fight. As a spectacle steeped in history that helped explain the mentality of a nation, it was interesting, and you had to respect its theatre. Some of the fighters had put on an amazing show; they were celebrities in their world. I was glad to have witnessed it, but I hadn't enjoyed it. It was impossible to escape the fact that it was animal cruelty, and an unfair fight. By the end, sitting in that big, bloodthirsty crowd as it judged kill after kill just felt barbaric. To my mind it was unfathomable to allow young children to experience that, but then again I am sure every culture has customs which seem like oddities to outsiders. I think I now understood bullfighting as a cultural event, but I couldn't like it.

Ahead of me was 400 miles (650km) to the Pacific, across the Sierra Madre Occidental Mountains, an extension of the Rocky Mountains. I was soon passing between 10,000ft (3,000m) peaks. On average I was descending, but for the first time in Mexico I now also faced some long and steep climbs. Mexicans tend to build their roads straight up hills rather than follow a more twisting alpine ascent. I was in very green farmlands in the lower terrain and cactus-peppered ranchlands higher up. It was beautiful compared to the weeks I had just come through.

The first day I rode 85 miles to the town of Tabasco. The name seemed to have nothing to do with the hot sauce, which is made in Louisiana. However, I did enjoy eating fifteen quite spicy tacos from a rather surprised street vendor. A normal portion was five, so when I went back for my third plate he gave me a hearty thumbs-up and joked that I needed it to stay tall.

I called home, and heard that my global circumnavigation had been voted by Guinness World Records one of the top 100 significant world records of the decade. I celebrated sat on a bench outside the town church, drinking a can of Coke, trying to chat to an old man about cycling.

The next morning I couldn't find my way out of Tabasco so I stopped to ask a young man. He told me to wait where I was and raced off. Before long he returned with his car and insisted on escorting me for about 5 miles, well into the countryside. I cycled along behind him worrying about why he was doing this, what he might want from me. When he stopped he explained that he had lived in Chicago for the last five years and was just home visiting his parents. Given that, his English was poor, but he was very friendly. He wanted to give me some money or food. I couldn't understand why and insisted that I didn't want any, with thanks. He replied that he really wanted to help me on my travels. I couldn't take his money and didn't want to lose more time over a meal, having just eaten, and in the end I managed to keep going. It was just one of the many kind gestures I had experienced already in Mexico, and I reflected on how rarely that had happened to me in Europe or North America.

The scenery got even better. I cycled down long avenues of shady trees, and passed fields with what looked like giant aloe vera plants. Out of the farmlands it was just as green, with little gorges, water-falls, and some colourful rocky outcrops and caves. The map I was using was now far too large-scale to indicate such contours. It was also missing a lot of the smaller towns, which meant I would head out on what I thought would be a long lonely stretch stocked up with food and water only to pass a succession of communities. It was my favourite part of Mexico so far, but I was suffering from a cold so could have been enjoying it more. Maybe the tequila hadn't been very helpful.

The next day I reached the city of Guadalajara, a much bigger place than Zacatecas. To get there had involved the biggest day's climbing yet. It was now constantly steep, and I was left using my lowest gear for the first time. I had two 15-mile climbs followed by a final 10-mile slog, and I averaged just over 8mph all day. The greatest reward was one 13-mile descent, even though the whole way down I knew I would be climbing back up the other side. For the first time it was also starting to get humid. The valley bottoms were beginning to look very tropical with jungle foliage, while at the top of the climb I would move back into ranchlands. I'd made only 65 miles but was rewarded with views of an immense tumbling waterfall on the city's outskirts.

The climbs were great fun compared to the frustration of my day off in Guadalajara. I had two couriered packages to pick up but they had been delayed somewhere in customs. It took a day and a half to figure out what had happened to them. I was almost out of memory cards to film on to, and there were no cards of the right quality to be found locally – and I tried everywhere. I was eventually told that one package had been sent back to the UK as it had included needles for my first-aid kit.

I rationalized the situation by telling myself that the time off the bike would stop me getting more ill, but I still felt keen to make up lost ground. Just before I left the other package did arrive, with a replacement stove and cycling shoes. I left the city on a four-lane highway, sure that I wasn't allowed on it but unsure of my alternatives.

I planned to reach the town of Colima, 140 miles (225km) down the road, by the following afternoon. With the runaround in Guadalajara, I'd failed to plan ahead properly and wasn't carrying many supplies. After an hour and a half the road reduced to two lanes with a hard shoulder. This was better riding, but the problem with being on a toll trunk road, apart from it being against the law, was that there were no stops, nowhere to pick up supplies. By late afternoon I was back on a normal road but still without food, and looking ahead I realized there was no way I could make the next town. At 4,500ft (1,370m) I was now crossing the Laguna Sayuta, two large dry salt lakes. By 7.45 p.m. it was almost completely dark and I had only just started to cross the second plain. I didn't mind wild-camping but there was little cover so I had to rely on nightfall to hide my tent. I had been looking for a spot for over an hour and was getting a bit worried when I spotted a small side road and pedalled up it for a kilometre before ducking off to the side. I camped on the gravel and ate some emergency rations, but was still hungry.

At 5.20 I woke with a fright to the sound of a loud crack. There were no lights shining on the tent and the noise had come from some way off. It had sounded like a rifle. I switched my head torch on – I always slept with it round my wrist – and listened tensely. Nothing happened, so I told myself it was unlikely to be a rifle, and even if it was, it still wasn't anything to worry about. I fell back asleep.

When I woke at seven I saw just how exposed my camp was. After quickly taking it down I found a dry pastry and a few biscuits before heading out across the salt lake. I stayed hungry till lunchtime, by which time I'd made it to the other side. After feasting ravenously at the first place I found, I headed back into the hills, facing a stiff headwind for the last stretch to Colima.

I woke the next morning to find the biggest volcano in Mexico shrouded in cloud, which made filming it a bit tricky. I also soon figured out that there was no human story attached to it. The obvious damage to lots of buildings in the town of Colima was related to earthquakes, not the volcano, and the prevailing wind was northerly, so ash rarely made it to town, despite the volcano being only 30 miles away. When I asked some locals what life was like here, I realized that the volcano was incidental.

Some of the best sequences I had filmed since Alaska had been entirely spontaneous, things I had happened across. Others had been well researched by my production team back in Glasgow, who needed to ensure that I wouldn't cycle past potentially brilliant storylines unknowingly. On this occasion I had raced for days to meet Carlos Navarro, a local volcanologist, only to find nothing worth filming. Carlos was a lovely man, though, and I was glad I'd met him.

Over some food he asked where I was heading next. When I explained my route down the Pacific coast past Acapulco, his expression changed. 'You know about Michoacán coast?' he asked. I didn't. In my mind, the Mexican Pacific was a paradise of beaches; the name Acapulco certainly conjured up such images. Carlos explained gravely how dangerous the next region was, how there was major marijuana-growing there largely controlled by a mafia group called La Familia. But the danger to the traveller didn't come from them, it came from the high level of petty crime. Due to the insecurity in the area, and in spite of its incredible natural beauty, there was almost no tourism and little investment. This lack of jobs and legal business had kept most of the rural communities in absolute poverty. Carjacking, mugging and other road crimes were now a major problem.

This was a very different risk to the high-level kidnapping and extortion risk in the north. I called Glasgow before carrying on, to make sure they knew. They didn't, and called their local contact in Mexico City. Without the need for any research, she confirmed Carlos's concerns. We had all somehow overlooked this issue.

I hadn't wanted anything to change, I was just making sure that the team knew the situation on the road. The BBC weren't so relaxed. I was already back on the bike when I got a message to say that I was being put back under escort. That was the last thing I wanted and I called back to put my case. Especially in an area of roadside crime, an escort would simply raise my profile, highlighting that I had something worth stealing. My producer understood, but maintained that the BBC couldn't be seen to have known of a high risk and taken no action. The only compromise was that a minder would shadow me, meeting every so often, at least ensuring that I was somewhere safe at night. This felt like babysitting and my every instinct reacted against such control. I again realized, with a pang of frustration, that this was not my expedition, but a major TV production. Some compromises needed to be made. Another briefly discussed option was to re-route, but leaving the coast and heading due east inland meant crossing the mountains and negotiating a sprawling Mexico City and its nearly nine million inhabitants, so I stuck to the original plan.

I was told that a man called José could reach me by five p.m. at a town called Tecomán, 40 miles down the road. I was there by two, and waited until nightfall for him to arrive. He turned out to be a tour guide, kind-faced and cuddly-looking, one of the least intimidating men I had ever met. He also drove a big white van with flash alloys so any hope of keeping a low profile had gone. Added to the frustration of this delay, I had an upset stomach and was in poor spirits.

The next day I realized that Carlos hadn't been exaggerating. The contrast heading down the coast was striking. None of rural Mexico had looked rich, but the remote communities here were by far the poorest I had seen, with a lot of makeshift housing. The gaps between villages were now significant, and most didn't have any shops.

Still, reaching the coast was definitely reason for celebration. The last time I had seen the Pacific was outside Anchorage, about 6,000 miles (9,600km) up the road. The view across rolling surf on a white sandy beach with palm trees swaying couldn't have been more different.

The road didn't hug the ocean for long, weaving inland through a tunnel of trees. Some more cooling ocean breeze would have been welcome as it was now very humid and the road was constantly undulating. It never climbed or fell very far but it was still leg-sapping progress as I skirted the foothills of the Sierra Madre del Sur. I couldn't drink fast enough to offset the amount I sweated. Just standing still it was like I was in a sauna. When sweating no longer does the job of cooling you down, your body feels bizarre, like your head is swollen and pressurized, your limbs heavy. Every time I came across José he would get out of his air-conditioned van and immediately break into a sweat. For all my reservations, he turned out to be easy company, and I made use of the van to carry as much extra water as I wanted.

I did notice that, for all the concerns about crime, the area was strangely devoid of men. In each community I came across I mostly saw women and children. José explained that most of the men went to the US to work illegally, to get money to send home. That certainly explained why many of the few cars I had seen had US licence plates.

For the first time since the Chihuahua region I was coming across regular military checkpoints, and on some walls and road signs were scrawled anti-government protests. Like in the north, you could probably drive through without realizing it was a troubled area, but at bike speed I could see lots of telltale signs.

The last stretch before the city of Lázaro Cárdenas was especially tough. My back wheel wasn't feeling right for the first 30km of the day, especially when I really cranked on it. I eventually worked out that it was the same bolt coming loose that I had replaced in Coeur d'Alene. I stopped at the roadside the next time I saw José. A wooden shack stood there and a gaunt middle-aged man, stripped to the waist, was selling watermelons. I didn't pay him much attention as he started speaking to José, I just turned my bike upside down and tried to fix it. After a few minutes José, still smiling, said, 'The guy wants you to leave the bike – he needs it more than you.' I flipped the bike back on to its wheels, put the bags back on and pedalled away.

$1 million pesos reward *(left)*: roadside billboards remind me of the hidden turmoil in Mexico's Chihuahua region.

The dreaded chipotle *(left)*: millions of fiery chillies being toasted.

The friendship of strangers *(below)*: a group of enthusiastic roadies keep me company and test my endurance!

Zacatecas *(below)*: overlooking the ancient city a few hours before the main Independence Day celebrations begin.

A spectacle of death *(above)*: like an ancient gladiator ring, more theatre than sport.

El Toreador *(above)*: the fighter executes formal moves, while trying to avoid being gored or trampled.

An unnecessary end *(above)*: I appreciate the history but can't condone the cruelty.

Masked military *(left)*: soldiers in Mexico often work away from their home region and remain anonymous to minimize the risk of family kidnappings.

Saint Death (above): depictions like the Grim Reaper painted on the walls of a roadside shrine in southern Mexico.

A dark art (right): candles, flowers, prayers and beer are left to Santissima Muerte.

Following the Pacific (below): stunning, but humid and hilly riding just north of Acapulco.

Maya Bike *(above)*: a pedal-powered corn dehusking machine, one of many old bikes given a new use.

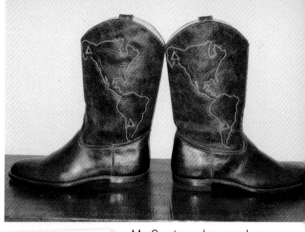

My Guatemalan cowboy boots *(above)*: detailed stitching showing my route, the Americas map, Denali and Aconcagua.

The Guatemalan national team mechanic *(left)*: the best man for the job gives my bike some much-needed attention.

Boy ranchers *(below)*: my first day in Nicaragua, meeting some cattle herders on the roadside.

Causing offence *(left)*: my visiting BBC cameraman quickly learns that some of the indigenous women don't want to be filmed.

The colours of Central America *(right)*: fresh fruit and bright clothes in the Mercado de Artesanias.

Stepping back in time *(below)*: two oxen plough a two-acre field in Nicaragua where white beans will be grown.

Sun-dried bricks *(right)*: hand-made and sold for $8 per 100.

A tricky border crossing *(above)*: La Unión, El Salvador, and my planned boat trip looks unlikely.

A break from the humidity *(right)*: racing through some cool, dark tunnels in Guatemala.

A dip in the ocean *(above)*: stopping briefly to go surfing in Sunzal, El Salvador.

Broadcasting to BBC Breakfast *(above)*: set up in a Costa Rican plantation, doing a Skype call to the nation.

Ngobe-bugle Indians *(above)*: at home with a family in their village, 15km from the main road.

Night-time in the jungle *(above)*: one of the characters I found in the Panama rainforest.

Yahoo the howler monkey *(above)*: relaxing with the rescue animals in Panama.

Land of the volcanoes *(above):* Concepción, a 1,610-metre crater as seen over Lake Nicaragua.

Monsoon season *(left and below)*: the tail end of the rains makes for some uncomfortable cycling through Central America, especially with big, fast traffic on some narrow roads.

The Crown Opal *(left)*: looking down from the bridge over the impressive 'bonnet' of my cargo ship as we transit a lock of the Panama Canal.

First sights of South America *(above)*: the shores of Guayaquil, Ecuador.

José caught me up a bit further on and explained that the guy had
been saying I was rich and had a van, so didn't need my bike. When
José had tried to make light of the situation, while warning me, the
man had walked off to make a call on a mobile phone. A semi-
clothed watermelon vendor in these parts wasn't someone I'd expect
to have a mobile, so this concerned me.

We were discussing whether we should move quickly on when
four men walked out from a small field at the roadside. One of them
was bleeding badly from his right shin. A dog had bitten him, José
translated. We sat him down at the back of the van and cut away his
ripped and bloodied tracksuit leg. It was a deep bite. Using a
wound dressing out of my first-aid kit we managed to stem the
bleeding and wrap a bandage tightly around the area. He needed to
get to a hospital but refused the offer, stood up with thanks and
limped off.

José looked shaken. This was beyond his usual day job of sightseeing trips with American tourists.

After that delay, I decided to keep on cycling. It was stunning
riding, surrounded by huge tropical ferns and creeping vines
around leafy hardwoods. At Lázaro Cárdenas, the road turned
inland, well away from the coast, for the afternoon and it thankfully
flattened out a bit. Near the end of the day I passed the biggest
military checkpoint yet. Thick rope was laid across the road to form
sharp speed bumps, too much for my bike. At the roadside a couple
of sandbag defences had been built around machine-gun posts. One
of these I saw was loaded with shells, each a couple of inches thick.
As a last defence, after the posts were a few very large strips of tyre
spikes on wires, ready to be pulled across. The masked soldiers
waved me on after asking where I was going and where I had come
from. I kept it local; there was no point in saying that I had
cycled from Alaska.

I was now heading into the Guerrero region of Mexico, where
there were signs of greater wealth and the people were noticeably
different, with darker skin and curlier hair. Late on that day I

stopped when I saw an unusual hut by the roadside. The small building had a metal-grated and padlocked door, and either side of it was a large yellow painting in black and yellow of the Grim Reaper. The white paint above the door showed the burn marks of a fire. To the side was a smaller hut, with an open front. This was an elaborate roadside altar, but unlike any I had ever seen. The brick shelves were covered in candles, flowers and, strangely, cans of beer. At the back of the smaller hut was a painting of another Grim Reaper character with the wording SANTISSIMA MUERTE. Picking up one of the candles, I was amazed to see writing in both Spanish and English.

> Oh mighty Father, Son and Holy Spirit, I ask for you to invoke the Holy Death, my white little girl . . . I want to ask from the bottom of my heart to break and destroy any darkness that is present in my person. Holy Death take all envy, poverty, lack of affection and unemployment away from me and I beg from the deepest of my heart for charity of your blessed presence to light up my house . . . Holy Death, pray thee our father.

The prayer went on for much longer, and the rest was just as chilling. The flowers at the altar were all fresh and had clearly been bought, an example of a wealth I hadn't seen in the roadside communities. In fact, people with money had built the entire shrine. The beer cans were all opened but left full. Inside the locked room were similar mementos, as well as bottles of tequila and some clothes. Maybe 'Holy Death' likes Modelo beer, I thought, trying to find some humour in this dark place, but in all honesty I felt a bit spooked and didn't want to be there when anyone else turned up. Someone had even left his identity card.

When I asked José, he explained that this Holy Death was a belief held by some people in this southern, coastal part of Mexico, who prayed for their enemies to be avenged. That wasn't what the prayer I had read said, but it left the same sinister impression. He seemed surprised to find such a public roadside altar, describing the followers as a cult within Catholicism that was feared by others. It was definitely a sinister-looking shrine, even if the prayer I had read was asking for redemption.

The local paper carried news that the Ciudad Juarez killers I'd read about in the *El Paso Times* the day before I crossed the border had been caught. I also learned that there had been a shoot-out between the army and a group of locals just a few blocks from where I'd stayed two nights earlier. The front-page photo was of one of the men who had been shot dead, with his wife leaning over him. I recognized the place.

Apart from this terrible undercurrent of crime and violence, it was such a stunning area. I could easily imagine it as a tourist haven. I wondered what it would have been like to travel through without the BBC keeping me up to date with all their concerns and without José to translate and describe what I was seeing. Maybe I would have remained largely oblivious to it all and just thought it was a poor but beautiful region.

In contrast to the poverty, I'd certainly ended up staying in a veritable palace in the town of Zihuatanejo. It hadn't looked much from the roadside and I was so shattered after a tough day on the bike that I hadn't noticed my surroundings when I asked for a room. An hour later, sat in a restaurant on the veranda looking out over the Pacific, watching white surf rolling over a beach lit by floodlights, it hit me, despite the rain battering relentlessly on the tented canopy above, competing with Sinatra on the speakers. Around me were four couples. The young, pretty waitress came over with a candle, joking that it was 'más romántico así', more romantic that way. The food was ridiculously good, and my room, which also overlooked the Pacific, had a big balcony with its own hot-tub and lounge. This was the ultimate beach escape for the residents of Mexico City, and a million miles from the poverty of the surrounding area. The temptation to rest there for a day was huge.

*

It took two more days of coastal riding to reach the outskirts of Acapulco. It absolutely poured down. It was the first time since Alaska that it had rained so hard. This time it wasn't at all cold, just miserable. Staying in the community of Papanoa the first night, I learned that it had rained every night for the last fortnight, and often during the day too. It was certainly set to get wetter as I headed into Central America.

Suitable places for putting up my tent in the close tropical vegetation were hard to find, and camping was uncomfortable in such humidity, not to mention the attendant dangers and nightly rainstorms. Rather unhelpfully, hotels in Mexico give themselves their own star rating, which was something I had only just realized. So, finding a very cheap room at a four-star hotel actually meant that I was probably about to stay in a cockroach-infested dive. I had spent the night in a few absolute holes along the coast, but that night's hotel was another great find.

The next day I found that the city of Acapulco was not all the glitz and glam I had always associated with the name. The touristy area stood along the waterfront with high-rise hotels, shops, clubs and restaurants, looking like a Californian boulevard. I even spotted a Starbucks, which looked very alien compared to the world I had just cycled out of. In contrast, downtown and the rest of the city were overcrowded, noisy and dirty. The roads showed evidence of the rainy season with potholes and washed-out sections. The majority of vehicles were either big US school-style buses or old-style VW Beetle taxis, all painted blue and white. Many of the buses played loud music, most streets had traffic jams, and when the vehicles did move the driving was erratic. The pavements were packed with street vendors.

Down on the shore, away from the tourist strip and the graffiti-strewn downtown, was a busy fish market. I spent a few hours trying to explore and film all this, but it was enough of a task to keep an eye on the bike and stay safe while cycling so I didn't feel relaxed enough to enjoy the place.

The road south climbed straight up steeply for a few miles until I was rewarded with a breathtaking view back down over the city. From the crest of this hill, the view down the beaches heading south was equally stunning. Once again I reflected on the extremes of this coastal ride, from crowds to isolation, poverty to opulence, crime balanced by real kindness, and plenty of rain and sunshine.

For my last stretch of Mexico it looked like I would pass through more towns and I made a conscious effort to start eating more when I did. The humidity was an energy drain unlike any other, and I felt too thin now. The Mexicans were still lacing my food with hot stuff, even though I had now left the chilli-mad north. I would often order innocent-looking food, for example a breakfast omelette, only to find I could barely eat it. I decided that my best option was to start an ice-cream diet, which simply involved stopping and eating one every time I got to a town. In terms of finding enough normal food, my process of trial and error had revealed that, contrary to my expectations, rustic and often dodgy-looking road-side stalls tended to have cheaper, fresher and less spicy food than proper restaurants. However, after a fast descent back to the Pacific I indulged in a family-sized Dominos pizza.

In the suburbs south of Acapulco, to my surprise, I cycled through an area of millionaires' mansions. The aptly named Diamond Point is home to many of the retired old guard of politicians. It was an odd place to take a call from my production team to say that they were extending my 'shadow' escort for maybe another three weeks. I stewed on this all afternoon, which was actually good fuel to make good miles. I understood my team's obligations and appreciated their concern but my spirit naturally rebelled against the idea of being babysat. Even with the best, most understanding escort my freedom to go at my own pace and explore fully was restricted.

I said 'my last stretch of Mexico'; it was actually eight more days' riding to reach Guatemala. I had always wrongly thought of Acapulco as near the bottom of Mexico; in fact this last section just went on and on. I noticed a considerable change in the people in the Oaxaca and Chiapas regions of southern Mexico, all of whom seemed far less guarded.

My only real concern now was the number of dogs. Every day I was chased. Every time I rode past a group of houses I would be alert for the barking to start, ready to give them a squirt of water from my bottle if they got too close. These were not mischievous pets that might frighten the postman, like in the UK, these were dogs that lived on the streets, semi-wild. Many looked in a very poor condition. I saw one that had no back legs, yet it was somehow still standing, balanced on its front two paws, eating something at the roadside.

I'd grown up on a farm with lots of dogs. It was not for a lack of compassion towards them that I was very wary. Mexican truck drivers carry small wooden bats to check their tyre pressure: they whack the bats against the tyre and check that the reverberating sound is the same all the way round. I came across a stall that sold these for the equivalent of about £1.50. They were beautifully turned pieces of wood, and very light. I bought one. It would be a last resort, but I didn't want to end up like that farm worker, with a dog bite down to the bone.

I mentioned this on my online blog, and got an unexpected response. Most people understood that this was an absolute last resort, that I'd only use the bat if I was attacked, but a few were exceptionally angry, accusing me of animal cruelty, even going so far as to post a link to a video of animals being beaten to death, saying that I should watch it and reconsider. A few people assured me that they would now no longer be following my journey.

Thousands followed me online; there was a real sense of community, a virtual peloton of support. Out of these great numbers there were only about five complaints, but they were venomous. Used as I was to sharing every move, it was easy to forget that others couldn't possibly fully share my rationale, my motivations and my understanding of any situation. All they knew is what I told them. So I regretted talking about buying the bat for defence. Animal cruelty is obviously a raw nerve, and so it should be. But if I were seriously attacked by a dog and I had a bat with me, I wouldn't hesitate to defend myself. Being an animal lover or not doesn't really come into it. But it wasn't a debate I was going to win, and the internet is the worst place for anonymous slander, so I apologized, learned a lesson and moved on.

A day south of Acapulco I was flying down a hill and round a sweeping corner when I rode straight into the path of a donkey standing idly in the middle of the road. Inches away from a massive and very embarrassing crash, with not even the time to touch the brakes, I managed to swerve and only skiffed its back legs with one of my pannier bags. The donkey didn't move, but it was now considering me quietly. I parked the bike, turned back and chased it off the road. It went very reluctantly. If a car had done what I did, it wouldn't have ended well for either party.

The next night I found a room in a very cheap hotel in a small town called Agua Fria, which, oddly, translates as 'cold water'. When I turned on the shower a number of large reddish-coloured cockroaches shot out of the drain.

In the morning I was setting out when an announcement was made through a system of speakers on telegraph poles. I didn't understand it, but José started laughing and translated for me: 'Can the boy who took the small brown dog last night please bring it back or we will come and find you.'

Acapulco had been the first sign of what turned out to be a VW Beetle explosion. They were now everywhere. The moto-rickshaw was also making its first appearance, reminding me of India. Near the town of Zanatepec I passed the narrowest point in Mexico, called the Tehuantepec Isthmus: here, it is just 142 miles (230km) from the Atlantic to the Pacific. The terrain was flattening out and the vegetation was thinner. Along the roadside I had seen a few monkeys and small parrots, which made me want to explore and document more of the wildlife. There was so much just off the road.

Secondly, I wanted to get into the Pacific. Having followed it for so long, it made sense to make it more than just a backdrop for the cycle. I kept looking for a good place to stop, but the ocean was so rough and I didn't want to risk it. It was certainly frustrating, sweating constantly in the humidity and not finding an opportunity to take a dip.

While the terrain was getting faster, the afternoon rains were becoming more predictable. On my third last day in Mexico it rained torrentially. At lunch I sheltered in a roadside café, looking out of the window at the deluge. There were quite a few truckers sitting at the next table, and as I got up to pay at the bar, one said loudly to his friend, 'The white boy's going to get wet!' He laughed. I laughed too. From his expression, he obviously hadn't imagined I would overhear his remark, let alone understand it.

I decided to stop early. There was no point in heading on as planned. It was dark almost an hour before I'd expected it to be, and the rain was reducing visibility. Vehicles weren't giving me much room and the trucks threw up a heavy spray. I am used to cycling in the rain, but this was something else, even heavier than I had experienced in Thailand and Malaysia. It was absolutely bouncing. I could hear it hammering off car roofs; it flowed in streams down the road.

After locking my bike and kit in a hotel room, I headed out for food. It was still thundering down. Straight across the street a taco vendor had abandoned his little stall and was serving just a few customers on some tables outside his own house, under the shelter of a balcony. It was a very rustic arrangement, for those times when he was rained out. The tacos were brought fresh from his kitchen.

A man called Roberto had taken over from José as my escort by this stage, and as we sat down and started to eat, a lady wearing a big rain jacket joined the table. My Spanish had improved a lot, but I hardly said a word. Roberto, however, was very chatty, obviously enjoying a chance to speak Spanish at some length again. When I went to pay, the owner offered to make us breakfast as well. His chicken and beef tacos had been wonderful, so I jumped at the chance to start the next day in such style.

The morning was clear and bright as Roberto and I sat down to eggs and grated potatoes with some meat and tortillas. Then, from across the street came the lady from the evening before, except this time she was dressed in a short skirt and strappy top, hair done up, make-up on as if for a night out. She sat with us again, me in my lycras ready to start cycling. Our conversation was again limited, but I did learn that she was a saleswoman for a PVC piping company. It occurred to me that she was dressed strangely for an industrial supplies salesperson. Then again, for all I knew dressing to kill helped the sell in Mexico.

It was a good clear day on the bike and I thought nothing more of the meeting until just before lunch a car pulled alongside and a young lady called out of the window. I didn't recognize her, but the driver of the car was the PVC lady. They pulled in a short distance ahead and asked if I wanted to stop for lunch soon. I did, so I waited for Roberto to catch up to let him know. Over a lunch of steak with deep-fried banana, avocado salad, refried beans and rice, I learned that the PVC lady's name was Gabby, that she was thirty-two, and that she lived in Mapastapec, the town I was heading for that night. Her friend was younger, very pretty in a flowery dress. Roberto again held the conversation as the girls didn't speak any English. Before leaving they insisted on meeting us for dinner that night. Roberto was obviously amused by the idea, but I didn't see any reason why not. It would certainly make for an interesting last evening in Mexico, and it would be good practice for me as so far I had probably managed a total of ten sentences with them.

Once they had gone, Roberto, now laughing, said, 'You know that they are after you, don't you?'

'No,' I replied truthfully. 'I can't even speak to them.'

'That doesn't matter,' he chuckled. 'It's get a gringo husband! You don't need to be able to talk for that!'

I didn't have a response to that. I had a scraggy beard, my clothes stank, and I was obviously not stopping in Mapastapec. I considered myself an unlikely candidate. Also, the conversation had almost exclusively been between Roberto and them, and he was an older married man. Nothing about our three meetings so far had seemed anything more than coincidences filled with friendly chat. My only observation was that they were slightly overdressed for selling PVC piping.

The afternoon rains returned. It was soon raining so hard that I couldn't look forward, only down, thanks to my contact lenses, with the occasional glance up to check for the many speed bumps, known locally as *topes*. I don't mind cycling in the rain but it was tough going after a while. The road was muddied and damaged in parts by the flash floods after the rains of the night before. I was relieved when the time came to stop for the day.

Dinner was one very long Spanish lesson. For nearly three hours I persevered. The greatest accolade I could take away is that my Spanish was much better than their English. Roberto just spent most of the evening laughing, talking to them in Spanish and trying to help my conversation whenever I ran out of words. We covered all the basic foreign language topics of conversation, including families, countries, jobs and hobbies. 'My father is a farmer and I have two sisters,' I threw together, along with other equally inspiring snippets. Ironically, it was also the sort of thing you might speak about on a first date, but the evening went well and wasn't at all awkward. Until we waved them off.

Annie, the younger woman, pulled me aside.

'Are you married?' she asked.

'No, I am not married,' I replied in English.

'You have a girlfriend?'

'Yes.'

I smiled. She had said these sentences in perfect English. She hadn't spoken any English at lunch or dinner, not a word.

'You do speak English,' I pointed out, happy to change the subject.

'No,' she said, and walked off to talk to Gabby.

I went off to chat to Roberto. It was very bizarre, like being in the school playground again, talking about who fancies who.

Regardless of ulterior motives, I had enjoyed my last day in Mexico and had learned more Spanish than in the whole of the previous fortnight.

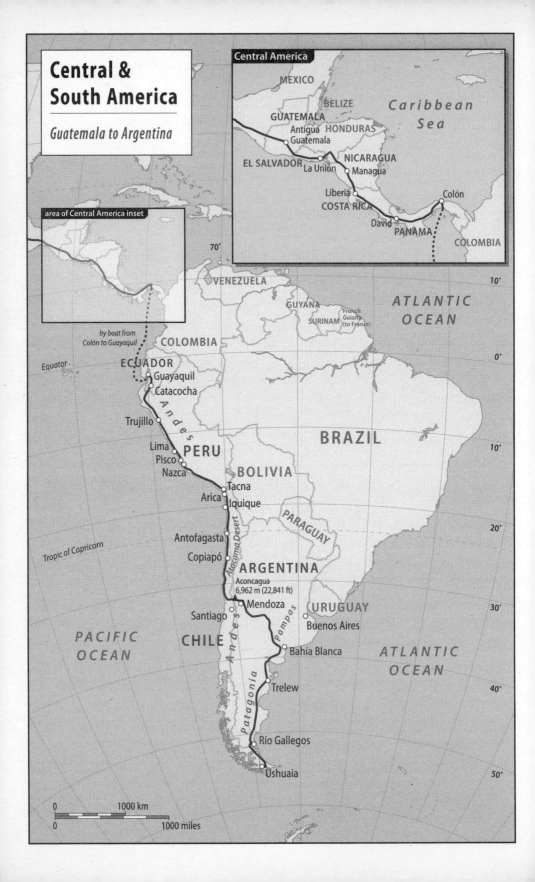

Central & South America

Guatemala to Argentina

Central America

MEXICO

BELIZE

GUATEMALA
Antigua HONDURAS
Guatemala

Caribbean
Sea

EL SALVADOR   NICARAGUA
La Union   Managua

Liberia   Colón

COSTA RICA

David   PANAMA

COLOMBIA

area of Central America inset

70°

10°

VENEZUELA

GUYANA

ATLANTIC
OCEAN

SURINAM

French
Guiana
(to France)

by boat from
Colón to Guayaquil

COLOMBIA

0°

Equator

ECUADOR
Guayaquil
Catacocha

Trujillo

Andes

BRAZIL

10°

Lima   PERU
Pisco
Nazca

BOLIVIA

Tacna
Arica Iquique

PARAGUAY

20°

Antofagasta

Atacama Desert

Copiapó

ARGENTINA

Tropic of Capricorn

Aconcagua
6,962 m (22,841 ft)

Mendoza

Santiago

URUGUAY

30°

CHILE

Pampas

Buenos Aires

PACIFIC
OCEAN

Andes

Bahía Blanca

ATLANTIC
OCEAN

40°

Patagonia

Trelew

Río Gallegos

50°

Ushuaia

0   1000 km

0   1000 miles

11

Crossing the Guatemalan border felt like a wonderful milestone. It was certainly very easy: the border guards stamped my passport without question and within seconds I was in Central America.

I was looking forward to smaller targets in the coming weeks after the three and a bit months and 6,500 miles through Canada, the USA and Mexico. Guatemala, El Salvador, Honduras, Nicaragua, Costa Rica and Panama looked like a fascinating tapestry of countries, as alike and yet as contrasting as European countries.

It was thirty-four days since I'd cycled out of Ciudad Juarez into a country I had completely underestimated, not least in terms of its size. I recalled how nervous I had been, and then how lost I had felt during my first few days alone without any means of communication, and then realized that I could now get by pretty well with basic conversational Spanish. This made a huge difference, and I entered Guatemala feeling strangely at home, certainly far more relaxed.

In contrast, Julio, my new escort, was anything but chilled out. José and Roberto, despite my initial reluctance to have any company, had been great and most of the time I had been able to ride as if they weren't there. They had also been brilliant at explaining about the world I was passing through, and given me far more information than I would have picked up. Julio was no qualified guide, he was the driver for an elderly lady in Guatemala City. As soon as I shook his hand I realized that he was very nervous at being taken off 'Driving Miss Daisy' duties in order to ensure my safety through Guatemala. In fact it wasn't long before I felt I was the one looking after him.

Back in the 1960s a massive flood of the Usumacinta River, which marks the border, permanently shifted its course, and overnight a big section of Mexico became Guatemala. Despite such a natural and seemingly fluid divide, the sense of being in a very different country was immediate. I cycled into the border town of Ayutla with that indescribable excitement of being in a new country, alert and playing a personal game of spot the difference.

There was a lot to look forward to. I had about eleven weeks to reach Aconcagua and start the climb. Put in those terms, it no longer felt that long. In the short term, I had a BBC cameraman joining me for five days. In other news, I learned that Barack Obama had won the Nobel Peace Prize. I was amused to watch hundreds of photographers turning out to take photos of the President's new pooch. When I checked on Twitter, many of the trending topics and feeds were related to *The X Factor*. In Ayutla, I felt a million miles away from these 'realities', and was left wondering if the situation in Mexico would ever make the world news.

The original plan had been to continue south-east on the same road, but there were now a number of strong arguments to divert inland towards the historic city of Antigua Guatemala. First, I was told about a project close to the city that recycled bikes into all kinds of machines used in the community, an enterprise I really wanted to visit. Visiting a city would also make better use of the cameraman joining me rather than just capturing endless miles of countryside. Finally, I wanted to meet an American called Clay Parker and a Dutchman called Harry Kikstra. Clay, a young Texan, had passed me on his old motorbike in southern Mexico, destined for Antigua; Harry had got in touch online, saying he was there having also cycled from Alaska.

Despite all these reasons I was still keen to stay on track for the sake of time, but my bike was in desperate need of a proper mechanic. A worrying click coming from between the pedals was quickly getting worse.

Alone on the bike I often find it hard to make objective decisions about changing my targets in terms of route and timings. Once a plan is set, everything else is worked back from this. You hang all your emotional highs and lows on breaking down the daily targets. Change these, and I find it easy to lose focus. But once I'd eventually convinced myself that Antigua was a justifiable detour, I set out with renewed energy – which was just as well as the ride immediately got tougher. The road set off in long steady climbs rather than coastal undulations for the first time in weeks. Narrower and in a worse condition, I couldn't figure out if the road was also busier or if I was just noticing the traffic more since I was now sharing the road with it and dancing around potholes when the trucks allowed me to move away from the verge. By the time the afternoon rains came I had climbed a long way and it was surprisingly cool, refreshing for the first time in ages.

Having Julio's truck hover around me all day simply caused more traffic. He refused to leave my sight. Anyone watching would have quickly noticed I was worth mugging thanks to his presence. It would have been very funny if I hadn't been so frustrated. I tried to tell him that he would be doing a far better job if he did far less, maybe disappeared up the road by an hour or so. Into my second day, I learned that everything I did or said was also being reported back to his boss, which was then emailed to my production team in Scotland. This really was a babysitter, and a nervous one at that.

Despite appearances, Julio surprised me with a remarkable life story over lunch in a roadside restaurant. When he wasn't 'on duty' he turned out to be good company. In his twenties he had gone to America to work illegally, like many of his friends. He had settled there for six years, married a lady from Panama, and planned to stay. All was going fine until one night they had a domestic fall-out.

Because of the shouting, their neighbours had called the police. When they arrived and he failed to produce papers, he was taken away and deported without being allowed to go back to his house. He had returned to Guatemala and had not seen his wife since.

I was surprised he was telling me all this, having only just met me. He chatted without obvious emotion about how he had just accepted what had happened and remarried a Guatemalan instead. I couldn't even begin to imagine just accepting something like this. Maybe only knowing the raw bones of the story made it harder to accept than the reality, but I was still stumped for a suitable response.

Guatemala means 'Land of the Trees'. The country shares an ancient history with southern Mexico that dates to the Mayan era. Just inland, in the highlands of the Lacandón mountains, lie many ruins from this early civilization. Nearly a thousand years ago the Mayans had sufficient astronomical knowledge to be using a 364-day calendar and were the first to use the digit 0, without which you can't count past nine. On a less progressive note, they also played a game roughly similar to basketball where the winning team was sacrificed to their gods. That dubious honour has got to affect your game, not to mention your motivation.

Still in the foothills, I passed mangoes, bananas, papayas, pineapples and avocados growing at the roadside. Both sides of the border shared a tropical abundance that belied the poverty in the area. Officially, 56 per cent of Guatemalans live below the poverty line, although in the countryside it looked like nearly everyone did.

Late on my second afternoon I took the pick-up on the mountainous roads to the small town of San Andrés Itzapa, where the workshop enterprise of Mayabike is based. It would have been a day's cycling in the wrong direction so I didn't mind the lift. The small team of local and international volunteers based here take shipments of old bikes from the US and create pedal-powered machinery for rural communities. It's a genius enterprise. Carlos, the founder, spent some time showing me his designs for bikes that were now used as water pumps, concrete tile makers, sweetcorn dehuskers, macadamia nutcrackers, food blenders, washing machines, and a lot more. Each of these machines brings a new level of efficiency to each task and can be used by those who cannot afford to buy and keep the petrol-driven equivalent.

On the rooftop of his workshop I found hundreds of scrap bikes waiting to be recycled, and a view across the town below me, surrounded by wooded hills. The old and ornate town hall, painted mustard yellow with white pillars, stood in contrast to the rest of the town, which comprised a lot of bare breezeblock buildings and rusted tin roofs. In the background, a red-and-white-striped mobile phone mast looked out of place. Women in traditional brightly coloured skirts walked along the streets. The few vehicles I could see were all battered old pick-ups.

It was early evening by the time I found my hotel in Antigua and went off in search of the touristy Bagel Barn, where I had arranged to meet Harry, his fiancée Ivana, and Clay. The streets were cobbled, with high kerbs and shuttered, dirty buildings. Take away the veneer of tourism – the internet cafés and hostels – and replace the vehicles, especially the old US school buses belching diesel fumes, and Antigua would look pretty much unchanged from centuries ago. The Bagel Barn was full so we headed off until we ended up in an equally touristy pizzeria, surrounded by back-packers and rich Guatemalans. It was an odd mix. If this was all you ever saw of Guatemala you might think it was interesting, even other-worldly, but in fact it was closer to American culture. I certainly flinched at spending a day's food budget on a pizza.

However, the company was exceptional. Harry is a cyclist second and a mountaineer and guide first, having climbed the highest peaks in all seven continents and written guidebooks for many mountains, including Everest, Denali and Aconcagua. Harry and Ivana had left Alaska over a year earlier and were planning on taking a further year and a half to reach Tierra del Fuego, cycling to every country in South America en route. We toasted the fact that I was the first cyclist to catch them after leaving a year later. Hearing some of their adventures, I grew envious of their freedom to explore. In turn, I could see that my mission to climb North and South America's highest peaks within the same season appealed to Harry's spirit of adventure. The grass is always greener . . . But he did nothing to dispel my concerns about the climb ahead of me. 'Aconcagua's one of the most underestimated mountains in the world,' he pointed out.

Clay's adventure was of a very different type. He didn't know Harry, and I had only met him for about twenty minutes at the roadside a few weeks earlier. While travelling around Guatemala the year before he had come across a small town near Antigua where almost every shop was a boot-maker. He had returned to the US, worked until he had enough money to buy an old Suzuki 250cc motorbike, then driven south with a view to setting up a business selling boots into the US. Selling Guatemalan cowboy boots to Texans sounded to me like selling ice to the Inuit, but Clay was adamant that the craftsmanship and cost benefit were incredible. The fact that Clay barely spoke a word of Spanish and didn't have any background in the import trade was incidental to his enthusiasm. I agreed to meet him the following morning and to be his very first customer.

It was three weeks since my last day off, in Guadalajara, and I was glad to be in Antigua. It was the most interesting town I had explored since Zacatecas. To start with, it took a few hours to sort my boots with Clay, mainly because he had never done a fitting before. He drew around my feet on a bit of paper and made various other measurements, then I chose from a thick folder of leather samples. After that came decisions about the overall cut, heel and stitching. Having never worn or studied cowboy boots, I had no fashion guidelines to follow; Clay was a newfound expert and relayed as much knowledge as he could remember. Down the side of the boots I decided to have an outline of the Americas stitched in white, with the two mountains inlaid in darker leather, and red stitching to show my route. On the scrap of paper, the design looked hopelessly elaborate, but Clay was confident that it was possible and asked for US$50. It was absurdly cheap; I decided to pay him more to help start his enterprise. With a shake of the hand he promised they would be waiting for me when I returned to Scotland. I had no receipt and no way of knowing if I would ever see Clay or my boots again.

That evening Nick, the BBC cameraman, was flying in to meet me, so I spent much of that day off catching up on blogs, doing some washing and backing up filmcards. Nick was bringing a new bottom bracket for the bike, and the mechanic wasn't coming till the morning, so it would be a late start.

At six p.m., all the lights went out. I was in the city centre walking down a pavement when the streetlights went black. There was still enough duskiness to see a little by and I stopped, unsure what to do, watching candles being lit hastily in the restaurant opposite. At the end of the street, I turned left. The whole city seemed to be in darkness. For over an hour I walked the streets. Candles flickered from some windows, chatter wafted from open doors, people walked around as usual. I began to distrust everyone, looking over my shoulder after them. The city in darkness suddenly seemed a place of secrets. I went back to the same restaurant as the night before. This time shadows danced on the walls, and drinkers sat on high stools around the bar in semi-darkness. What had been a brash tourist hangout now seemed like a medieval tavern.

By the time Nick arrived the lights were back on, though not so much for him. It was seven a.m. UK time and he was jetlagged to the point of making little sense. I actually knew Nick fairly well: he had last filmed me from the back of a motorbike as I rode into Paris at the end of my cycle around the world.

At breakfast, a somewhat refreshed Nick commented that I seemed out of sorts. I hadn't meant to seem antisocial. On the contrary, I had for a while now been looking forward to seeing a familiar face from the past. But as I sat there and listened to Nick talking about everything he needed and wanted from our four days' filming together my gut reaction was to cycle off and be alone again. I felt agitated, ill-adjusted to company; I felt as though my routine was being disrupted.

Somehow, the BBC's Guatemalan fixer had managed to source the national team mechanic to fix my new bottom bracket. Not that I have ever heard of the Guatemalan cycling team on the world stage, but still, I assumed he must be pretty handy. He arrived mid-morning and would have replaced the part in minutes if it hadn't been for the need to film every stage.

It's a fine balance in observational documentary-making, to capture things as they naturally happen and at the same time capture enough to be able to relay events fully. This means you sometimes have to re-do or re-say to allow for a change of shot. On my own I tend to do this very little, but I understood that whenever a cameraman joined me for just a few days he would want to film everything. I now had to accept that we wouldn't be leaving till the following morning. The long-term targets of staying on time and the immediate checklist of things to film weren't going to equate for a few more days.

Just behind a busy bus terminal we discovered the Mercado de Artesanias, Antigua's main market, a bustle of over a hundred colourful stalls selling everything from fruit and locally made wares to black-market CDs and other tat. It took some getting used to not being my own cameraman, and I felt very self-conscious of the attention Nick's much larger camera attracted in the busy market. Local women sat on the ground in colourful dresses and wide-brimmed hats selling fruit. One had her baby wrapped in a shawl across her back. As soon as Nick turned his camera towards them they covered their faces and looked away. It was clear we were causing offence.

Learning from our mistakes, we explored elsewhere. I wanted to find somewhere for lunch. Many of the stalls had food, but much of it could have lain out all day. To make sure it was fresh and good I wanted something cooked in front of me.

At the side of a stall laden with bananas I eventually spotted a very small woman frying with a wide pan. There were no seats so I asked cautiously if she could cook for me. *Para llevar* was one of the phrases I used every day to ask for food to go. I towered over her and her deeply wrinkled face beamed back at me. She seemed to smile more from the eyes than her mouth as she paused for thought. 'Sí,' she laughed, and beckoned me inside.

I was invited to sit on an upturned crate as she put some meat in the hot oil and pushed it around.

'Is it chicken?' I asked in Spanish.

'No, es fileto pescado.' She laughed a bit more.

A fillet of fish. I now had the horrible thought that I was about to eat her lunch.

To my left, behind the piled-up fruit, sat a much younger lady, maybe in her late teens, with a baby in her lap. As I watched she pulled her top down and clamped the baby to a swollen breast. A customer walked up and the mother stood, placed a bunch of bananas in a bag, took the money and chatted away, all the time breast-feeding her infant.

My fillet of fish was served with plantain, the savoury banana that comes with every dish in the American tropics. It was delicious. As I ate, the old woman peered over at me, still beaming. Her face was etched with a lifetime of hard work and optimism. I was sitting down and she was barely taller than me. I paid her the equivalent of a dollar for lunch. She seemed delighted.

When I made it back to the hotel I realized that my wallet was missing. The last thing I had paid for was the food. After that I had spent half an hour wandering through the busy market, soaking up the amazing colours and the bustle. My pockets were deep, there was no way it could have fallen out, but there had been plenty of pushing people, opportunities for wandering hands. I kicked myself for not being more careful. I always split my wallet three ways for this exact reason, so I had two more cards to rely on before I was out of money, but that did nothing to dispel my mood of frustration. I wanted to get back on the road, wheels turning.

I got my wish the next morning, and was rewarded with very dusty, busy and polluted roads. I didn't care; there is no better therapy than progress. The filming had been a success so far and in the end Nick and I had enjoyed an evening exploring Antigua. I was starting to relax into his company, but it was bizarre being so acutely aware of my own awkwardness, my subconscious fight to be left alone.

It made sense to cut back towards the coast on to the CA2 highway, the traditional Pan-Americas route. My research suggested that it was the best road through Guatemala while avoiding the big cities. Julio was now Nick's driver and he seemed happier in this role than as my minder. Considering the amount of filming we did we made good miles, reaching the city of Escuintla just before dark. The road flattened out as I pedalled out of the foothills of Guatemala's central highlands and on to the Pacific coastal plain where the temperature hovers around 30 degrees throughout the year.

After Antigua, Escuintla, a city with industry at its heart, felt charmless. Statistics suggested it had the lowest unemployment and poverty levels in the country, but it wasn't obvious. It felt very tired and edgy. It's no more than a stop-off for any traveller, but even that proved tricky for us. On our third attempt we found a hotel with one room left. The tiny space had just enough room for two beds, my bike and Nick's film gear. A broken air-conditioning unit was the only decoration. Julio reassured us that he would find somewhere else. If not, he'd be back to sleep on the floor.

Much later, we were sorting through kit in the room when we heard two loud cracks outside, a pause, then a hollow bang. We stopped, listening intensely. The sounds had come from fairly close, maybe a few blocks away. After a longer pause there was another snap of what sounded like a handgun, which was echoed by what I knew to be a twelve-bore.

'Let's eat in the hotel tonight,' I suggested lightly, trying to find humour in the situation.

'Agreed,' said Nick.

*

The rains had finally broken a camera, despite my constant efforts to keep everything dry. The humidity caused the cameras to automatically shut down, and when the rain bounced angrily off the tarmac, even in waterproof bags things sometimes got wet. For two weeks my mobile had been working only sporadically, with a permanently broken number 4 key. It had been a good test of my personal thesaurus to try to keep the Twitter feed going without ever using the letters g, h and i. Sometimes I just let the followers work it out for themselves: 'Fone key after DEF now not respond*n* so you w*ll see t*at t**s text *as none!' Nick had brought out replacements for these, and many other supplies, more than I could hope to carry. At least for the few days I had support I could eat chocolate and energy bars till I could eat no more. In terms of energy I felt good after the two days off in Antigua, very keen to up the pace as soon as possible.

Ever since I had committed to a journey down the Americas, there had been the question of how to cross the Darien Gap, the 100 miles of near impenetrable jungle and marshland that divides Central America from South America, between Panama and Colombia. It is the only section of the Pan Americas route from Alaska to Tierra del Fuego that has no roads. The Gap is an imposing natural barrier, not to mention home to FARC (Revolutionary Armed Forces of Colombia) guerrillas.

There had been a few recent British endeavours in the Darien Gap. Horticulturalist Tom Hart Dyke went to the region in 2000 to look for rare orchids and was kidnapped for nine months by the FARC. Karl Bushby, an ex-paratrooper, had better luck in 2001 and successfully crossed the Gap on foot as part of his Goliath Expedition to walk round the world from Tierra del Fuego to England via Alaska; he is planning to reach home at some point between 2012 and 2014. When I was interviewed back in Whitehorse, Canada, by CBC Radio, the same interviewer had spoken to Karl on his walk north. Apparently he wasn't in great spirits at the time, already many years into his journey.

For good or bad, I didn't have this kind of time on my side and never gave the Gap serious thought. If there was no road I would just need to find a way around it. It had never occurred to me that I also wouldn't be able to go through Colombia. Discussions about my route ahead had been going on with my production team since central Mexico. As far as I had been able to gather, nothing had changed for the worse in Colombia recently, but the official advice was to avoid it.

The conversations we had about Colombia reminded me of when I was in Iran discussing the risks of cycling through Pakistan. Once again I was certain I could carry on, that continuing was not an unreasonable risk. But, as I pointed out before, when I carried on into Pakistan it was my decision to make, given that I had privately funded that expedition; this was a BBC-funded expedition, and accountability for the decision fell on their shoulders, not mine. I felt pretty helpless on the road, knowing that people were meeting in London and Glasgow to decide which course my expedition could now take.

I didn't blame any of my team back in the UK, their hands were tied, but it's impossible to describe my frustration at the thought of having to miss a section of the route south. Just a month before leaving for Alaska I had been sent on a week-long 'Surviving Hostile Environments' course held by ex-Special Forces soldiers. It was the most intense practical week's learning of my life, with full kidnapping scenarios played out with actors in the Welsh country-side. Having been through all that, I reasoned that I should be able to risk riding through the sorts of places this course had prepared me for.

It was still a few weeks away, but I learned that an arrangement had been made for me to join a cargo ship at Colón, in Panama, to pass through the Panama Canal and go ashore in Guayaquil, Ecuador. There was no world record on the horizon this time, so no list of rules to follow. If I had been going for the Pan Americas record I would have had to start from the top of Alaska, miss the mountains and go a lot faster. Nonetheless, being told to miss Colombia was a huge personal disappointment.

It was easier to accept that I couldn't cycle through Honduras, given the military coup of 28 June and the continuing political fall-out there. I was reliably informed that I could simply get a boat along the coast from southern El Salvador to Nicaragua, a three- to four-hour crossing that would bypass about 200km (125 miles) of Honduran coastline.

It was my fifth day in Guatemala and I was already heading for the southern border with El Salvador. I had just started to feel familiar with the country, and by sundown I'd be leaving it. My journey through El Salvador promised to be even briefer.

As the road gradually converged with the Pacific again, it descended into more farmland. It wasn't as insanely muggy as the jungles of southern Mexico, but still humid enough to make sweating a futile and uncomfortable reaction to the conditions. Nick spent a fair amount of time filming out the back of José's pick-up, and it was a small consolation that he seemed to be suffering more. Even though he wasn't cycling, this was a major climate shock for him, having come from an October Glasgow.

Near the town of Taxisco I came across a garage on the opposite side of the road, and immediately pulled on the brakes. There were no cars in sight, nothing for the four attendants to do, so they were all dancing. An old-fashioned boom-box sat on the tarmac beside the petrol pumps, music blasting out of it. The three girls and one young guy, all dressed in bright yellow shirts, were salsa-dancing with great gusto. The girls threw their hips, swinging their arms above their heads, dancing around each other with wonderful abandon. I stood there watching, and wishing I lacked British reserve and could make myself go over and join in. Instead I just applauded, which encouraged an encore. When a car did arrive, the girls went about cleaning its windscreen still in time to the music.

Throughout Guatemala I had heard a lot of music wafting from rustic roadside houses, seen women and children working with smiles and a skip in their step. Despite the evident poverty, there was a warmth here that I hadn't seen so much of in southern Mexico. Many Mexicans had warned me that it was dangerous in Guatemala. For sure there are bad people – I'd had my wallet pinched – but, like everywhere else I have ever travelled, those people are hugely outnumbered. The north-to-south pecking order is an interesting phenomenon that I became aware of as I cycled through, the USA patronizing Mexico, Mexico patronizing Guatemala . . . Panama must be an absolute pit, logic would suggest. Or else it was all nonsense.

For lunch I stopped in a small roadside shed under a thatched roof for another meal of *riz* (rice), *frijoles* (refried beans), tacos and *queso* (cheese). I liked this diet, thankfully, as it was pretty much all I could ever find, and I needed an abnormal amount of it. Most food seemed pretty similar to Mexican food, although when I raised this observation with the shack owner I was firmly corrected. The *muy picante* chillies certainly weren't so fashionable, which was excellent news. One less palatable change was the preference for corn tortillas over flour tortillas. Flour tortillas do the job of a simple, fairly tasteless parcel whereas corn tortillas are like wrapping that same meal in cardboard. It's certainly hard work to eat lots of them. The food was also noticeably cheaper than it had been in Mexico, and it hadn't been very expensive there. I could now live for a fortnight on what it had cost to feed myself for a day in parts of Alaska and Canada.

Most meals were now served with a few slices of a soft white cheese called *queso de capas*. Just before the border I passed through a town where roadside stalls were selling this. An enthusiastic local showed me a couple of old cooler tubs inside, sat on a makeshift bench. Without electricity or means to refrigerate, the rounds of cheese were floating in tepid water. For less than a dollar I bought one. Having stopped to have a look, I felt obliged, even though I knew there was no way I could eat it all before it sweated to bits. I ate some and donated the rest to a roadside restaurant a short way down the road.

More practically, the man also had fresh coconuts. Not the hairy brown ones we buy in Europe but the larger, green, fresh type; they were stacked in a large pile on the ground. Taking a machete he swiped the top cleanly off one, placed a straw in the hole and handed it to me as a present. The sweet milk was the most refreshing thing I had tasted since entering the tropics, the perfect drink for the climate.

Further down the road I saw a young boy pushing a wheelbarrow lose his balance and tip the load of gravel into the road. He looked about ten years old and was wearing worn trousers, a dirty T-shirt and sandals. As I pedalled past, he pulled the barrow upright and started shovelling. It was heavy manual work, and he paused to look at me curiously. He was so young, yet he acted older, having already started his working life. I was struck by that self-conscious pang when you realize that someone is looking at you as a window into another world. Like in Mexico, I was very aware here of how relatively few working-age men there were in the rural communities I was passing, how the manual work was left to the young and old.

Later on I crossed a bright yellow metal bridge over the Paz River and entered El Salvador. An imposing whitewashed and blue concrete building stood as the official entry point, dusty trucks lined up on either side. Still, if I hadn't asked a guard where to go, I wouldn't have been stopped. He waved away my passport – a universal gesture that meant I wasn't important to him. Without a stamp and without paying anything I cycled into Central America's smallest country.

12

Nick left the following morning to fly home. His camera was rolling until the moment he drove off, late, for a plane he very nearly missed. We had filmed enough in five days to make an hour-long documentary, though it would probably boil down to less than ten minutes on screen in the end.

One of his last ideas was to film me cycling down a deserted Pacific beach at dawn (this would eventually make it as one of the final shots of the second programme). For sure it was stunning, and a lot of fun, but a serious diversion from the main road. Only the narrow strip of sand where the waves lapped in was firm enough to ride along, which inevitably meant getting pretty wet. As a cyclist first, film-maker second, I would never have thought of a shot like this as it wasn't really part of the natural journey, but I had to agree with Nick that it looked spectacular.

And the diversion showed me a side of El Salvador I would otherwise have missed. The dirt road that wound down to the beach took me through small fishing hamlets in a forest of large palm trees. The houses were little more than beach huts, divided by hand-made wooden fences. Shallow wooden boats, large enough for just a few men, were pulled on to the sands along inlets that wound in from the beach. Few people were stirring so early. Life seemed very simple and wonderfully relaxed. I am sure statistics would say these communities were living in abject poverty, but they were thriving and smiling. Real poverty is far more complicated than just pennies in pockets; here was proof that other factors include climate, level of subsistence, and strength of community.

For a while now my handlebars had been slowly seizing up. I had no idea what the issue might be as I hadn't adjusted anything. When it finally became so bad that I could barely turn left or right, I unscrewed the Allen key bolts on the stem to look inside the headset. Being a fairly average mechanic, I wasn't expecting to see anything I could recognize as wrong. To my dismay, but also amusement, a ring of tiny ball-bearings – meant to aid the free movement of the bars – fell on to the ground, still partially held in shape by a completely worn ring of metal. I had thought the headset was an enclosed unit, so it was alarming to see small bits falling out of it. Before anything else could drop out I put the top back on. The good news was that I had my steering back; the bad news was that there was now movement in every direction caused by a gap between the forks and the frame that I couldn't close. Over any big distance or rough roads I was now worried that the constant impacts my frame would be taking would cause it to break.

I was riding in farmland now, but further south the main road met the coast again and started weaving erratically, following every cove with sharp climbs. I hadn't made a single 70-mile day since Mexico and was desperate to make up lost ground, despite the slow terrain. Back in a dense tunnel of foliage, it was unbelievably hot. For five days there had been little afternoon rain. Of course this was a relief, except that I had wanted Nick to experience the full force of the tropics, even if he was unable to film it, to understand what I had been facing.

That night I met Mike and Alanna in their Russian motorbike and sidecar for the second time. They had had puncture issues and were tired, with frayed spirits, but were just as boisterous. It was certainly a long way from Soldier Summit in arid Utah. They had taken a far less direct route south, which accounted for my staying ahead of them. They had been to Las Vegas to interview Elvis, a rabbi and a porn star and Los Angeles to meet a movie star and some swingers. Passing through Mexico City they met one of the capital's bishops and a wrestler called 'Crazyboy', 'a weird and wonderful collection of people with opinions on lasting love'. We were both filming, but they took the road to wherever a story interested them, whereas I tried to find interesting stories along a fairly set road. Alanna had now endured nearly five months of being coupled up in a sidecar, waving like the Queen to the gawping world they passed. If they had stood out as eccentric in the US, they looked positively otherworldly in Central America. But they didn't care, and had the bravado to carry it off. I also soon found out that they had the lingo, fluently, which was impressive.

With the luxury of more than a roadside meeting this time, we sat up till gone midnight sharing stories from the road. They were the palest adventurers I had ever met, looking as much the Londoners as the day they left England, but they made up for that with some wonderful accounts of the absurd and the unknown.

In the morning I woke at six to try to get some morning surf before a day on the bike. The town of El Sunzal was the first touristy coastal town I had seen, and I woke to perfect waves rolling in. I had been looking for a spot like this for weeks and wasn't going to miss the chance. A shop was already open and I rented a long board and borrowed a pair of shorts for a few hours. The water was like a cool bath, and I watched quite a few surfers on the break about 50 metres out, silhouettes in the early morning light. Having only ever surfed in cold places it felt odd to be in swim shorts as I lay on my vast board and started to paddle out. For the next few hours I got bundled time after time and spent all of my energy swimming back out to try again. Of all the sports I can't actually do, surfing ranks as my favourite. I did manage to stand a few times, all too briefly, but they were glorious moments, gliding effortlessly down the wave, before being ejected back into the washing-machine.

It was just gone ten when I walked back to the hotel and found

Mike and Alanna getting up. After sharing a second breakfast it was hard to get on my bike, not just because of the company but because I felt exhausted in a way I would never experience after cycling. I had also managed to rip off a toenail on the reef. It was sorely tempting just to go back to bed.

My perseverance was soon rewarded. I turned one corner to see a small crowd gathered at the roadside. I stopped and followed their stares to see a man climbing a large tree on the opposite side of the road. He looked in his fifties, maybe older, but had a haggard face, spindly legs and arms, and a thin mop of black hair. He was dressed only in what looked like a baggy loincloth, though it could have been ripped shorts, and he had bare feet. The speed and ease with which he climbed was incredible; he practically walked straight up the trunk, throwing a loop of rope repeatedly upwards to hold himself. Every now and then he beamed down at his audience, baring a few buck teeth in a gummy mouth. Once in position, he drew a long, heavy-looking machete from his waist and started cutting branches. For the next half an hour he moved around the tree cutting more branches, showboating to us by jumping across any gaps and at other times hanging upside down on the rope. I can't imagine many tree surgeons could have done what that man did, yet if you met him walking down the street you would think he was too frail to work. I was keen to keep going but remained where I was, amazed by his agility, until the job was done.

It was breathtaking riding after that – and not only in that the humidity made it hard to breathe normally. I spent the day trying to peer into the jungle, wanting to explore beyond its dense veil. Many of the trees formed a canopy overhead, and their vast trunks were lined with giant stabilizing roots that formed deep ridges, like sinews, straining under the bark. Creeping vines wove webs on every branch across this structure, a symbol of the interdependence of the jungle. Whenever I came near the Pacific there were patches of tourism, beachside bars and hotels, flashes of relative wealth. It was certainly a busy coastline. Despite being less than a third the size of Scotland, El Salvador has the same number of people, the densest population in the region. In the afternoon I cycled into a succession of tunnels, the longest about half a kilometre. The immediate cool was bliss and I relished the goosebumps, caused partly by the relative chill and partly by the thrill of blasting through without lights on, whooping loudly into the din as trucks passed. I emerged from each smiling, immediately slowing down as I hit the wall of heat.

The following day was my last in the wee country of 'The Saviour', my first good mileage day since southern Mexico. I was heading for the port of La Unión. Research suggested that from there it would be fairly simple to get a ferry across the Gulf of Fonseca to the port of Potosi in Nicaragua, thus avoiding Honduras.

Along the roadside the typical house had a small dusty courtyard, often occupied by one or more dogs, maybe a pig and some hens. They were as rustic and homemade as imaginable, but most seemed very well kept. The wooden walls matched the earthen ground. In one, a little girl of about five stood, waving silently at me. Everything around her was brown, yet she was wearing a bright pink dress. I waved back, at which she smiled widely and started waving with both arms right above her head. It was the sweetest thing.

Later, I passed a police car. Even before it did anything I knew I would be stopped – it was that sixth sense that detects when some-one has taken an interest in you. I pedalled on, but sure enough a siren broke the silence. I looked over my shoulder to double-check it was me they were after. I pulled on the brakes and stopped but stayed mounted. Both officers got out of the car. One looked typically local, quite short, dark hair, a moustache; he stayed quiet. The other was taller and had lighter skin and brown hair, obviously partially Caucasian. He approached me, carefully important.

'You have a problem,' he said slowly.

I fought the urge to laugh – as often happens at the least appropriate times. It had been said in the style of Schwarzenegger's 'I'll be back' and it was obvious that he spoke very little English. I wasn't about to help him by trying to speak Spanish. Whatever he had stopped me for, I knew it would be a money-making venture. I leaned down, unclipped my pannier bag and took out one of my cameras. Smiling, I spoke in English, just dropping a few words in Spanish so that he would understand: 'I am from Escotia and I am filming a documental for the BBC.' It was a practised approach, making it clear that I wasn't American, and making them think that I was a journalist so not worth bribing, as it would get reported.

It didn't seem to work. The officer pointed to his head then gestured towards me. 'No . . .' He didn't know the word for helmet, so stopped. 'Casco' – he used the Spanish. 'You must pay.'

There it was, straight to the point. I had seen hundreds of cyclists on the roads in Guatemala and El Salvador and not a single one had been wearing a helmet. I was absolutely certain it wasn't the law to use a helmet. Still on my bike, I turned, unclipped my helmet from my rear pannier and fastened it on. 'OK, thank you, gracias,' I laughed as if it was all sorted out, and pushed off, cycling between them. I didn't dare look back for about 50 metres, expecting a shout or the siren again. Instead, when I did look back they were still standing there, staring after me. I had probably saved myself a dollar or less, which seemed a bit silly when I reflected on the event, but it had been a premeditated response to try to stay in control of the situation, and I was pleased that it had worked.

La Unión had a rough feel about it from the moment I reached the outskirts. Pretty much freewheeling all the way down to the main market street, I then turned left and at the far end of a smaller road I could see the water's edge. It wasn't the ferry terminal I had been hoping for and I approached carefully, feeling far more self-conscious than usual. People were taking notice of me. The street was narrow and dirty, with old pick-ups and cars parked along the kerb. I couldn't say exactly why, but it didn't feel safe. I turned round and left, resolving to get a room and come back in the morning. It was too late to get the ferry that evening anyway.

I remained hopeful about the ferry, despite my first impressions of the port; I was mainly concerned about news from the other side. José, a Costa Rican driver who was meant to be meeting me on the Nicaraguan side, got in touch to say that the road from Potosi was dirt for nearly 50km. He had thought I was coming across that afternoon so he'd set out to meet me, but it was the wet season and his van had soon got stuck in the mud. It had taken him five hours to get out and backtrack. If I did get across I would be cycling on this road, or forced to get on the local buses, which had off-road truck wheels, in order to get back to the main road.

I woke thinking it would be an interesting day whatever happened.

It was back downhill to La Unión port. It was early in the day but there were already a lot of people about, all men and boys. The small harbour's walls ran a few hundred metres into the bay and the tide was still out well beyond them. The only boats in sight were simple wooden hulls, maybe about 25 feet long, with outboards. The seven I could see were lying beached a short distance out. The bay beyond was topped with white horses to the horizon and a strong wind gusted onshore. Julio stayed close but looked as out of place as I did, and even more nervous.

A few men immediately approached, beckoning for money. I couldn't understand everything they were saying. All around eyes followed me and I made sure not to meet any of them.

It took a while to identify some people I trusted the look of. It then became clear that there was no ferry. It had sunk a few years ago and not been replaced. 'So I'll explain,' one of the men continued. 'You need to wait for a while because he does trips over that way. He goes every week but they're sporadic, that's the problem.' I had no idea who 'he' was, but it was clear that the only way across was on one of the open wooden boats, and that no one had any idea when they went.

My heart sank as I looked back out and watched as barefooted men unloaded one of the boats and carried sacks up the beach. As a foot passenger this would have been an adventure, but wading to the boats carrying the bike and five bags with expensive film kit would be crazy, not to mention trying to keep track of it all and make sure it was safe on the ocean in a crammed boat. Even if I could pay extra to charter a boat, it promised to be a rough crossing to an unknown road on the other side. A deciding factor was that I'd also picked up some food poisoning and been quite ill in the night. I was fine to keep going, but the idea of being stuck in the confines of a rocking boat at sea . . .

I tried to think through my options, but the attention I was receiving was uncomfortable so I decided to move along from the main harbour to a blue building belonging to the Salvadoran Navy. It wasn't much of a national armed forces headquarters but it was the smartest building around, and no one followed. I called the UK. Production were still of the opinion that I should go by sea, but they weren't looking at what I was looking at. I couldn't rationalize the ocean trip as less risky than making an overland dash through Honduras. It took some convincing from me, but in the end they agreed the land route was the better option. I reassured them that if all went well we could clear the country in just a few hours. On four wheels, not two.

I threw my bike in the back of the pick-up and was relieved to leave the port behind.

Before heading back to the Pan American highway I asked Julio to go back down the main street to an ATM I had seen. El Salvador uses the US dollar and I wanted more international currency as a back-up. I had entered my pin and was just hitting the amount when two men came and stood very close behind. I didn't have to look back to sense them. It was too late to cancel. I waited for what felt a long time for the machine to start whirring. They were still right behind me on the pavement. As soon as the notes appeared I whipped them away and walked off, around the corner and into the waiting pick-up. My heart was still racing as we drove off.

It didn't take long to reach the Honduras border and it was very simple to get through. I didn't even have to leave the vehicle. As soon as we'd set off again I realized I hadn't waited at the ATM for my bankcard. There was no way we were going back now. I kicked myself for getting spooked so easily, for losing my cool after a morning of feeling on edge. Having been pickpocketed in Guatemala, I'd now left a back-up card in El Salvador. I was down to my last option. I needed to be doubly careful of my wallet now or I would run out of money.

It took two and a half hours and paying off policemen at check-points to reach the Nicaraguan border. The road was very straight and the roadside more open and farmed than southern El Salvador. It was very pretty, and I gazed out longingly, wishing I wasn't going at 60mph, seeing it all through glass. I never said anything to the police, letting Julio do the talking. Behind the wheel he seemed a different man than on the street, laughing and joking, seemingly unworried. At the first checkpoint he'd wound down the window and leaned casually on the frame as the policeman stepped forward. You would have had to be watching pretty closely to notice him palming a few notes. With minimal pleasantries we were off again. I looked at my driver with a new respect. He seemed in his element. About an hour later, we'd approached another police stop. This time we barely paused. It was like paying those US-style road tolls where the skill is to throw your money into the bucket without stopping.

The last stop had been trickier, and I thought for a moment Julio might have been tripped up by his own confidence. As one police-man came to his window, another came to mine and looked in. I didn't touch the window as it was still wound up and looked left instead, towards Julio. My heart sank as I watched the policeman on his side wave away the bribe. Trying to pay off any official is a risk, and it appeared Julio hadn't waited long enough to calculate if it was appropriate. I assumed there would be an issue now. Instead, the policeman stayed calm, took out a pad of paper and started a conversation I couldn't keep up with. I was referenced, but Julio answered for me. After about ten minutes the notebook was put away, and Julio stretched into the glovebox and handed something over.

We were allowed to go soon after that. My nerves were frayed; Julio just laughed. Apparently the policeman had been giving us a ticket for not wearing seatbelts, even though we both obviously were. The initial bribe had been waved away not because the cop was straight but because it wasn't enough.

I was mightily relieved to see the white banner BIENVENIDO A NICARAGUA. Street markets and borders seem to go hand in hand in Central America and we wove past lots of large tricycle taxis, each with a huge parasol, and many colourful stalls. It was with un-reasonable glee that I clipped my bags back on to the bike and pedalled into this new country. The short absence from the saddle and recent fast-forward travel made me immediately revoke any and all damning thoughts I had recently harboured about bike travel. What freedom!

Nicaragua was immediately welcoming and intriguing. The road was now following the Central American Volcanic Arc, earning the region's largest country the title 'La Tierra de Lagos y Volcanes' – 'The Land of Lakes and Volcanoes'. I had seen a number of volcanoes in the distance in Guatemala and El Salvador, as well as the invisible one in Colima in Mexico, but never so close or in such numbers as on my route through Nicaragua.

After the day's delays and travel I managed only two hours until I found myself pedalling into the sunset. When you spend months on a bike you get used to wonderful sunsets – and, when keen enough, sunrises – but that first evening in Nicaragua was past adequate description. In the foreground to my right were a few hardwoods and a verge of very tall grasses. Far off were two volcanoes: the larger was San Cristobal, a near perfect cone which was partially eclipsed in the foreground by Chonco's untidy hump. The sky hosted lots of blue-grey cotton clouds on a background that looked like molten lava. The reds and oranges were so intense and complete that the sky looked as solid and permanent as the volcanoes themselves. It was fierce and beautiful, and I stood there for a while, mesmerized. I'd go so far as to say that those first few hours in Nicaragua rate as the most striking and memorable impressions of a new country I'd ever experienced.

José, who was my age and normally a tour operator in Costa Rica, was much easier company and immediately agreed with me that his job was slightly unnecessary, that Nicaragua was a relatively safe place. Out of the four escort drivers I had been with, he was the first who I felt treated me as an equal rather than as some rich traveller. From the outset we spoke as mates would.

The next morning I was just setting out when I spotted a herd of cattle approaching along the wide verge accompanied by two young boys and an older teenager on pony-back. The eldest had a shotgun slung from his saddle. José pulled up in the van and explained wild cattle herding to me as I watched. They didn't own land so had to keep moving, and cattle theft was common, hence the firearm. I didn't feel we were in danger, and José agreed.

As they drew close, the younger boys allowed the cattle to graze and rode towards us. One wore a holey light-grey T-shirt and dirty white baseball cap, the other was bare-chested with a green shirt tied around his neck; both had dark shorts and sandals. They looked about twelve years old.

'How old are you both?' I asked after getting off my bike and exchanging *holas*.

'I'm fifteen,' said the second boy.

I turned to the other. 'And you?'

'Thirteen.'

The boy with the bare chest turned to his friend: 'I don't understand. I don't understand the way gringos speak.'

'He's not a gringo,' José tried to help out, 'he's from—'

'I'm Scottish . . . from Europe,' I cut in.

'Now I understand,' nodded the boy.

I turned to José and in English commented that there was no way the bare-chested boy was fifteen.

'Are you fifteen years old?' José asked the boy again, who was now walking over to my bike.

'Yes,' he said, and he held up ten fingers, then five fingers.

'He is the smallest fifteen-year-old I have ever seen,' I said to José. The shirtless boy was now examining my bike.

'I'd like to learn to . . .' he began. 'I'd like to learn to speak English, but to speak it well, like a gringo, as well as you do. I'd like to learn.'

I told him that I would like to learn more Spanish.

He pointed to the bike. 'How do you turn it on?'

'It's not a motorbike!' I laughed.

'But how . . . but . . . so do you just pedal quickly like this?' He stood on the spot spinning a leg around frantically.

'I know how to ride a bicycle, but not this one,' the other boy said.

'Me neither!' muttered the shirtless boy, who was now prodding the saddle, which was at chest height for him.

'Have a try,' I offered.

'What?' The boy looked suspiciously at me. 'I try?'

He could just about reach the pedals once he was on the saddle, but there was no chance of him pedalling anywhere. The other boy was now back on his pony. When I stood near them I was taller than both.

They then wanted to show me their cattle. The one already on the pony rode off, whirling a rope above his head before throwing it in an impressive arc over a grazing cow's head.

'Look how he's going to grab the cow, he's going to grab it very skilfully,' the bare-chested boy commented. 'I know how to lasso cows too. But these cows are not mine, mine are those on the other side. If you like, I will teach you how to lasso cows.'

We walked down the verge together.

'Chico,' he called out to his friend, 'can you lend me the rope? Look.' He ran off, looking back to check I was still watching.

'Do you have to be strong?' I called over as he threw the rope.

The cow he'd lassoed started walking away, at which the boy lay flat on his back. He was slowly dragged along the grass until it stopped.

'Is it difficult?' It certainly looked painful.

Standing up again, the boy nodded. 'Sí.'

Without any encouragement they then both got on their ponies to demonstrate their riding skills, galloping up and down, stopping and turning fast. The ponies were bridled simply with rope, the saddles were bits of rug, the foot loops leather. The shirtless boy then jumped up on to his saddle and started walking up and down the pony's back.

Those boys were tough for sure, but also friendly and bright. They were mature beyond their years, hardened to life on the fringe and a livelihood that only they would defend, but ultimately they wanted to be liked, to learn, to be happy like any other child. But before long they would probably lose that remaining innocence. Certainly the older, armed kid never approached me.

I shared some food and left them with a bottle of water before pedalling off.

All day I passed wide fields to my left, framed by the peaks of not-so-distant volcanoes. They were certainly close enough to see the scorch marks on the upper cones. On some, trees seemed to hug to the old lava flows which were like gutters between grassy ridges that tapered up the sides. Other dormant peaks were more rounded and completely covered in trees. A few of the larger cones seemed to have a wispy cloud hanging about their peaks, which added to the magnificence; I couldn't work out if this was a stream from the craters or real cloud hovering at the mountaintops.

Later I spoke to some young men who were standing outside their home at the roadside. Contrary to my understanding, they explained that the lava was toxic and that crops wouldn't grow in the aftermath of an eruption. Volcanic ash could decimate their crops. I asked why they lived so close if it didn't help them, to which they replied that their land and house were hardly worth anything. If they sold, their only option would be to move even closer. They insisted they didn't live in fear, that they were actually proud of the volcanoes. But they also accepted that if there were a serious eruption, they wouldn't survive. As I cycled on from them I passed large volcanic boulders at the roadside – evidence of the power of previous major blasts.

It was easy riding, mildly undulating but nothing challenging, until the following afternoon when I skirted Nicaragua's capital Managua as best I could, wanting as ever to avoid the worst of city riding, its pollution and dangers. From the suburbs the road rose sharply, at first lined with expensive-looking properties, before climbing into the countryside. It was relentlessly steep and the rain started about halfway up, pouring down my face, obliging me to stare down at my front wheel rather than up at the next turn. I was soon in the cloud, so when I did peer up I could see less than 20 metres ahead. I could hear trucks labouring up behind me, sounding like prolonged thunder. From the other direction they appeared out of the veil of cloud like runaways, owning the road; they had no time to react if anything was in the way. It was a narrow gauntlet to run, busy at times when traffic met, and I shrank into myself, listening to my own tempo, trying to ignore the discomfort. It took over two hours to reach the long ridgeline at an elevation of about 860m (2,820ft) at the town of El Crucero.

The roadside was often lined with fences made out of branches, homemade wonky constructions compared to normal fence posts. I was also amazed at how small many of the fields were, and how much of the land was arable, assuming grasslands and grazing would be easier. Then I spotted a farmer turning a field. He had two oxen harnessed to a heavy-looking wooden brace on top of their thick necks and tied to their wide horns. Between the oxen was mounted a 10-foot swoop of wood with a metal blade fixed at its lowest point. It was the most basic hand plough I had ever seen, let alone seen used. The man steered the plough with one hand while holding a long stick to direct the oxen in the other. He wore a dirt-coloured short-sleeved shirt buttoned just once at his waist, and a cap so faded it was now sun-bleached grey. Another man was standing by the fence, and when I stopped to film he explained that he was the farmer and had contracted this man to come in and plough the 2-acre field for the price of $7. He had buckets of white bean seeds at the fence line, ready to hand-sow once the field was turned. Get rid of the baseball cap and absolutely nothing about this tradition had changed for centuries. I stood there, watching those oxen turn within a metre of where I stood, with the very real impression that I was watching the past.

But in Central America, lots of things we take for granted in Europe are still manual tasks. I had passed a number of brick factories before plucking up the courage to cycle into one and ask to see it. The last time I had seen such places was in Pakistan; they were obvious from the high chimney above the baking furnace and the huge mounds of baked bricks. Here, as in Pakistan, the bricks were all red, despite the darker soil.

A lady, maybe in her early thirties, came out of the small house. She seemed shy. A young girl of about seven followed her, barefoot, wearing a simple dress. In the space in front of the house were many wet bricks, laid out in rows, drying in the sun. They were corner bricks, slightly rounded, for building chimneys and curved walls. I tried to ask where the boss was, and if I could look around. She seemed unsure of the question, of why I would be interested, before saying that she was the boss.

She was very sweet, smiling as she walked about her work, showing me the process. Dropping into a mud pit under a tiled canopy and adding more water to the clay-like mix, she squelched about with her bare feet before picking up a dollop, dropping it into a mould and using a trowel to remove the excess, smoothing out the top. Gently, and very slowly, she lifted the frame off, leaving behind a perfect brick to bake dry. The young girl played off to the side, sitting in a wheelbarrow, throwing bits of dirt about. The furnace was nearby; it had a pit about 5 metres into the ground into which logs were fed through a hole. A broken handmade ladder lay against the pit wall. Smoke billowed out from every crack near the top, scorching the walls black.

It was hard, heavy work, and I didn't find a way of asking where her husband was. She explained that they sold the bricks for $8 per 100. There were piles of them all around, but selling them all still wasn't going to make a lot of money. From one pile she picked up a roofing tile with a chipped corner and told me she gave ones like that away to local school projects.

After her initial uncertainty she had grown in confidence, obviously very proud of her work and home. I thanked her. It was a fascinating process in itself, but more than that it had been another great example of the warmth of the people and the culture here. Nicaragua had quickly become my favourite country in Central America.

The lady left saying that it wasn't hot enough today to sun-dry the bricks, but it was plenty hot for cycling. I had now been suffering from minor food poisoning for two days as well and had been taking antibiotics but I was still fairly uncomfortable on the bike.

The next day I reached the border with Costa Rica just before dark, blasting out the final 30km in an hour and fifteen minutes. It was a big mileage day and utterly stunning, still following the Ruta de los Volcanes. The south-west of the country is dominated by Lago de Nicaragua, or Cocibolca, the largest lake in Central America, covering over 3,000 square miles. My road hugged its west bank, along the narrow strip of land between it and the Pacific. Despite this geography, the lake drains into the Atlantic side – a far greater journey – and I was impressed to learn that despite being freshwater the lake is home to lots of bull sharks. So despite the sweltering heat and my lunch stop on a gravel beach, I refrained from taking a refreshing dip. The biggest island on the lake, Ometepe, hosted two of the most impressive volcanoes on my route, Concepción at 1,610m (5,280ft) and the slightly smaller Maderas.

Both looked like they rose straight out of the water, and were crowned in a cloud of steam that hid the craters.

A few miles before I got to the border I reached the lorry queue. After all the bullying I'd endured on the narrow roads it was bliss to pedal past them all. The drivers were obviously prepared for a long wait: many had slung a hammock underneath their trailers in the space before the rear wheels and were dozing. It was the coolest place to be when driving an archaic truck without any air-conditioning. Into the woods again, I spotted lots of green parrots on branches, each with a dash of orange on its head.

From this long tailback I should have guessed that the border was going to be tricky. The buildings were the same chipped off-white concrete, but there were a lot more of them than at other borders I'd been at. I had to queue and pay an administration fee at two places before being allowed through. This alone took an hour. For a driver it looked like a lot of bureaucracy, with many stages of stealthy costs. However, José, whom I caught up with here, knew the system, and after a few quick conversations with the right people he was through quicker than me.

The next day was 23 October. Just about a month since I had cycled out of Colima under the watchful eye of Mexican José it was now my last day with Costa Rican José; the team back at Auntie Beeb deemed Costa Rica safe – Pura Vida, as the locals say. He had been very good company. The son of a trucker who knew the ways of the road, he had loved the adventure as much as me, although he would be the first to admit he was in no shape to try to cycle it. Despite having resented the idea of being shadowed, and while it hadn't been without its frustrations, I had grown to enjoy the banter, the company, whenever I stopped cycling. From here on in I was alone again; it would feel odd to go back to having my meals on my own.

On my last evening with José we ate in a roadside truckers restaurant, a wonderfully rustic place. All the men ate in silence, except for the odd outburst at the TV in the corner that everyone was watching. The show was *Latin America Idol*. It was amusing and odd to watch these burly men being so passionate about teenage pop.

After the meal I showed José my BBC website which at that point featured a fundraising campaign my team and I were running for Children in Need called 'Catch Me If You Can'. The challenge I had given followers back in Scotland was cumulatively to cycle as many miles as I had since Alaska by Children in Need night in November. I had done a few radio and online bits to launch this campaign, but because I couldn't meet the press directly we'd arranged for Katharine Brown, Miss Scotland 2009, to get on her bike and launch the campaign on my behalf. I was delighted with this arrangement. José also enjoyed this story, but when I showed him the launch photos he seemed quite disappointed.

'She is the most beautiful woman in Scotland?' he asked.

'Well, that's a matter of opinion, but she is certainly stunning.'

I felt a strange loyalty to this girl I had never met, as José sat there judging the beauty of Scotland by her.

'Yeah, she is nice,' he conceded, 'but no bum.' He paused, looking closer. 'She is too thin.'

This led on to a very amusing conversation about what he found most attractive in a girl. I soon felt less put out by his initial impression of our beautiful Miss Scotland as it became clear that he thought the whole world should share the Latino taste for big bums. He explained that there was such a fascination with the big booty that bum implants, or buttock augmentations to use the proper term, were becoming increasingly popular in Costa Rica, as disposable incomes increased.

I had no answer to that.

13

It was a gradual climb, but nothing taxing, to the first main Costa Rican town of Liberia, where I was really hoping to find a cash machine. I was very low on money, having made it through Nicaragua without renewing funds. I had not used my last remaining card since leaving the UK six months earlier and I spent a few days quietly concerned that if it didn't work I would soon be quite stuck. I only had British sterling and Guatemalan quetzals left and could find nowhere that would change this. Thankfully, I did find a machine, and the ATM whirred enthusiastically into life. My whoop of relief slightly startled the two ladies behind me in the queue. 'Lo siento,' I apologized, and beamed at them.

It rained on and off all day, but mainly on, and I was cycling through an area of trees and wild grasslands with the odd stretch of roadside being claimed for farming. I was now six hours behind the UK, and at 11.30 a.m. I'd arranged a live video call to the Scottish evening news programme *Reporting Scotland*. Considering the landscape and weather I was now very concerned about how this would work. I needed to locate somewhere far enough from the road to avoid loud traffic noises while also finding an interesting background and ensuring it was dry.

Since Alaska I had been doing a weekly call to BBC Radio 1 to speak to Greg James, regular updates to BBC Radio Scotland, as well as a number of TV link-ups. On each occasion there was the challenge of how to make the link and ensure a secure line. The satellite phone had a bad habit of dropping out mid-call, which had led us to use it only for pre-recorded interviews. For this video call there was no chance I would be anywhere with wifi so I would be relying on the BGan satellite dish I was carrying. This was an amazing bit of kit, tough in adverse weather conditions, but my laptop wasn't.

At eleven I stopped, having made reasonable mileage, when I spotted an open field. I had been looking for somewhere better, somewhere with a view, but I was out of options. It was some kind of orchard, with young trees planted at regular intervals in proud mounds of dirt. Thankfully the rain had stopped. About a hundred metres up a tractor path, I set up. The BGan weighs a kilo, as does the Panasonic Toughbook laptop, so they are considerable bits of kit to carry. I connected them with a 3-metre internet cable, then clipped a laptop web-camera to the top of my tripod. I then set up the bike as a backdrop, so that I could sit in front of it for a decent framed shot which also showed suitably nondescript countryside.

The BGan quickly found a GPS fix so that it could tell me which direction and elevation to be set at in order to get the best line of sight to the geo-stationary satellites. As these were all round the equator, in theory my connection should be much stronger here than it had been in the far north. Usually, when uploading photos, checking the website and replying to emails, I would stream at the lowest rate, where you pay per kilobyte. However, if you want a very secure link with high usage you can pay per time, per second. I didn't dare ask the production team what the highest streaming cost, but it certainly gave me brilliantly fast internet – remarkable considering it was kit I could carry on the bike and use absolutely anywhere, so long as I could see the sky.

I opened Skype and saw straight away that the techie team were online, so I settled down and placed the call. I sat on the earth with one earphone in and one of the camera microphones now coming out of the laptop, all ready for the interview. There was by now less than ten minutes before the live broadcast.

They picked up.

'Hello Scotland,' I joked.

There was a long pause, then a 'hi', followed by some muffled noises. Sitting in the UK studio, they obviously weren't as excited about taking this call as I was making it.

'We can hear you fine,' the technician said, 'but the picture is very over-exposed.'

We spent a few minutes trying to adjust the camera settings, with no improvement. I looked at my watch, then at my surroundings, feeling slightly frantic.

'OK, I will try and find somewhere darker.'

The only shade in sight was cast by a large hardwood tree back near the road, and back near the noisy traffic. I switched the BGan off, closed the screen, bundled everything up in my arms and ran across the field. For a couple of minutes I struggled to find a fix through the branches, and eventually took the BGan out on its full wire to see the sky. While it was logging in I sprinted back and got my bike, then set up the shot. Log in, dial up . . . I was back to the studio by twenty-seven minutes past.

'That's better,' the technician commented as I sat there sweating profusely, trying to think about what I was going to talk about. 'I'll pass you through to the studio.'

A brighter, female voice said, 'Hi Mark, how are you?'

I was so buzzed by the manic rush and haphazard set-up that I went straight into a spiel about where I was, about my first impressions of Costa Rica, and—

'Mark,' the voice butted in, 'this is the producer speaking. You'll be going live in about five minutes, we're running a bit late.'

I sat back laughing, and knocked over my bike. After recovering it and myself, I sat there for a few minutes listening to the talking heads in the studio before my bit. It went well, live to the nation for a few short minutes, and I answered their simple questions about where I had been, where I was going, the highs and lows, etc.

Despite the successful transmission, I always came off these

Finding new camera angles *(left)*: in the flatlands and banana plantations of Ecuador.

Morning roast *(below)*: filming the whole process of coffee making in the high Andes.

Another very long climb *(above)*: what goes up, must come down!

The view to Peru *(below)*: looking forwards to a stunning descent to the border town of Macará.

Travesia de Los Andes *(below)*: Lazaro on his 8,000km push across South America.

A Peruvian feast *(above)*: rice, steak, plantain, fried eggs, potatoes, noodle soup, onions and coffee.

No Ciclistas *(left and below)*: 'Why?' I wanted to find out. That's why! A red lorry illustrates the price for losing control on this extreme section of Pacific road, El Serpentin.

NO CICLISTAS

Maria and her family *(above)*: living in the shanty-town of El Molino, near Pisco.

Walls of shame *(above)*: one of the many fronts that have been built to hide the lack of reconstruction after the massive earthquake.

The start of the Atacama *(above)*: considering the short descent and long climb back out of a deep valley.

Southern Peru *(right)*: big hills and vast deserts.

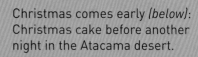

Christmas comes early *(below)*: Christmas cake before another night in the Atacama desert.

Salar de Pintados *(above)*: like a vast concrete ploughed field, I struggle to find somewhere comfortable to sleep in this salt plain.

Leaving the Atacama *(left)*: celebrating having made it through one of the driest places on earth.

First sight of Aconcagua *(below)*: South America's highest peak, as seen from the road.

Rested and ready *(above)*: Damian, Sebastian and myself prepare to climb Aconcagua.

Playa Ancha, the 'wide beach' *(above)*: on the long walk into the mountain, I get to know my new team.

Mulas *(above)*: the incredibly sure-footed mules that carry much-needed equipment to Base Camp.

Plaza de Mulas *(left)*: the second-largest base camp in the world, after Everest. A busy village of climbers.

Camp life *(left)*: Sebastian and me sitting out the storm at Base Camp.

High Camp *(right)*: as we set out for the summit, looking back down on our tents.

Our tents at sunset *(below)*: camp two at 5,400m.

The shadow of Aconcagua (left): an imposing sight as we climb out of High Camp.

Hoping for the weather to hold (right): already high above the surrounding peaks, just a few hours from the summit.

Top of the western world (left): my second major summit, once again in a blizzard!

Valentine's night *(above and right)*: a lonely bus shelter is a welcome break for a night out of the relentless wind in Patagonia.

Under the road *(left)*: this viaduct proves to be my best option when my tent blows down.

Tierra del Fuego *(above)*: the weeks of cycling through featureless flatlands give way to stunning snow-peaked mountains, lakes and trees.

The End of the World *(right)*: arriving on the beach by Ushuaia, the southernmost city in the world. The end of my journey.

broadcasts wishing I could do more than just another travelogue. I wanted to share more about the making of the documentary, what it was actually like to carry all this kit, film my own story, make my own broadcasts. There was no reason for the audience sitting at home to assume I didn't have a film crew setting up this broadcast. This strand about 'how I was sharing the story' was now a big part of the whole picture, as most days on this expedition I was spending hours filming, photographing, blogging, uploading and broadcasting. In that sense it was such a different challenge to the simple focus racing around the world had been.

After packing everything back into my pannier bags, I still had 50 miles to cycle that day.

The next day it rained and rained and rained. I was used to this by now, but it's still so hard to get going when it's bucketing down. The end of the wet season was doing nothing to ease the saddle sores. Until the tropics I hadn't had anything worse than mild bruising, but being unable to regularly clean and dry shorts that get soaked every day is a fast track to bad rashes and open sores. It was manageable, but it was the most uncomfortable I had been on the bike on the journey so far. I ended up cycling well into the dark, which was dangerous on narrow roads with heavy traffic, but I could only stop when I found a room. This certainly wasn't camping territory yet, with lots of thick jungle.

In the early afternoon I'd skidded on a wet ridge of tarmac, immediately losing control. Instinctively unclipping my pedals, I'd found myself running down the road, with the bike falling on the tarmac. It was one of those falls you could never recreate. Luckily no cars were coming, and I was unhurt, so I carried on, having notched up my first little crash of the journey. Later in the day I realized that dropping the bike had somehow broken my pump. So I was fine unless I got a puncture.

When I did get back to the more open sections along the coast I was amazed to find them very developed, with large billboards, mainly in English, at regular intervals for condos and beach houses. It seemed that Costa Rica was a popular second home for Americans, something I hadn't seen anywhere else. Even the very small pockets of surfing tourism in El Salvador had been the domain of the rich locals. I saw a lot more wildlife down the roadside, too: monkeys swinging through the trees above the road, and huge red macaws and smaller green parrots flying around.

Back in Scotland, it usually fell to my mum Una to sort out logistics. In less than a week she had managed to source the spare part for the bike's headset and courier it out to Costa Rica. Mike and Alanna, the Ural bikers, had been recruited to intercept me again and deliver the bits. My BBC team knew how to make the production, but it was Mum who had fifteen years' experience of getting me out of tricky situations the world over when on expedition. She is tireless in her research and reliable, as only mums can be. It had been her role to do most of the route research, and much of the logistics on the road. If all went well I would have the new part in the next few days.

By day three in Costa Rica I was back on the coast heading for the town of Paritta, skirted by banana plantations. Hungry, I stopped at a large open-air restaurant for a second breakfast, only to be told by a very grumpy lady that she wouldn't serve me as my tour bus was about to leave. Bemused, I turned to see a line of mainly overweight gringos slowly tackling the steps on to their coach.

'Tengo un bici,' I said to her, pointing to my bicycle parked at the roadside on its stand.

She remained frosty, but at least she fed me.

The further I travelled into Costa Rica, the more I witnessed this change of attitude from the rest of Central America. In Guatemala, El Salvador and Nicaragua people had seemed pleased and intrigued by the arrival of a gringo, whereas many Costa Ricans acted like it paid to tolerate tourists. And I can understand if there is some resentment. The appearance of gated communities, and oceanfront real estate being snapped up for foreign holiday homes must provoke a love/hate reaction; it brings wealth to some but dilutes the culture and community for the many. If all you ever saw of Central America was Costa Rica you would probably think it very wild and wonderful, but from what I was seeing it felt rather westernized and less friendly.

Despite the mixed welcome, it was some of the most stunning riding yet. I was often just metres from girls in bikinis bronzing themselves on the golden sands, with a backdrop of yachts anchored in the shallows. At times it was like cycling through a picture postcard, yet I kept on pedalling. It was Monday and my boat through the Panama Canal was scheduled to arrive on Saturday, which didn't leave much leeway.

I was surprised to find a long section of gravel track as I cut south of the town of Uvita. I persevered, because I knew the inland detour was considerable, hoping to find tarmac again soon. After a short while I was down to a single lane, unsure if this was a road in the making or if it was being rebuilt. Either way, the wettest months of the year didn't seem a sensible time for roadworks. Then I spotted two dark creatures playing at the roadside. They were the size of a labrador but with a shape somewhere between that of a badger and an anteater. I wasn't fast enough to get a photo. Later I went online to try to identify them but they didn't match any description of the tapir, tamandua, opossum, coatimundi or any other exotic animal native to tropical America I could find. Over lunch I chatted to a South African lady about her efforts to rescue sloths in the area. All this amazing wildlife redoubled my desire to explore and film before leaving the tropics.

I was back on the Pan American Highway and it was raining again when I came round a corner to see a couple of touring cyclists sheltering under a tree across the road. Having not seen any other touring cyclists on their bikes since the US I was absolutely delighted, and I crossed over. They were German and didn't seem as delighted to be meeting another cyclist. They were very wet and miserable, but were friendly enough until they asked where I had cycled from.

'I started in Alaska in June and am heading to Argentina,' I explained.

'What a waste,' the man replied, making no pretence to be polite. 'You miss everything going so fast.'

His girlfriend or wife smiled in agreement, as if it was a conversation they had had many times.

It was a hard one to respond to as we all stood, dripping wet, under the tree. It felt like a poor defence to mention that I had gone much faster around the world and that in fact I was enjoying having more time to explore a bit. But then, as I started trying to make light of the awkwardness, I got annoyed. It would never occur to me to judge someone else's journey like this. It always surprises me when travellers who see so much can maintain such narrow views on what is right and wrong.

'Well, I'd better keep going,' I said, and left them to their doom and gloom. Ironically, a few hours later I received news that Scott Napier, another Scot, had just finished his cycle from Alaska to Tierra del Fuego. We had left Alaska in the same week and had nearly met on the road early on. I was still in the tropics while he had already pedalled the whole of South America, setting the new Guinness World Record for the Pan Americas at 126 days. Scott's incredible effort made my journey look wonderfully pedestrian. With my hearty congratulations to Scott I tried to shake off the grumpiness caused by the meeting with the German cyclists, but such events always bother me longer than they should when I'm alone on the road because there's so little to distract your thoughts.

On the food front, fresh fish was a wonderful change from chicken and beef. My only quibble was the now ubiquitous papaya. Every plate featured generous slices of it. In my opinion there is no excuse for putting a piece of papaya on a plate of tacos or at the side of a piece of fried fish. The natural abundance of tropical fruits did make a very welcome addition to my diet, with the sole exception of this soapy-textured, bland-tasting fruit. Apart from fish, my other source of protein came from cycling into the dark most days and therefore eating lots of bugs. The rest seemed to get caught in my beard. I often felt the sensation of wriggling, until I ran my fingers through it to get rid of them.

It didn't stop raining the next day, which at least kept the insects away, but it was so heavy that I was forced to stop cycling a couple of times. On the second occasion a tiny wooden shelter, which may have been a bus stop, was the only place to hide for nearly an hour. The trucks thundered past, throwing a wave of water to each side. It was too dangerous to cycle. Torrents of water washed across the roads.

I decided to stop an hour earlier than planned, as it was already dark as well. I was in the little town of Rio Claro, where Mike and Alanna eventually managed to track me down. They were as close as I got to teammates on the road and we shared one of the most awful meals of either of our trips so far, which simply added to the hilarity of the conversation. I was certainly hugely grateful for their delivery of bike bits and a new bankcard.

Leaving Costa Rica was easier than entering it had been, no doubt helped by my still damp clothes, which I could smell, so it must have been pretty awful for anyone close to me. Thankfully the Panamanian guards didn't see this as reason enough to refuse entry. I was across in time for an early lunch, or second breakfast – my favourite meal of the day.

As I sat in a small garage eating, I got a call from a researcher at the BBC who had found a place to film in the rainforest the following day, if I was keen. Despite the race for the boat, I wasn't willing to miss this chance. I couldn't wait. *I will make up the miles*, I told myself. It was becoming my favourite catchphrase.

From there it was a good climb, then a long descent to the town of David. The road was now a double lane, with a wide hard shoulder, and so far there wasn't a cloud in the sky. First impressions of Panama were good. Mum had found the names and addresses of two bike shops in town so I raced to get there in good time.

I reached the outskirts at five p.m., just as the afternoon rains started. It took a while to find my way in and ask for directions. The first shop sold everything from freezers to a few basic bikes, but didn't have a workshop. It was gone 5.30 by the time I found the second place and they were closing at six so they said they weren't doing any more repairs that day. I stood outside in the pouring rain, wondering where to find a room, when I spotted some bikes outside what looked like a garage just up the street. Dashing over, pushing the bike, I found a single-room workshop with about ten men in it, some working on a few bikes, most just chatting, standing around the open door. There was no sign, no shop, no till. It was a very basic workshop.

I explained the issue as best as I could, not knowing any of the vocabulary for bike bits or knowing who was in charge. There were some general nods of enthusiasm, although I was sure none of them had seen a bike like mine. They gathered around, leaving the jobs they were doing, and started talking about the problem. I was left on the outside. I pushed back in, suggesting I should take the bags off. There was no floor space left in the workshop so we were all on the pavement outside, underneath a narrow section of roof. The rain was streaming off this and literally bouncing off the road in the growing darkness.

It took a while to remove the bars and slide the new ring of bearings into place, mainly because there was so much conversation involved. This still left a gap as the frame and forks wouldn't join snugly, and it took them a while longer to figure out that there were some broken remains of the old ring of metal still in the way. These were completely stuck, having been hammered fast in place over the hundreds of miles since the breakage in El Salvador. By this time it was dark and they were talking loudly to hear one another above the rain.

I was out of the loop, so I was alarmed to see one of them pick up a chisel and start hitting away at the broken piece. He paused just long enough to say to his friend, 'If we damage it, it's going to cause a lot of trouble,' which I am glad I didn't understand at the time. I got the translation from the film clip later on.

It was clearly a case of too many chefs, but I was still grateful for their apparent enthusiasm, until I heard more of those translations, which revealed that they were mostly bantering about things other than my bike. All the while I stood to the side, assuming they were diligently grafting on my bike, which was lying in bits on the pavement, in a rainstorm, in the darkness, in an as yet unknown country.

It was obviously going-home time for a local school as boys and girls were running up the road, trying to dive for cover under the roofed section just outside the garage. This, too, was a constant distraction for the men, who shouted out and whistled at the groups of older girls, all soaked through in their white shirts.

It was way past seven by the time I left, having never made it inside the workshop. Their shared efforts cost me five US dollars and the men seemed pleased with their handiwork. I can't aptly describe how heavy the rain was as I cycled around town under the glow of streetlights to reach my hotel. I didn't care. My bike was fixed.

The next day was the 150th of the expedition. At seven a.m. I was collected in a bashed old pick-up by a man called Steven. An Englishman, he had spent much of his life in Africa and Australia, working with animals. With his wife Michelle and teenage son and daughter he now had a 40-acre plot of rainforest in Panama where he ran a monkey sanctuary. A few miles uphill on a very rough track off the main road we turned into the entrance to his lodge, which he had built himself. As soon as I opened the truck door a small black monkey launched itself on to my leg and clambered up hand over hand. Steven walked off, another two climbing on him.

I had never been close to a monkey, let alone had one climbing on me. He or she had the cutest little face, and eyes that peered at me, and long fingers that grasped tightly. Forget dogs, these were the most affectionate animals I had ever met.

My new friend was called Google, and his friends were Yahoo and Mona Lisa, or just Lisa; there were a few others I never got the names of. They had all been rescued from accidents or mistreatment and were now semi-domesticated, spending some of their time with a troop of wild howler monkeys that lived in the area.

After managing, with difficulty, to leave the monkeys at his small house, we set out into the forest. A maze of paths led all over and within ten minutes I would have been unable to find my way back. We were mainly climbing. Vines and branches sprawled through the air in all directions; some seemed alive, others decaying. The ground was a similar mix, with bright fungi sprouting from old trunks and huge ferns spreading upwards for any light in the shadowy sub-canopy world. Steve showed me army ants with incisors the size of their abdomens marching along a path in their thousands, an amazing-looking bright-red plant called Shampoo Ginger, and a couple of spider webs with brightly coloured owners that he assured me could kill me. I walked along with my arms close by my side, not wanting to brush by anything in this teeming and potentially lethal world.

At the top we came to a clearing where banana trees had been planted. I could now see all the way back down to the Pacific, a spectacular view. More significantly, I could also look across to his land boundary on the far hillside. There was a distinct line where rainforest now met a bare landscape, completely cleared of trees.

'This is what we are trying to protect,' Steven explained. 'The locals just come in to chop and burn. They no longer respect this environment as it's not worth anything to them. They know that if they clear a space like this and grow banana trees then they can sell them. But if this island of rainforest that we just walked through was cleared, it would take hundreds of years to recover.' He was sad about the situation, but determined to make a difference. Despite the ongoing damage he was adamant that working with the locals was the only way to ensure that this ecosystem had a future.

Back at the house, we made a plan for the rest of the day. Steven was pretty keen to go back into the forest later, and that I should spend the night in there. That left us enough time to take his jeep deeper inland for a few hours.

The road got increasingly bad and in sections we clambered along steep washed-out tracks before slewing through muddy pits that came up the wheel axles. Few vehicles came this way. Within a few kilometres we passed a young lady dressed in a traditional long pink dress, walking with her husband. They were Ngobe-bugle Indians on the four-hour walk back to their village from the main road. Steven stopped and they clambered into the back. She was carrying a young baby. The road continued to be bone-jarringly rough, and we were all constantly thrown about, yet the woman kept her baby clamped to her bare breast the whole time. I felt fairly broken by the time we had done 15km inland to their village, and I was very impressed with the driving.

As a thank you, the young couple invited us into their hut. It was built on a frame of wooden poles, about 7 metres by 4 metres, with corrugated-iron sheets on the roof and some wooden slats boarding part of the walls. Most of the space was open, with a string hammock hanging over the dirt floor and clothes hanging from the roof poles. A duck was tethered by one of its legs to a table leg, and a few metres away from the hut a pig was roped to a large log. The parents looked younger than me, yet there were five children and the mother was heavily pregnant. Four of the children were girls; they all had long jet-black hair, were dressed traditionally, and their feet were bare. There was no easy way to communicate but, using the camera, I showed each of them pictures of themselves, which made them laugh. The father then came over holding the baby. I didn't know what he was asking, but Steven took the lead. He blew on the baby and drew a cross with his finger above him. 'Do the same,' he said quietly. I leaned forward, blew gently on the baby and traced my index finger over his tiny face.

Once we'd left, Steven explained that they believed that white people were strong and that we would give good health to their sick baby. I felt uneasy about not having done more.

We drove slowly back through the village, which had no electricity or running water. He explained that in the past the Indian communities would have been mainly self-sufficient, but now they were trapped in dependency on a capitalist society without any industry or much income to support themselves. They lived in absolute poverty without an obvious way out. We were only about 200km from Panama City, considered the Hong Kong of Central America, a mecca for trade and commerce.

As night fell we armed ourselves with powerful lamps and headed back into the jungle. It was a very different place now. The beams, normally capable of shining a quarter of a mile, now penetrated less than 10 metres into the dense foliage.

'Watch out for vine snakes,' Steven warned airily, 'they're pretty nasty.'

'And what do they look like?' I questioned.

'Like vines,' he laughed.

Vines hung everywhere and were thick underfoot. I kept close behind him, genuinely nervous. Steven seemed wonderfully at home, but I couldn't stop thinking about how stuck we would be if our lamps failed.

Flashing the light around, I could pick up the whites of eyes looking back at me. It's no exaggeration when they say the rain-forest comes alive at night. We spotted a few more spiders, and some bark scorpions; Steven was very disappointed not to find a snake. He had seen a fer de lance recently, the cause of more human fatalities than any other American reptile, and was keen to show one to me. I was fairly keen that he didn't.

About a mile into our trek we came to a place where he knew there was a tarantula nest. Instead of a web, these huge spiders have holes in the ground and lay trip-wires for passing insects and small rodents. Steven had brought a skewer of wire and some bait to try to lure the tarantula out. He explained that the spider was a female, so very large, the size of a side plate, and about fifteen years old by his best guess. Crouching in the undergrowth, I handed my lamp over so I could have the film camera in one hand and the skewer in the other. My heart was racing but I tried to breathe quietly as I lowered the small clump of food into the utterly black hole. Nothing happened. I pushed it down a bit further, my hand now within a foot of the hole. The wire tightened. Silently, she had grabbed hold of it. It felt like having a fish on the line. I slowly tried to move the wire back out. It was stuck. Steven took it from me. After a few minutes, two hairy legs appeared. They looked an impossible size for the hole. I took the wire back and kept trying, pulling until her pincers were visible. But then it got stuck again. I could pull back on it hard to no avail. The spider was stronger, braced against its hole. Eventually the bait came loose and she disappeared back inside. In awe and still very nervous, I followed Steven back down the weaving path, utterly lost. I hated being so dependent on someone else.

In a wide clearing Steven had already set up some netted jungle hammocks. With whispered assurances that nothing could get me in there he bid me goodnight. I clambered in, zipped the net closed around me and tried to sleep. Inevitably, I kept waking. The forest was impenetrably dark and loud with noises – creaking, rustling, scurrying, the voices of countless unknown living things. I felt fairly safe in my hanging sanctuary, but very exposed as well. At one point something walked right underneath me and I tensed involuntarily. My sense of hearing was ultra-heightened; my head craned towards every noise.

I did sleep for most of the night in the end, but didn't feel particularly well rested the following morning. After a quick breakfast and plenty more howler monkey cuddles, Steven drove me back to David. I was cycling by nine a.m.

I spent that day peering even closer into the roadside jungle. In the north of Panama by the Caribbean coast and to the east by the Darien Gap are vast and nearly impenetrable areas. Steven had spoken about wanting to stage an expedition by foot into these areas, carrying only a hammock, a machete and a few weeks' supplies. Despite feeling so ill at ease in there, when I was back on the bike I spent several hours imagining what that would be like.

Without a hammock I knew it would still be tricky to find any space to camp. Thankfully it was at least dry for the second day. By 4.30 p.m. I reached the small community of Chiriqui, having accepted that I wouldn't make the next big town, Santiago, by nightfall. But the clocks had gone forward another hour at the border – I was now five hours behind UK time – and it didn't get dark till 6.30. I wanted to go further, so I stopped at a small garage to buy some food and ask what there was up ahead.

The customers behind me were dressed in dark blue uniforms and had both arrived on a motorbike. They immediately asked where I was cycling, and I explained as best I could. My Spanish still wasn't great, but this was at least a practised conversation.

'Where do you sleep?' one of them asked, in Spanish.

'Sometimes in a tent.' I gestured towards the bag on my bike. 'But I would like to find a room tonight. Do you know anywhere ahead?'

'You can stay with us,' he said, as if it was obvious.

I had no idea who they were, but they seemed nice guys, and on second thoughts it was crazy to go on for another few hours just to sleep in the jungle.

'Dos kilometros,' he explained, 'and you will see us.' With that they got on their motorbike and disappeared.

Sure enough, within a couple of kilometres I spotted them standing at the roadside. Behind them was a group of about ten other men, all in uniform, and a few big red trucks. They were the Cuerpo de Bomberos, and I had been invited to stay at the fire station.

They were all very welcoming, and there didn't seem to be any fires to put out, so everyone was on cleaning duty and chatting to pass the time. I had been there for an hour when I got a text from Mike and Alanna to say that they were hot on my trail again, asking if I had found anywhere good to stay. I felt a bit awkward. It would look odd if a few hours after I'd turned up alone two crazed-looking Evil Knievel types appeared on their Russian motorbike. I told them where I was, but I couldn't find the Spanish to announce their arrival.

The black Ural eventually turned into the station and the firemen's reaction was, unsurprisingly, one of bemusement. Thankfully, Mike and Alanna were better able and more used to defending their eccentricity than I was, and they had none of my reserve. In fact Alanna was on particularly boisterous form, immediately nicknaming all the firemen as if they were part of a calendar. 'Así, debe ser el Señor Febrero' – 'So, he must be Mr February.' They seemed amused and intimidated in equal doses, but at least I no longer needed to worry about introductions. Very soon the offer of accommodation was extended to my London amigos and we were shown through to a large room with bunk beds and lockers, like army barracks. Most of the men were on duty for the night, and we would be bunking down with them.

Alanna, with little diplomacy, insisted I take a shower, claiming that I smelled unimaginably bad, and that my horribly stained, sweaty cycling clothes reeked of pee. I tried to defend the fact that lycra and polyester can become pretty unpleasant and that I hadn't had any kind of accident. But the more you defend such a ridiculous accusation, the more it sticks, and I didn't have the Spanish to check that the firemen knew that Alanna was joking. I took small comfort from Mike's encouragement to ignore her.

That night it was us three and eight firemen sleeping in the bunk beds with an air-conditioning unit that kept the room far colder than outside. I slept fairly well, but every time I woke I could see that my fellow travellers were restless. Alanna was significantly more subdued in the morning as we packed up and headed off. The firemen had been great hosts. If all went well I hoped to catch up with the loony lovebirds again before the end of our travels.

I was now south of where I needed to be as the cargo boat I was due to join was leaving from the town of Colón, on the Caribbean Sea. In fact every mile in Panama was on average an easterly tack, not southerly. From coast to coast the Americas is at its narrowest at this point, hence the 48-mile Panama Canal, so it was a relatively short northerly commute from Chiriqui to the Atlantic coast.

It took two days, during which time I left the rainforests behind and entered vast and more commercial farmlands. It also rained, unsurprisingly. Nearing Colón, I stopped in an underpass to shelter from a deluge to find another cyclist, a middle-aged man, doing the same. He was carrying only a few small pannier bags yet explained that he was near the start of a very long cycle. His name was George Sitra, and he came from Brazil. We huddled over a map as he traced out what he planned to do, visiting as many countries as he could in a decade. He had books of detailed notes already, which he flicked through, dropping wet splodges on each page as he did so. He was heading north so we shared a few bits of advice about the road before heading back out into the rain.

After all the rush, I then received news that the shipping arrangements had changed and I would have two days to wait in Colón. I wished I had known earlier and spent more time in the rainforest instead. Colón didn't feel very safe to explore alone; in fact it boasted the highest crime rate in the region. From what I'd seen it differed hugely from the rest of Panama, much of the population being of Afro-Caribbean origin: they had remained after being brought in to build the canal in the early 1900s. I did manage to find a replacement bike pump and some spare inner tubes, but apart from that it was nice just to pause and recover briefly. I spent the forty-eight hours mainly sleeping and eating.

I had no idea what to expect for my voyage to South America. Una had managed to track down a shipping company in London called Star Reefers, which didn't have a ship of its own in the area but had arranged with another company to take me onboard. All I knew was it was to be a banana cargo vessel, and that the journey through the Panama Canal and down the Colombian coast to the Ecuadorean city of Guayaquil took about sixty hours.

And so I waited.

Early on my third day in Colón I bundled the bike and pannier bags into a taxi and was taken to the port. Being a cargo port, it wasn't set up well for passengers, and it was unclear how to go about passport control. Having got through without a problem I was led by a man who didn't say a word to the water's edge where a 20-foot pilot boat was waiting. Another man onboard gestured for my things to be handed over. Wishing someone would speak to me, I leaned out with my bike, then the bags, before jumping onboard. Still in silence, we pulled away, cruising slowly past rows of cranes and mountains of containers, and underneath tankers being loaded. It was a vast scene of industry, the home of one of the western hemisphere's biggest tax-free ports.

Once away from the harbour, the pilot opened up the engines and we shot forward. The bike and bags weren't tied down on the flat decking and I was worried about them, but my pilot and his friend seemed oblivious so I stood quietly, holding on to the railing. They both had lifejackets, I didn't.

After about five minutes with the throttle open we were a good distance out into the bay and getting closer to a large cream-coloured vessel. CROWN OPAL, PANAMA was emblazed in black across the stern. The pilot throttled back as we drew near and down her starboard side. Her hull rose vertically for at least 5 metres above sea level and a rope ladder was hanging overboard, stopping just above the waterline. I looked up and saw three faces peering down, all wearing crash helmets. Then a rope was thrown down, which the man who had met me caught and started tying to the bike frame. I rushed over to check the knot before it was hoisted slowly upwards. Next my bags were taken up, in three separate bundles, which left me, holding my film camera.

'Go,' the pilot called out in English, still at the helm. It was the only word he had spoken.

The pilot boat was bobbing, so the rope ladder moved in and out of reach. Glancing up again, I wished I wasn't holding my camera, and that I had a lifejacket. I unscrewed the microphone from the top, stuffed both parts into my trouser cargo pockets, and reached up. As soon as the small boat lifted in the water I grabbed hold of the ladder and put my right foot on the lowest rung. Pulling upwards, I had just placed my left foot when the pilot boat moved away, coasting for a few seconds before opening up and racing in a wide arc back the way it had come. I was left standing on the bottom rung, a foot or so above the open ocean. I glanced up again to see a few faces still peering down at me. Slowly I climbed, reminding myself to keep three points of contact. Before too long I was pulling myself over the side.

I stepped into a group of men, all dressed in overalls and hard-hats. Without any introductions I was led between rows of containers, off the deck, inside and up a couple of narrow flights, through some heavy metal doors, and into a cabin. I had no idea where my bike was, but my bags soon appeared, carried in by some young sailors.

And so I was left there, unsure what to do next. My crew seemed to be Russian, and lacked that Central American warmth I was now used to. I looked out of the small oval window, then explored my small but comfortable cabin. In two and a half days I would be in South America, and given my impressions so far, it promised to be an interesting journey.

14

I woke, my contact lenses dry on my eyes. The cabin was shaking very slightly and there was a deep rumbling noise. I sat up and tried to wake up properly, laughing at myself. I hadn't meant to drop off and could have been asleep for days, considering the way I felt. In fact it was just gone two p.m. and I had been out for less than an hour. Through the window the horizon was now moving, slowly. We were off.

I didn't know anyone onboard, or where anything was, but I couldn't spend over two days alone in my cabin so I fixed my contacts and checked that I looked vaguely presentable. I'd found a machine wash in Colón, and it was bliss wearing properly clean clothes for the first time since northern Mexico.

I opened my door and saw that I was at the top of some stairs. I could only go down, or through another door opposite. The CREW ONLY sign made me think it wasn't another cabin. I hesitated. My first impressions hadn't been particularly welcoming. I knocked. No reply. I turned the handle and pushed. It was open. A man in a short white shirt with collar stripes turned, and to my great relief welcomed me in, introducing himself as Captain Viacheslav. There was no smiling, but he had at least shaken my hand. A few of the men who had shown me onboard were also in there, now without helmets, and they introduced themselves quickly as Poliakov and Tkachev, names I continued to forget.

I had inadvertently walked on to the ship's bridge and now had a complete view down the whole vessel. The banks of dials and equipment all looked *circa* 1970. I later read that the *Crown Opal* was built in 1997, so I can only assume all cargo vessels are built to look like factories. There was certainly no luxury or styling in sight.

We were underway but it would be 16:00 hours, according to Captain Viacheslav, before we reached the first locks of the canal, so he offered to take me to lunch. We went down two steep metal flights of steps to a galley that was a little more luxurious. We sat in faux leather chairs and ate some dark meat in gravy with mashed potatoes and broccoli – in silence.

Back on the bridge I noticed there were two doors leading out to a railed platform that ran down each side of the ship. On the starboard side this came past under my cabin window. I realized that I must have one of the best cabins onboard.

An official Panama Canal pilot master was brought onboard to steer the 152-metre vessel through the eight-hour transit. As we made our approach, the mood on the bridge was one of quiet tension – not surprising when driving with a 128-metre bonnet, using a steering wheel smaller than a car's, with just a few metres to spare on each side. I had taken a sailing boat through locks before so I understood the theory well enough. We would be lifted up through one lock system, with a few big steps, before transiting a series of lakes and dropping back to sea level at the Pacific end of the canal through two more series of locks. But the scale of each process was stunning, probably the most impressive feats of engineering I had witnessed so close up. The Crinan Canal on Scotland's west coast just doesn't compare.

Thick ropes were attached to heavy locomotives that pegged the vessel at each corner before pulling us forward. I set up one of the cameras on the railings, locked off for the next few hours, so I could capture what would be a cool time-lapse. At the second step up, a huge cruise liner was passing in the other direction. As our water rose, theirs sank. Each cabin on the pearly white floating hotel had its own balcony, with deckchairs. Many of their occupants stood less than 20 metres away taking photos and waving enthusiastically. I felt strangely proud of my ugly brute of a ship, with its huge cranes, dirty great chimney and stack of containers. My new Russian and Ukrainian colleagues weren't inclined to wave back, and I wasn't about to break rank.

The international nautical language is English so all the crew had to be able to communicate in it. They could too, very well, about anything to do with shipping; most other conversation I found quite hard work. It was a case of understanding all the words but being left with little idea about what they were actually trying to say. This maybe comes from speaking English only with people who are not native speakers. And the majority of the time they just spoke Russian to one another.

They were hardy men for sure. There were no jokes, no banter, and they didn't exactly make it homely for themselves. The only luxury on the bridge was a kettle, a pot of coffee and some sugar. And it wasn't even proper coffee, despite its natural abundance in Central and South America: they subjected themselves to drinking Nescafé instant for six months at a time while at sea.

After Lake Gatun it was a narrow canal for many miles. Darkness had fallen by the time we floated under the imposing Centennial Bridge, the suspension bridge that carries the Pan American Highway that I had been cycling on. We eventually approached the locks of Pedro Miguel and then Miraflores, each time guided in only by green lights to the left, red lights to the right. Otherwise it was pitch black, with some lightning flashing on the horizon to the south-east. During the last lock we passed a car transporter going the other way. Capable of carrying five thousand cars, she utterly dwarfed us. I stood on the open bridge watching her in awe. The Russians didn't seem to share my excitement so I kept my reaction to myself.

I watched the pilot master climb down that vertical rope ladder in the dark, illuminated by a spotlight, on to a small launch boat, and motor away. We were out, under La Puente de las Americas, the Bridge of the Americas, and off into the Pacific, with the sky-scraping cityscape of Panama City lighting up the night sky behind us. It is easy to abuse superlatives, but it had been a truly staggering experience.

For the next two days we headed south at about 20 knots, staying around 80 miles off the Colombian coastline. There was absolutely nothing on the horizon most of the time, just the odd passing ship. It was a wonderful adventure and I spent much of my time on the bridge just looking out. This wasn't just for the enjoyment of it: I had an unofficial watch, like the rest of the crew, to spot fishing boats that were too small for the ship's radar to pick up and hard to see on the waves. We could crush them without even noticing. I watched the sun sinking for over an hour. Viacheslav came out on deck after a while to check up on me as I ran around taking film and photos. He seemed baffled by my interest in a sunset, but my enthusiasm did at least make him crack a smile.

On my second day onboard I rigged up the BGan on the deck and ran the cable through my window, so that I had internet. Despite the ship's rocking, it was a great connection, and I settled down to update the blogs, send photos and do emails until I made myself seasick and had to lie down for a few hours.

I now felt I was starting to get on with Captain Viacheslav, despite the very limited conversation, and he offered to show me around the ship. I agreed, but was quietly nervous about one thing. Back in the jungle, Steven had explained that the most feared spider in Central and South America is the Brazilian wandering spider. 'Be careful on that boat,' he had warned before explaining the creature's unique character. 'Its venom contains a toxin which gives men an erection, which can last until they eventually die. Those who survive are often left impotent.' Jokes aside, this priapism – the fancy word for what is basically a prolonged erection – was meant to be excruciating. The toxin is being developed for use in impotency medication. A quick Wikipedia search did nothing to dispel my concerns about what is widely considered the world's most deadly spider: it informed me that a common name for it was 'banana spider' because it liked to hide in banana bunches on plantations, and sometimes hitched a ride on ships. We were travelling empty, but due to load up with thousands of tons of bananas in Ecuador that would then be taken back to Europe. I raised the wandering spider issue with Viacheslav who assured me that all the units were completely sealed when bananas were onboard, so they didn't worry about spiders. But they weren't sealed now, and we were clambering around the vast wood-slatted holds in the ship's hull. They looked very clean, but also dark and wonderfully spider-friendly. I wasn't sad to leave them.

By the second night I was feeling very cooped up, desperate to stretch my legs. There was nowhere to walk in a straight line for more than about 10 metres. I again marvelled at these men's ability to do this for half a year at a time.

I woke on my third morning at sea to see land – my first sight of Ecuador. Guayaquil is positioned 40 miles up the estuary of the Guayas River so it took a few more hours to reach the port, mainly through thick mangrove forests that grew into the water on both sides. As we approached the city, I saw along the river's edge a shanty-town built on stilts. Hundreds of huts made of bamboo walls and iron-sheeted roofs stood on tall wooden legs so that the river could wash under them. The narrow beachfront was a landfill of litter, with people sifting through it. From the ship's bridge I could see over these makeshift single-roomed homes to more substantial houses behind, but they were still on streets of dirt, built with bare concrete blocks. Along one street I watched some children playing football. Despite the obvious poverty, it did look very green, with a sea of trees poking higher than the city. In the distance to the north the city was hemmed in by forested hills, and to the east I could see the skyscrapers of downtown.

Two big tug boats pushed the *Crown Opal* around in her own

length, shunting from the sides at the front and back, before we could pull into port. A concrete wall and prison-style barbed-wire fence divided us from the shanty-town area.

I went ashore to be met by a man called Xavier Romero, a contact of the shipping company that had been asked to make sure I got ashore without issue. He was quite a round man in his fifties, with short curly black hair and a very kind face. It was too late to get cycling so he suggested taking me for dinner, then taking me back to the ship. There was no point in getting a room when I could stay for free onboard. I accepted, surprised by the kind offer, having got used to the brisk efficiency of the Russians.

As soon as Xavier and I cleared the double-gated port entrance in his pick-up, he wound down his window and turned on a CD of Latino ballads at high volume. After a while he broke into song, tapping the outside of his door as we waited at traffic lights. I laughed, which he took as encouragement. I looked around, soaking up my first impressions of South America, with no idea where we were going.

After the decent but fairly military meals onboard, eaten in silence, it was wonderful to sit in a bustling restaurant and eat the best steak I could remember, chatting and laughing to a background of live music. Xavier's great loves were music, food and women, and he spoke at length about the depths of his passion for each. Being a lover ran in the family, he explained, and he had twenty-nine sisters and brothers. I couldn't get my head round this; I can only assume they didn't share the same mother. He told one story about a town in the high Andes where the women were the most beautiful he had ever seen, and how they had powers over any man. It sounded almost mythical. Later on another story alluded to the fact that a few years ago he had left his wife of many years for a woman from there. Xavier looked like an unlikely Romeo, but there was no doubting him. However, he had seen the error of his ways and gone back to his wife. 'Well, she still loved me of course,' he explained simply.

It was late by the time we left, too full to walk comfortably. Xavier insisted on driving back to the ship via his home so I could meet his children.

The next morning Captain Viacheslav called most of the ship's crew together for photos before I left. I hadn't realized that I was the first non-business passenger they had ever allowed onboard. No wonder they weren't practised hosts. Most of the deckhands were Filipino, with the Russians and Ukrainians in charge. It had been an amazing insight into life at sea, a privilege, and once used to their ways I felt I had got on well with the crew. They certainly gave me a great send-off, lining the bows and waving as I clipped my bags back on the bike and pedalled away.

It was good to be back on dry land, away from a world that constantly vibrated to the throb of a V12 engine the size of a small house.

Xavier was with me to make sure I cleared Guayaquil safely. He had brought copies of four CDs with him, a selection of his favourite music for me to take on the road. Quite tired of my current iPod selection, which was half filled with Spanish lessons I no longer listened to, I was grateful for this unexpected present.

I was now 2 degrees south of the equator, having crossed it while out in the Pacific. My legs felt very fresh, my cycling top was brilliantly white again, and my hair oddly sun-bleached now that it was clean. It felt like a fresh start after five days off the bike, and I had just six weeks to reach Aconcagua in time to climb. I had spent a lot of time onboard sitting in my cabin, reading up about the mountain. It was now a bigger focus than ever before, and I was slightly behind schedule. I would need to speed up for certain.

The first couple of days riding in Ecuador, until the town of Santa Rosa, filled me with confidence as I sped across a flat agricultural plateau. Ecuador is the biggest banana producer in the world and I was lost in a world of plantations. Now that I was out of the tropics I was keen to start camping again, but the vast Dole, Del

Monte and other commercial plantations didn't offer anywhere obvious so I spent my first night in the town of Naranjal. A room cost $12, so similar in price to Central America, and I was intrigued to see the receptionist working on a typewriter. Tap, tap, tap, slide and ting. It was lovely to watch. For a few more dollars I bought myself half a cooked chicken and managed to find my way on to the flat roof of the hotel, where they hung the laundry. I sat on the edge, looking across a sea of rooftops and aerials as the sun went down, and reflected on a good start to South America.

The next night, in Santa Rosa, I did the same. With all the flat roofs, it seemed the safest place to set up the BGan and do my blogging. As I worked away, the whole city went dark. The only light came from my laptop screen. A quick Google search explained the problem: Ecuador was in the midst of an electricity crisis, caused by the worst drought for forty years that had depleted water levels at the country's main hydroelectric plant at the Paute River dam. Only two of its ten turbines were working so the country was experiencing rolling black-outs for the foreseeable future. My rooftop was a very peaceful place from which to watch a country in darkness.

As I sat there in the dark I checked the news online and was shocked to read that El Salvador had been hit by severe flooding and mudslides, killing nearly two hundred people, displacing an estimated fifteen thousand, and blocking well over a hundred roads. The same low-pressure system I had felt the serious effects of in Panama had caused over 400mm of rain to fall in some parts of the country. I had cycled through some of the worst-hit towns just three weeks earlier.

I woke at 5.30 the following morning to the sound of torrential rain on the window, so I reset my alarm for 7.30. I thought I had left the rainy season behind. Sunrise was at six a.m., and being near the equator sunset was predictably twelve hours later, so I was keen to get early starts, just not in heavy rain. By the time I wheeled the bike out it had stopped and I raced back into my room to get the bags. The door was quite low and I forgot to duck. I didn't pass out, but I barely remember falling down. There was no one around and I must have been too shocked to call out anything. Instead I remember curling up and cradling my head, still lying on the ground. I had caught the crown, which swelled into a good lump.

About twenty minutes later I started out, very slowly. After a few hours I was feeling nauseous and very weak so I stopped for a second breakfast. I knew I was concussed, but I was also sure I could keep going.

The road now started climbing into the Andes and my target was to reach the village of Olmedo at about 4,000ft (1,220m) by the following morning so I could film at a coffee plantation. I knew it wouldn't be a straight climb, that it would have some good ups and downs in between, but I never expected it to be what it was. I left after that second breakfast at 10.30 a.m. and by two p.m. I had covered just 45km – a new slow record. And then I slowed further. The road steepened so that the average gradient was between 8 and 12 per cent. The sun burned through the cloud and it was hot work pedalling uphill at walking pace. The nausea had thankfully faded by the afternoon but I was left with a cracking headache that felt like something stabbing behind my right eye. As I climbed, the tarmac grew patchier, so whenever possible I had to cycle down the middle of the road. There were soon fairly long sections of gravel, which were often ridged where water had run.

It wasn't going well, and I wasn't enjoying it, but I had to get my thoughts together for a satellite call with BBC Radio Scotland. At the scheduled time the trees were close on both sides and I was climbing so it was harder to get a satellite fix. However, once connected, the line seemed good and I managed to call the studio and chat to the producer for a minute. The presenter came on after I had been holding for about five minutes, by which time I was confident about the line. Apart from the expected slight delay, the conversation started well. Then, as he began a second question, the line went dead.

All the morning's frustrations boiled over and caught me by surprise. 'F***!' I yelled. I felt like I could cry.

Satellite phones don't cut out like mobile phones do, and often reconnect after a pause. I hadn't hung up. Horrified, I quickly hit the red button. Had I just uttered that expletive on drivetime national radio? I quickly dialled my home number and Mum picked up.

'Hi Mum, what was the last thing you heard?' I asked.

I shall be eternally grateful that the quick-fingered producer had cut the link as soon as the line went dead. With no real harm done, I had the first laugh of the day and carried on.

In the middle of the afternoon I got a rear puncture. I took the bags off, turned the bike over and set about the simple repair only to find that the new inner tubes I had picked up in Colón didn't work: their valves didn't fit through the wheel rim. Thankfully I was still carrying three old tubes, as I had been concerned about the new ones. All were patched at least once and I didn't have many unused patches left. I fitted one of these, but only got about 50 metres down the road before the tyre was flat again. The second repair worked better and I carried on, being as careful as I could on the rough gravel sections.

In the early evening I arrived in the very pretty mountain town of Balsas, just in time to watch a highly competitive game of volleyball in the town square. Except it wasn't like volleyball as I know it, with three instead of six players. I later found out it's considered by some to be the national sport and is played with a heavier ball than normal volleyball. For such a small town, a huge crowd had gathered, and I enjoyed the atmosphere and entertainment after a day of personal battles.

Wheeling out the next morning, I found the rear tyre flat again. It was gone eight a.m. by the time I finally left. Ahead of me was a 350-metre climb, then a 500-metre descent from Brisas on beautiful tarred mountain roads. Once across the whitewaters of the Rio Pindo I started climbing again, now mostly on gravel roads. In the late morning I punctured yet again and used my last patch to fix it. There was something wrong with them for sure, they weren't strong enough, but the condition of the roads with so much weight on the bike wasn't helping. It was just over 20km to the next village of Chaguarpamba and if I punctured again I would be walking.

The climb was beautiful and took in a few huge switchbacks. These weren't alpine-style hairpins but detours of several kilometres as the road searched for a reasonable route upwards. It's one thing knowing you will be climbing all day, it's another actually to look up and see the road you'll be cycling on in an hour's time, as long as you keep that leg-sapping rhythm going. But the bike and I weren't enjoying the loose gravel and relentless gradient. It was too heavy with all my film and communications gear for this sort of riding and I was soon sick of the clouds of dust from passing vehicles.

I had meant to be in Olmedo by lunchtime, yet it was mid-afternoon by the time I reached Chaguarpamba, still 15km short. Late or not, I had to eat, and stopped in the first place I could find. I had just sat down to a bowl of rice and chicken when a man walked over. Dressed in a shirt and trousers, he was far too smart to be a local. He also spoke perfect English, and he seemed to recognize me. As luck would have it, he had just left the coffee plantation I was heading for and had overheard the owner on a phone call to my mum that morning, talking about my delays. I could have hugged him. It was so nice to speak to someone in English. He was a journalist from Mexico, and he joined me for lunch.

Things were looking up. My new friend was able to call Angelino, the man at the coffee plantation, so that he could come and meet me here. I could get by in face-to-face conversations, but over the phone Spanish was tricky. While we waited, we set about trying to fix my bike. Inevitably there was no bike shop in the village, but my journalist friend asked some locals for someone to help. The restaurant was in a fork in the road with the main road carrying straight on, and the high street running off this. We were directed back up the main road to a very basic workshop that fixed car tyres. It took half an hour, but the little old man in charge was able to fix all three inner tubes with what have to be some of the largest patches ever used on a bike; he also gave me a tube of rubber glue and about thirty new patches to take away. Remote places are always good at improvising, and I was massively relieved, still hundreds of miles and a country away from the next bike shop.

While he worked, Angelino arrived and the journalist left. Angelino mentioned a few times that it was a good road and not far to the village of Olmedo and that I should follow him there. I paid the man in the garage and packed up the bike again, but Angelino had gone, without telling me. I had been in the workshop and had no idea where he was. Unworried, I set off up the road, which continued to climb and climb, gravel for most of the way. After an hour and a half the road came to a bend and I saw a village in the valley far below me. I crossed over and looked long and hard over the crash barriers at the scene below, then studied my map. That had to be Olmedo, but where was I? There was no obvious way down there. The road continued upwards for another hour, by which time the sun was sinking. The consolation for this unexpected climbing and mileage was that the view across the mountains from this altitude at sunset was utterly breathtaking.

I was caked in dust from passing trucks and exhausted when I came across a steep track down to my left. I was now well beyond Olmedo, having skirted the valley around it. This track was very steep indeed, and I struggled with the heavy bike on the loose dirt. Eventually, in the gloom, I found myself in the tiny village.

It transpired that the road to Olmedo was directly along the fairly flat valley bottom, accessed down the high street of Chaguarpamba. Nobody had told me this, and the main road I had followed was new, not shown on my map, hence my confusion as to how I had gone wrong. I had cycled an extra 16km uphill on a dirt road. As I was staying in Angelino's house I decided to bite my tongue and not ask why he hadn't come to find me when it was obvious what I had done. Maybe he thought I knew what I was doing.

It had been a long day, but Angelino had a wonderfully welcoming home. The kitchen-cum-living-room area was lined down one side with large hessian bags of coffee beans, a large coffee filter jug on the table was replenished regularly, and bottles of coffee liquor sat at the side. About eight of his friends and neighbours were there and they spent most of the evening with us. His wife was the local primary school teacher and he proudly proclaimed that she taught English. Maybe so, but we soon gave up and just spoke Spanish. I was the only person not drinking coffee, although I did try some of the coffee wine, which was surprisingly good. Even his two young teenage daughters sat at the dinner table drinking straight black coffees. I love coffee but I was ready to sleep and didn't want anything to spoil that.

At the crack of dawn we got up and went out to see the plantation behind his house. It seemed an unusual place to try to grow anything, but Angelino described, with great passion, the advantage of coffee growing at altitude. The plantation was at about 4,500ft (1,370m) which meant the coffee was given the coveted Café Altura tag, making it more expensive. Because the beans mature more slowly at higher altitudes they become harder and denser, the flavour and strength more concentrated. The youngest shoots looked like bean sprouts, while the larger plants, under a canopy of bird-proof mesh, looked more like a cannabis plantation.

After the tour, Angelino suggested we make some coffee. Still shaking off tired legs, and with all this talk of great coffee, I was keen for a cuppa, but I didn't realize how literal he was being. It took us over an hour to de-shell the beans using a 4-foot mortar and pestle, dry-roast them slowly over an open fire, then hand-grind them. The process was fascinating and the smell of the cooking beans as they went from their raw light tan stage to nearly black cooked was wonderful. A braying donkey and someone chain-sawing made filming a bit tricky (you couldn't orchestrate worse background noises), but I still ran around trying to capture the scene.

The resulting cuppa could have woken the dead. Angelino drank it like water, but I rarely have unsweetened black coffee, so while I could appreciate it was excellent I struggled slightly. I hadn't eaten yet and soon felt wired. It was like being given cast-strength malt when you're used to drinking watered-down blends. I don't know the terminology, but I would describe that homebrew as a full-bodied, deep and meaningful roast with a kick of adrenalin. If I were in marketing I would call it the Morning Glory, or something equally inappropriate. It was certainly a rude way to start the day. With my cyclist's hat on I turbocharged myself with another mug over breakfast before accepting Angelino's offer to drive me back up to the main road.

Thankfully, from near the turn-off they seemed to be building a new road just for me; so much so that long stretches of fresh, perfect tarmac were only down the right half of the road. This was ideal, until the traffic coming the other way decided that it preferred this to the bumps on the left-hand side and I was pushed off the road. Despite this game of bulldog I made much faster miles, still climbing. It was a further couple of thousand feet up to the village of Velacruz, where I turned south-west towards Peru. It was surprisingly cool but the views were brilliant, spoiled only by road-side rocks daubed with political graffiti, which looked odd in these wild highlands. I finished the day in the beautiful town of Catacocha, with its steep, narrow streets and pastel-painted houses with tiled roofs.

I woke just a few hours after falling asleep, and was violently sick. For the rest of the night I only dozed, getting up at least every hour to be ill. At dawn I got out of bed and took a very slow walk outside, trying to get some air and shake it off. My head ached and I felt like my kidneys had been thumped. After being sick again

I gave up the idea of cycling anywhere that day and went back to bed. I hadn't felt that terrible since getting water poisoning in Iran. I lay there curled on my side; I couldn't turn on to my back as my stomach was so cramped. The messages of support from friends and online were wonderful. I felt a long way from home, but being ill simply redoubled my determination to make up for lost miles.

I thought back, trying to figure out the cause. It could have been a few things. Angelino had given me some yoghurt at breakfast, which tasted homemade, probably not pasteurized, and then I had eaten some meat at dinner in Catacocha which wasn't very hot. I'd considered sending it back, but decided that the place looked decent. I lay there and calculated that I needed to make up nearly a week to reach Aconcagua on time.

By mid-afternoon I'd managed to get up and go out for a bowl of soup and some water with powdered dioralyte. The next morning I set out again, feeling pretty weakened but determined to regard this as the start of a new leg. This was the big push for the mountain.

I spent the day thinking about my route options ahead and decided that I would be willing to miss Bolivia if it was necessary to reach Aconcagua on time. Una was already researching this, and it was proving a tricky decision. Rerouting through Chile was certainly more direct, but it posed its own challenge: the Atacama Desert.

Despite spending the whole time feeling hungry and a bit ropey, it was one of my favourite days of the entire ride. Words can't aptly describe such mountain scenery. Despite dropping by nearly 5,000ft (1,500m), I also spent much of the day climbing, including one spectacular two-hour ascent. At the top I stood on the road's edge looking out over what must have been 30 miles of mountains, my road a tiny line winding up the valley below me. I laughed out loud, victorious.

I then punctured again, but could easily fix it now. In doing so I met my first stick-insect at the roadside while under the watchful eyes of a herd of goats, lazily chewing their cuds. A bit later on I was amused to pass a group of about ten middle-aged men and women, stripped to their underwear, bathing and washing their clothes in a roadside stream. I stopped, and one of the larger women beckoned me in, much to the hilarity of her friends. I waved but carried on.

The sun was setting and I was still quite high when I crested a hill and saw a flood plain far below and many miles ahead of me. Just before the haze obscured it I made out a river. That was the border with Peru. Shouting in celebration, I spent nearly an hour freewheeling fast downhill, entering the border town of Macará in the near darkness, my eyes still streaming.

15

The next morning I had just a couple of kilometres to go to reach the river. The border was easy but involved lots of waiting around and paper stamping. First impressions of Peru were that, in contrast to Ecuador, it seemed arid, despite still being in the shadow of the mountains. The vegetation was sparse and scrubby, with small purple and yellow wildflowers on the roadside. Some of the trees looked like acacias. They certainly had the thorns but were smaller than ones I had seen before.

Once again I had no idea what the new currency was; bearing in mind this was my tenth country of the journey (if you exclude Honduras), I should have got better at finding out. The first place I stopped at accepted US dollars, the currency of Ecuador. Then at the first main Peruvian town of Tambo Grande I saw a police car so I stopped it and asked if there was a bank near by. There wasn't, or it wasn't open, or they didn't want to take me there. But they beckoned for me to follow them. They took me to a small roadside restaurant and shop where they introduced me to the owner, a large man with a similarly sized character who produced a huge wad of cash from his pocket and offered to change as much money as I wanted.

Later, I found myself in the middle of absolutely nowhere and was excited to push my bike a few hundred metres off the road through the sandy soil and set up camp. I had really missed my tent.

Cheap hotels lose their charm quickly and are often far dirtier. As I sat outside my tent having some food, I watched some turkey buzzards with their ugly red heads considering me from a scrubby thicket nearby.

It's much easier to get going early when camping, especially when your sleeping-mat is punctured and you've been sleeping on the earth all night. I was off at sunrise. I felt that I had only just got used to the idea that I was in the mountains, and now I found myself in the desert. Peru was nothing like I'd imagined. I was travelling due west towards the Pacific in a dogleg that would turn south again by lunchtime at the town of Sullana, and within a few hours the wind started to pick up from the south-west. I wasn't in brilliant spirits as I headed out south, aiming for Piura by mid-afternoon. I hadn't had to cope with any headwinds for a long time and I kept wishing I was back in the hills where you at least got some pay-off for hard work.

Any thoughts of self-pity were short-lived due to my next encounter.

A couple of bright rickshaws and a group of men were gathered around something in a sandy lay-by, under some trees. I was already cycling past when I spotted a sports wheelchair. Intrigued, I turned round. There was a man on the ground with a bright yellow bike helmet on and he looked up, smiling broadly under a fine moustache, as I approached. His name was Lazaro, he was from Colombia, and he was fixing a puncture. The other men didn't seem to be helping much, mainly because they weren't needed. Lazaro was wearing a red polo shirt and tracksuit trousers with the left leg tied up. He had no left leg. I read the print on his shirt: TRAVESIA DE LOS ANDES 2009. I offered to help, but he declined with thanks and kept chatting cheerfully, explaining that he was on an 8,000-km (5,000-mile) push across South America. Still sitting on the ground, he lifted the wheel back on to his chair and pulled himself into the seat. The other men started to disperse, having lost interest, but Lazaro and I kept chatting.

After swapping contacts and taking a photo, he pushed off.

'Adios!' he yelled happily. 'Vaya con Dios!'

I walked to the side of the road, filming. He was soon a dot on the very long straight I had just cycled down.

In Sullana I'd eaten a big plate of rice with a rather tough, salty steak, a fried egg and some plantain before asking for another three of these for the road. It was over 200km to the next guaranteed supplies across the 'Desierto de Sechura', so I also bought some more biscuits and 7 litres of water. But having changed just $40 at Tambo Grande, I was finding that having bills that were worth more than $5 was as good as no money at all as no one had change for something that big. So I decided it was best to backtrack into the centre of Sullana, find a bank to withdraw a bit more, and get everything broken down into small denominations. I couldn't find a bank until I recruited the help of two motorbike policewomen. They were very helpful, and more to the point looked fantastic, dressed in knee-high black boots, jodhpur-style trousers and fitted jackets.

Shanty-style houses, many of whose walls were made from what looked like some kind of wicker, some with animal pens attached to the side, extended for miles into the desert. Trees and big shrubs survived, but in between was sand, now, not arid soils and hard-scrabble. I passed a few large herds of goats, two young barefooted girls riding a donkey that was also dragging pieces of wood, and a horse and cart, the man holding the reins sitting on top of a high pile of foliage. The roadside communities thinned out but never ended, and as the hours passed I began to wonder where I could hide away and camp.

It was getting dark when I pushed my heavy bike off the road and it took a lot of effort to get it just a few hundred metres through the sand, which was very soft; in fact it wasn't long before the wheels no longer worked and it needed dragging. Putting up the tent was the next challenge as the pegs wouldn't hold at all. Borrowing a trick from fixing snow belay anchors with ice axes, I collected some branches and dug deep trenches in the sand before laying a T-shaped anchor, with a couple of other branches as deep vertical pins. It was still saggy, but it worked. Dinner of cold steaks was like eating shoes, but I was famished so enjoyed the lot.

ZONA DE DUNAS read the yellow warning sign as I pedalled into the desert in the morning. And the reason for these dunes was the wind, which I could tell always blew from the south-west as the trunks and branches of the few trees that survived all pointed north-east, bullied permanently into odd shapes. It wasn't hot, maybe in the mid twenties, but when the wind picked up from mid-morning onwards I soon felt blasted, which felt like sunburn.

The following morning I made it to the small city of Chiclayo and stopped briefly to explore the witchdoctors market. I was slightly disappointed, having anticipated something wild, to find that the *brujos* I saw all looked rather normal, and none I spoke to could predict the future, which I'd thought might be helpful. After deciding that hallucinogenic cactus wouldn't help my cycling, I kept going.

The next 25 miles was the first stretch of complete desert, with large dunes and no trees. Large concrete signs in the sands warned that around me was Ministry of Defence land, PROHIBITO EL INGRESO, PELIGRO DE MORTE so I pushed on to the town of Mocupe. It would soon be dark so I planned to get food quickly, then carry on.

When I spotted a wooden handwritten sign outside a small house with the word COMEDOR on it I stopped and pushed open the door. Inside were three small tables in a very dark room. No one was there and I was about to leave when an elderly lady walked in and said something that I didn't understand, but it didn't seem friendly. Maybe this roadside diner wasn't open. It didn't feel right, so I apologized and started to leave.

I was getting back on the bike when a younger lady, maybe in her forties, came out of the door and asked if I needed to eat.

'Sí, gracias,' I replied. I felt I couldn't really say no.

'¿Dónde viene?' she asked.

She'd asked me where I came from but I misunderstood the question and told her I was going to Argentina, but then joked, 'Esta noche, voy a la desierto!'

'No, no puede,' she said, shaking her head. 'El desierto es peligroso.'

Half an hour later, having accepted her advice that the desert would be too dangerous when it got dark, my tent was pitched in the yard behind her house, and I was sitting in her kitchen having dinner with her son, and her mother, whom I still couldn't understand. They were very poor and the place was dirty, but they were charming company, the food was excellent, and they wouldn't let me pay. I tried to teach her son some English, while he laughed at my poor Spanish. In the morning she cooked an excellent breakfast and I managed to leave some money on the table.

I was soon back on another desert stretch, this time surrounded by large rocky outcrops several hundred metres high, with sand dunes carved into arêtes and crumpled like waves nearer the desert floor. In the early morning light, dark shadows added a dramatic effect to this already spectacular scenery.

As the wind picked up, it started to blow the sand across the road in a constant stream. Never gusting, this foot-deep layer of flying sand slightly obscured the road, not so that it made cycling more difficult but so that it gave me the impression that I was floating along.

Out of the sands, while passing the next town, Pacanguilla, I came across a couple of cyclists coming in the opposite direction. They were on an absolute high, full of stories of being blasted north by a tailwind for many hundreds of miles. I crumpled a little inside. The man was also wearing the most indecent pair of cycling shorts I had ever seen. They weren't much more than black boxer shorts. Apart from bearing bad news and wearing bad shorts, Olivier Peyre was in great form and it was nice to share some adventures from the road. His partner, who indicated that she wasn't his girlfriend, despite being cool with the shorts, didn't say much. The Frenchman was on a four-year world cycle, carrying a small paraglider that he used as a sail wherever possible.

The next day was 20 November, Children in Need night 2009, and I was expected to do a live TV broadcast to conclude the 'Catch Me If You Can' challenge. I had cycled just over 10,000 miles (16,000km) since Anchorage and would find out when live to the nation if my followers had managed to match those miles and raise lots of money.

I set out just before six a.m. so that I would arrive in the city of Trujillo by midday. I needed to reach a town for a good internet connection, and it was far too bright, sandy and windy in the desert to do an outdoor broadcast. The link worked a dream this time, but during the one-way process it was strange to try to look enthusiastic and normal when I was basically speaking to my blank computer screen, knowing that millions were watching my every move. Some 21,000 miles had been logged, and £4,946 donated – a great commitment from a lot of people in a short period of time.

I felt shattered afterwards. I normally was after broadcasts. Nerves do strange things to you.

I had by now decided to reroute through Chile instead of Bolivia, and Scott Napier, he of the Pan Americas world record, had been helping with lots of information about the road ahead. One of his top tips was to find a man called Lucho Ramirez d'Angelo in Trujillo. Lucho runs the Casa de Ciclistas, a free hostel for long-distance cyclists. It isn't in the guidebooks, and backpackers aren't welcome, but any cyclist can stay and fix their bike in his workshop. Lucho was my only chance of finding spare inner tubes to back up the patchwork ones I was on as no shops in Peru were likely to stock the ones I needed. He had piles of old inner tubes left by other cyclists and it took us a while to dig out a few that fitted. The only thing that came more highly recommended than Lucho's workshop was his chocolate cake, which I never saw, but for the price of a modest donation to the hostel I was very grateful to be back on the roads with spares. It would have been crazy to head into 600 miles of the Atacama Desert without them.

Next stop was the laundry. I was averaging one proper clothes wash per month since the USA. Here, even after laundry and a shower I continued to find sand everywhere.

Last stop was the post office. It was time to get rid of everything that wasn't essential. I needed to speed up, and I wanted more space in my bags for food and water for the desert ahead. Having sent home a number of packages I was already down to the minimum of what I thought I needed, so it was time to get ruthless. It took a while to go through everything, but it was well worth it: I ended up sending home a 4.3kg package that included my camp stove and a pile of electronics.

Enjoying the lighter bike, I climbed steadily out of Trujillo for a few miles. Halfway up I was lost in my own world, spinning away at a good cadence, when a man came striding past me. He hadn't even stayed on the verge, but overtaken me in the middle of the road. Being overtaken by someone running was a bit embarrassing, especially when I couldn't catch him until the road flattened out. I had to laugh. Maybe I wouldn't be that much faster than before.

My map didn't show much detail, but over the next few days there turned out to be more roadside villages to get supplies. I was also delighted at the regular appearance of chips in the diet, proper fat potato wedges, something I hadn't seen for a long time. When it came to drink, it was hard to avoid the Inca Kola, a bright yellow soda that is a national obsession. Peru with its Inca Kola and Scotland with its Irn Bru are the only countries I have heard of where Coca Cola isn't the top seller. Fuelled by chips and liquid sugar I set a four-day target of reaching the capital, Lima. I was getting earlier starts and, aside from some saddle sores, I was feeling good on the bike.

Day two of the four was a Sunday, and it was still quite early when a big group of road cyclists shot past me; some others had

already passed. They were the first roadies I had seen since Mexico.
Right at the back, three young riders were slightly off the pace. As
they passed me one slowed to say hi. I assumed he would soon race
off to catch up with the others, but he stayed, and his friends fell
back to go at my pace. They were all about twenty years old and
riding decent entry-level road bikes. None of them spoke any
English so I chatted away as well as I could in Spanish and they
were good company to start with.

After about 10km at a decent pace for me but a slow pace for a
race bike, we reached a long climb and I said that they could go on
if they wanted. They stayed. I geared back, settling into a climbing
tempo. The same guy stayed on my shoulder talking and talking
and talking, not seeming to worry that I didn't understand most of
the time and wasn't wanting to answer anyway while climbing.
After about twenty minutes we were still climbing and I could tell
that the silence and the pace were getting to him when he asked for
the third time if I was all right. Without being rude, I repeated that
he and his friends were welcome to go on. He took this as the right
time to give me a cycling lesson, demonstrating how to sit back on
the saddle while climbing, and how to breathe. I ignored him. He
meant well, but I wasn't in the mood to be patronized. After more
silence he leaned over, put his hand on my back and tried to give me
a helping push up the hill. I quickly brushed his hand away, and
after that he got the message and stopped trying to teach me. I was
seriously tempted to offer to switch bikes for a few miles and see
how fast he was then, but I bit my tongue. Once on the flat we
chatted more about his furniture making and my cycling around the
world, but after two hours I wasn't sad when they said they needed
to turn back.

That afternoon I found myself on some very exposed desert
stretches, and that night I wrote in my diary:

Biggest headwind yet kicked up for a few hours and I stopped at
one point and just put my head on my arms on the bars. It is all

I could do as the wind buffeted me. For the first time it was head on, so strong. The gusts almost stopped me or pushed me around and at best I was going at walking pace. Had reasonable target to finish the day but with that wind I lost so much time.

At 4pm I was at km 347 and saw a restaurant (called Playa de Gramita). I wasn't carrying a meal so stopped to eat one quickly and get one to go. Was met by Clemente – an older man – who looked out the door at my bike, smiled and showed me to a table. I was the only one there. After agreeing to fried fish and chips he brought out two guest books and proudly showed me all the people who had stopped by. The first he showed me was Karl Bushby in 2000, who had left a hearty message of thanks, like many others.

Clemente didn't speak much English but was obviously used to conversing with travellers and mentioned he knew of Casa de Ciclistas. He sat with me as I ate and asked lots of questions about family and Scotland. A lovely guy – his mannerisms were so friendly and open. When I was done I wrote a message in his book and went to pay. He wouldn't take anything and insisted, saying when he comes to Scotland I could look after him. But he had never travelled. He just seemed to love helping travellers and now had friends all over the world. One of the most welcoming men I have ever met. We got a photo outside and he gave me a hug goodbye. It brought a tear to me as I cycled off and made me miss home for the first time in ages. An amazing man who I shouldn't forget. A great example of a true world citizen.

It was a hard slog from there but at least the wind had died a bit. My left knee is a bit sore. Very beautiful day, but the toughest of stretches so far in the wind this afternoon.

Late that evening I reached the Pacific again, and for the next few days it was odd to see how the desert met the ocean. When I was very close it sometimes felt like I was cycling along the beach itself, especially where the dunes encroached on to the road. At other times, when I climbed inland a bit, the views were over a mini mountain range of rocks and sand dunes. Early and late were the best times to experience this world, like a lunar landscape of greys, yellows and browns.

On the final stretch before Lima, from just after the town of Chancay, the road split, but it wasn't immediately clear why. Both ways stated that they went to Lima but the main road headed inland, up a big climb, and the sign indicated it was further than the smaller road that stayed on the Pacific. Keen to make good time – I was due to meet a BBC correspondent in Lima at lunchtime to do some radio pieces – I turned off along the coast road.

After a few kilometres I passed a small round sign with a red line through a bicycle: NO CICLISTAS. I debated the quandary with myself for a few minutes. The road was in excellent condition (all Peruvian roads seemed to be), I was already committed, and there seemed no good reason why this road wasn't suitable for cycling. I didn't want to turn back without good reason.

It turned out the sign was there for a good reason.

My road started to climb to an elevation of a few hundred metres. At the same time the land to my right started to disappear. The result was that I soon found myself committed to a road high above the Pacific with no verge, just steep cliffs dropping off directly from the edge, for as long as it lasted. To my left the terrain reached far above me to a top I couldn't see, shrouded in cloud. In essence, the road had been carved into the side of what was a mountain rising straight out of the ocean. It looked like sand, especially because it lay in deep furrows, maybe weathered by coastal rain, but it must have been rock at that gradient. Some sections were truncated, broken off above the road, but I couldn't stop anywhere to explore.

The drops to my right were often staggering. There were moments when I felt my breathing shorten and my jaw set as coaches and trucks laboured up behind me. There were barriers on some sections, but not others, and I felt very vulnerable. Still, it was very exciting. At one point I spotted the remains of an articulated lorry lying about 50 metres below the road, precariously perched about 100 metres above the crashing waves, having clearly driven straight off the edge. I imagine it will always be there, as a reminder.

After a few hours the terrain eased, allowing the road to pull back from the cliff edge, and I eventually descended into the outskirts of Lima. As I turned on to the bigger road I looked back for one last glance at the most memorable stretch of road since Hatcher Pass and saw a sign that read EL SERPENTIN – The Snake. It's a great name, which the authorities need to signpost at the northern end.

Ironically after this experience, Dan, the BBC correspondent in Lima, gave me a full escort across the city, which was deemed dangerous to cycle. Home to a third of Peru's population, it was certainly vast, and I didn't mind the company. Dan took me for the poshest meal of the expedition. I felt like a tramp sitting in that salubrious restaurant, being introduced to ceviche, a local delicacy of fresh raw fish marinated in citrus juice, spiced with chillies, and seasoned with onion, salt and pepper. It sounded like guaranteed food poisoning to me, but Dan insisted. It was surprisingly good, but I did find a full plate quite hard work and left wanting some proper food for fuel.

Apart from doing some radio and seeing me through the city, Dan was meant to have a package that had been sent out for me: a new sleeping-bag, new inner tubes, a tyre pump and some SD cards to film on to. However, when Dan had gone to pick it up and produced his passport, which said 'Daniel', they'd refused to believe this was the same name as 'Dan', fined him on the spot and refused to hand it over. I was annoyed by this, but not surprised. None of the couriered packages that had been sent to me anywhere south of the US border had got through on time. Some hadn't got through at all. I was starting to understand the true meaning of bureaucracy, but people here seemed to me to take it for granted.

The next morning I rode about 15km before I could find any breakfast. They're always slightly harder miles when you have to get going before any food. At a tiny shack at the roadside I enjoyed a plate of rice, some unidentifiable meat, a pile of yucca, which is like a stringy potato, some scrambled egg rolls and, of course, some coffee. Unusually, Peruvian coffee was almost always served on the table as a bottle of treacle-like concentrate alongside a mug of hot water.

Throughout Central and South America I had passed more traffic accidents than anywhere else I had ever travelled, including India. So I didn't slow down when I saw a crowd of people on the road ahead. It was mid-afternoon now and I was barely paying attention as I got close, assuming it was a broken bus or something similar that I could cycle past.

It was, in fact, a demonstration. I was in the middle of the crowd before I figured this out, and I was immediately worried. I started cycling back the way I had come but people were strung right across the road behind me now. I couldn't retreat or carry on. I surveyed the scene. It was impossible to count, but there were maybe a few hundred men, and many of them wore balaclavas. So far no one was paying me much attention, just rallying round me. It was a very strange place for a dispute, in the middle of the countryside. A few metres away a man started spray-painting a road sign, while others stood around cheering.

Then I spotted a black van a short distance ahead and a small TV crew filming. I pushed the bike towards them and introduced myself. I was with them for about ten minutes, trying to stay safe by association, and also filming what was going on myself. It was exciting and confusing. A line of riot police, dressed in black with large shields, tried to push the crowds off the road; the protesters stopped a number of trucks and clambered on top. I eventually saw a space in the crowd, thanked the kind cameraman and managed to cycle through and keep going.

My adrenalin was running on high after this, but I reflected on the fact that I hadn't actually been threatened at all. I had, however, stood out, mainly for being tall and certainly for being the only lycra-clad person there. The reporter had explained that it was a dispute between regions about work, but that was as much inform-ation as I got.

The headwind subsided for a few days south of Lima and I made much faster miles. Late on 27 November I reached Pisco, which was a bit off my main route but a place I really wanted to see. On 15 August 2007, the town was near the epicentre of an 8.0 magnitude earthquake that destroyed over 80 per cent of the city, leaving about six hundred people dead. It had been arranged for me to meet volunteers from an organization called Pisco Sin Fronteres, and then to meet local people who had been affected by the disaster.

I got a bit lost on my way in and found myself in the town centre. The main street was lined with red brick walls, but the door and window spaces in them were empty. I stopped and looked through one of these to find a small shack in the space behind. The wall wasn't part of any building, it had just looked like a building-front from the road. The streets were still strewn with piles of rubble. Dave, one of the English volunteers, explained later that the locals call them the 'Walls of Shame'. They are superficial walls, built to give the impression of the government's commitment to rebuild Pisco.

As we talked, we walked over to a small makeshift community where seventy families lived on land smaller than a football pitch. A young mother showed us around, explaining how there were no toilets so they just had to throw excrement into the surrounding fields, which meant that disease was now a problem. I filmed, which was difficult, but made great fun by the hordes of children running around, fascinated by the camera. One man was building a house out of wood and cardboard which he explained would take three days.

I had the option to stay overnight at the volunteers' centre but really wanted to find out more about the shanty-towns, so I asked if I could stay there. Many of the helpers seemed to find this a strange idea, saying that it was dangerous in these communities at night. But I insisted, and Dave agreed to make some introductions.

I changed and got some absolute basics for a night in El Molino, a much larger and more established community, with thousands of families. The volunteers advised me not to take any valuables, but I later wished I had taken photos of my family and a bit more money, which I could have left there. It took a mototaxi about fifteen minutes to get there and it was nearly sunset when we arrived, so we didn't have much time for introductions before the volunteers left me.

Maria, one of the community leaders, agreed to have me stay. It was hard without enough Spanish but Maria was very kind and patient. She took me for a walk around the area near her small home before introducing me to some of her family. She had seven children. Her eighteen-year-old daughter was there, breast-feeding a one-year-old, along with her thirteen-year-old daughter and a handicapped teenager whom I didn't really get to see. Maria's house had concrete floors and was built with proper joinery, which was better than most, plus it was painted, which made it stand out. We all sat in the small front room on stumps of wood, but there weren't enough for the people who kept coming in, so most sat on the floor.

I felt like a giant in their midst, clumsy both literally and in terms of conversation, as I tried to talk about the earthquake and the situation they now found themselves in. Maria's eighteen-year-old daughter lived about 20 metres away in a shack made of wood, plastic sheeting and hessian sacks; they had found one sheet of corrugated plastic to put over their bed to keep dry. Everyone was very friendly and there were lots of smiles, but when I chatted to Maria alone, her anger, sadness and resignation were obvious. She talked about how the majority of international and federal aid promised had disappeared, about the corruption and neglect of the government. Maria's greatest fear was that the earthquake would happen again.

I had planned to film how they made dinner, but then a black lady arrived with a small plastic plate of chicken and chips, plus a mug of a strange hot drink which was like a thick and very sweet tea. I didn't understand what was happening, and tried to pay, but she refused and left. Maria said it was her friend and insisted I start eating. I did – it would have been rude not to – but kept offering the food around to the family. They refused. There wasn't much and I ate it all, assuming theirs would be coming. Half an hour later the younger daughter went out and came back with a bag of dry white bread rolls. I watched with horror as they sat on the floor eating them, with nothing but water to drink.

Later, Maria brought a mattress through and made up a bed on the floor. I asked her why they didn't eat chicken. 'Because we can't afford it,' she said simply.

I went to bed but could hardly sleep, and was up at five a.m. A light stayed on in the other room all night and there were regular voices. I half-woke at one point to see someone at the canvas door looking in at me.

I thanked Maria as best I could, wrote a note on a scrap of paper and left her 30 sole (about £12), which is all I had, apart from the half a sole it would cost to get the mototaxi back to town. On that bumpy ride back to Pisco I was absolutely desperate for the loo, having had no idea where to go in the shanty-town.

By eleven a.m. I was cycling out of Pisco, saddened by everything I had seen, feeling very unmotivated and tired. My challenge didn't seem so important compared to such a basic fight for existence. It was a hard experience just to move on from, to count as just another episode of life on the road. I didn't want to film anything else that day, just to get some miles done, keep going, but production had stressed that I should film some *cuyes* whenever I got the chance.

Around lunchtime, hungry but nowhere near a town, I passed a sign saying CHICHARRON DE CERDO CUY. A few hundred metres further on I stopped and with now-or-maybe-never reluctance turned back to explore.

Peruvians eat about sixty-five million guinea pigs a year. Having grown up in Scotland, I naturally think that eating them is slightly taboo. There is no logic to this, it's just a cultural aversion. I am sure Peruvians would find the haggis, sheep's stomach stuffed with spiced grain and offal, slightly odd.

A few plastic tables were set up at the roadside under a bamboo shelter, in front of metal gates. Inside, I found the farmer, who welcomed me and led me to a large shed. Inside that were hundreds of low brick pens with thousands of guinea pigs. A radio on the wall was playing music. The farmer described how they were timid animals, to the extent that if someone walked in or there was a loud noise, a few would suffer heart attacks. But if he left the music playing, they were fine.

'Would you like to eat some?' he asked.

I still wasn't mad about the idea, but agreed, with thanks. As I said, I grew up on a farm so there is nothing about the process of killing and preparing animals I'm squeamish about, it's just that these guinea pigs were particularly cute and I was feeling more sensitive than usual.

We chose one, and I helped prepare it. From shed to plate took about half an hour; it was served battered and deep fried with potatoes on the side. Sitting back on my own at the roadside, under the bamboo shelter, I ate my lunch. The meat was wonderfully tender and delicious, but there wasn't a lot of it and there was a lot of skin and bones. It reminded me of when I worked on farms in the south of France and we used to buy large bags of frog legs as it was the cheapest meat. They, too, were tasty but rather unsatisfying, so I decided not to make eating guinea pig a habit.

There was my stomach to consider too. It hadn't been right for over a week. I often felt full when I hadn't eaten, had sore kidneys, and other unpleasant symptoms. I doubt the guinea pig made much difference, but I continued to feel gradually worse over the next few days. It was very uncomfortable, in wide open and often barren desert scenery, to have to keep running off to the roadside.

Near the town of Ica I passed the steepest sand dunes yet, straight out of the Sahara, with billboards advertising sand-boarding and desert 4×4 tours. For a tourist visiting here there would be absolutely no way of guessing what was happening just up the road. Even most Peruvians in Lima think that Pisco has been rebuilt.

I was soon battling the headwinds again and getting utterly battered. My face and especially my lips felt wind-burned and raw. When I spotted a tiny green shack ahead, a wooden booth in the middle of nowhere, I decided to stop, hoping they would have something to drink. As I got close I was surprised to see another cyclist there. His name was Doug Gunzelmann, from Boston, and he was on a fully laden mountain bike. Initially I thought this an odd choice for the excellent roads, until he explained. He had spent the last three months cycling 6,000km (3,700 miles) across the Amazon jungle, the majority of which had been on dirt tracks. I therefore assumed he was a veteran explorer, but he explained that he was a laboratory scientist who had never done a bike tour before, never travelled alone, never been to Brazil, and hadn't been able to speak Portuguese. It was a brilliant story full of encounters with panthers, eating piranhas and relentlessly tough cycling. I loved his style. We chatted for a while, glad of the sun-warmed drinks that were on sale.

A little girl, maybe about seven years old, the daughter of the señora who had served us, was playing behind the counter. After a while she caught our attention and pointed at the almost indistinguishable remains of roadkill on the road behind us.

'Perro, mi perro!' she laughed.

I looked at Doug, making sure I had understood what she was saying. That was her dog. Neither of us could think of a suitable response, we were simply left commenting that they raised them tough out here. Doug suggested that the landscape probably put some gravel in her guts.

The day finished on a better stretch, near the town of Palpa. The main highway followed a long detour inland while a much smaller road, signposted for cars only, looked shorter. Following this, I made a short climb through a very narrow, roughly carved and low tunnel for half a kilometre before emerging into a breathtaking view over a wide green river plain, far below, with sandy mountains around. The road remained narrow and patchy but it was a most exhilarating switchback descent. My brakes were making a horrid noise by the time I reached the flat.

The 50-mile stretch to the south of Palpa is a high, arid plateau called the Pampas de Jumana, home to the world's most famous geoglyphs. I hadn't heard of the Nazca Lines and wasn't brilliantly excited about seeing some drawings in the sand in the flattest, most featureless stretch of desert yet. But it was in fact surprisingly intriguing. In the middle of nowhere stands a viewing tower at the roadside, which for the princely sum of one sole you can climb in order to look down on some of the hundreds of depictions across the area of people, animals, birds and reptiles that have survived for over 1,500 years. For me, more interesting than how they were made and what they meant was the period of world history they had endured while never seeing any change. It was a humbling line of thought.

From Nazca the road turned back towards the coast, which I followed for the next three days. When I first reached the coast there was a 10-mile stretch where the drifting dunes threatened to swallow the whole road. Sand blew everywhere and I was forced to stop and push the bike through. Where it was a thinner layer, I tried to cycle through. It was good fun, but slow going.

Once out of the beach, the hills to my left became steeper and closer. I was amazed to find myself in a green world again, for the first time since Ecuador. At first there was just the odd coarse grassy patch, but I then spotted cattle grazing on the hillside. I was still in a world where it almost never rains so I had to ask a few locals to find out that the *garúa*, or ocean fog, that gets trapped by the hills is enough to fuel a mini ecosystem and these green oases. It was a wonderful change, but along that narrow coastal road I had a few days of very rough camping.

The road followed a spectacular cliff-top route, with good drops at times and very few crash barriers. I wasn't quite ever as high or exposed as I'd been on El Serpentin, but it was much longer and more undulating. At one stage for a few hours I found myself in a thick *garúa*. Vehicles appeared and vanished in an instant, with eerie silences in between. By the roadside on this section were a startling number of small memorials dedicated to those who hadn't survived the drive. Where the road left the cliffs, I found a small chapel, a place for drivers to stop and say a prayer for their safe journey. It was noticeably warmer inside with so many candles burning and I stopped just long enough to get shouted at for filming it.

While I much preferred this interesting coastal stretch to the seemingly endless desert riding, I was in a real mental slump, one I couldn't seem to think my way out of. I had no problem keeping going, but it felt robotic. I couldn't find much passion in the cycling or interest in the world around me. I had given myself a few serious pep talks since Ecuador, each time to get motivated for the daily miles I had to do to reach Aconcagua by Christmas. That was now just over three weeks away, and though I was on the go from before six a.m. every day till six p.m. I was clocking poor mileages. Every time I stopped, I felt unmotivated to start again. A quick meal would often become a few hours off the bike. I knew that the key to getting my focus and optimism back was sorting my stomach out. I was still ill, and it was—

Twang!

I was going around a corner, but not fast, lost in my thoughts, when I heard the unmistakable sound of a spoke breaking. Incredibly, it was the first of the journey; 10,000 miles without any wheel problems was a personal record. But I was surprised to see that it had snapped right in the middle. I had never seen a spoke break in the middle before.

That night I found myself a room at the unwelcomingly named Hotel Turistas, took the bike up to my room and set about repairs.

Midway through, still truing the spokes, I fell asleep, slumped over the wheel. Whatever stomach bug I had was sponging up a lot of my energy. I was worried.

Production asked me to phone a nurse in the UK, who simply told me to go and see a doctor. After persuading her that wasn't possible, I was prescribed some Cipofloxin, a general-purpose antibiotic I was carrying. Unconvinced with this diagnosis, Mum checked with a family friend who assured me that the gut wall wouldn't absorb Cipofloxin, that it would do no good. Dan in Lima had by now managed to get my package released from customs so he was tasked with getting the correct prescription.

It was another four days to the border with Chile. Four more days in the Peruvian desert, up above 4,000ft (1,220m) on some big climbs. This sometimes sheltered me from the winds, but it was still tough going. Whether flat or hilly, the story of the Peru I'd seen was one of sand, but more than that huge winds. I have since spoken to a number of cyclists who had been equally surprised by the harsh climate. In geographical terms, of all the countries I've ridden in Peru remains the most different on the ground from what I had expected, just like Iran remains the most different culturally speaking.

Apart from those daily miles, there was the real mountain climb to plan for, which meant daily discussions with Mum, the production team, and my sister Heather, who is a climber, about kit choice and logistics. It was peculiar to sit in a tent in a hot and sandy world chatting on the satellite phone about the cold and snow.

A few days from the border I woke in thick fog at five a.m. and sat at my tent door eating more white rice. Good fuel, though I always found I was hungry again very quickly. It was now 190 days since Alaska, and I reflected that at the equivalent time on the world cycle I was speeding over the Pyrenees on my way to the finish line in Paris.

Within an hour, up a gentle climb with more sandy horizons (the fog had burned off), a Landcruiser passed me and stopped. Out stepped four men from the Arequipa Cycling Club. I had passed the town the day before. A rather windy and desolate place to get into road cycling, I thought, but they certainly all looked the type. And for me, Christmas really had come early: José Antonio, the president of the club, his younger brother and a couple of friends had my package. No courier company would agree to this delivery, so Dan from Lima and Mum had figured out this solution. The cyclists explained how one of them had tried to catch up with me the night before on a motorbike, but I had got much further than they expected so he had turned back. They had all set out at the break of dawn to find me. They had also brought a dozen bananas, three big tubs of yoghurt, a big tub of electrolytes and lots of snacks. It was a vast amount of food, far more than I could carry.

'Yesterday, at lunch, you ate three *lomo saltado*,' José teased me, and his friends laughed, making gestures for being fat.

I was completely bemused. How did they know what I had eaten? *Lomo saltado* was my new favourite, a standard southern Peruvian dish of sliced steak with thick chips in a gravy sauce. It was delicious, and I had indeed had three plates of it the day before.

'It was in the local paper,' José clarified.

I was still bemused. I hadn't spoken to anyone over lunch, so whoever had reported me would have had little chance of knowing anything about me, except that I cycled and I ate a lot.

So, based on Mum's request to bring me a few supplies, and on reading what must have been a rather vague newspaper account of a hungry gringo, they had come to find me with a vast quantity of food. I was immensely grateful, it was an incredibly kind thing to do. I was with them at the roadside for over an hour, unpacking my new kit and stuffing supplies in every possible space. They wouldn't accept anything for the food or their petrol. 'We are cyclists, you are a cyclist,' José kept repeating.

A few hours later I reached the region's capital town, Moquegua,

walked into a roadhouse to get lunch and was aware of eyes following me, more than usual. As I took a seat a man walked over, wrung
my hand, said something I didn't catch and made a gesture about a
person's figure. It seemed that my eating habits really had made the
news in these parts.

That night I pulled in behind a large sandbank and decided for
the first time not to put the tent up. I couldn't see the point. It
barely got any cooler at night and it didn't look like it had rained
for a very long time. I was by now accustomed to sleeping on my
punctured sleeping-mat, stuffing spare clothes under my hips and
shoulders inside the sleeping-bag to cushion things a bit. Sand is a
surprisingly firm mattress.

I woke at first light. As the sun crept over the horizon I sat with
my sleeping-bag wrapped over my shoulders, spooning back a *pollo
saltado*, a chicken version of the tasty *lomo saltado*. It was magic.

16

The reality of those last four days in Peru was so many subtle shades on a theme, and yet it is hard to relate with much distinction. Just describing more mountains and more sand would miss the starkness of this strange other world with its Martian landscape; it wouldn't do justice to the suffering of long hours spent climbing or the thrill of some magnificent descents. On only a few occasions did the road drop into lush green valleys, fed by a river that dropped out of the Andes far inland, before climbing back into the desert. Like snow, I now knew the many ways sand could be shaped by the wind, how it looked on vast plateaus and on mountains, how it comes in every shade. Southern Peru is not for those who suffer from a sense of space sickness. It's a part of the world that makes you feel very small.

By now my lips were swollen, especially my lower one, as if I had been punched. It stung painfully when eating anything salty. I had tried to be careful to use sun cream, but the relentless dry wind had left the skin cracked, red and very tender. It was a concern. My stomach was feeling slightly better, despite the fact that I hadn't yet started the medication the cyclists had delivered, as I had been told not to take it while food was scarce.

For all these reasons, it was with trepidation that I woke on the morning of my last day in Peru. My own poor research had informed me that Chile was where the desert, in the form of the

Atacama, started; I had overlooked the fact that this entire re-route through coastal Peru would also be desert. The fact that the Atacama was larger, drier and presumably windier wasn't easy to look forward to.

The last Peruvian town on my route, just shy of 40km from the border, had a reputation for being one of the most patriotic in the country. I had grown increasingly aware of an anti-Chile attitude since Lima. For fifty years, until 1929, Tacna was controlled by Chile, during which time Peru's southern neighbours tried to persuade the Tacneños to forget their Peruvian roots. Inevitably, they didn't.

As I left my cheap hotel that morning, set on getting to Chile quickly, I found the central streets of Tacna filling with people. Intrigued, I left my bike at the hotel and followed them to the large central square.

It was 8 December, the Feast of the Immaculate Conception, a Catholic celebration that is a national holiday in many countries, including both Chile and Peru. Some sort of parade was about to take place. I thought it would be a good idea to try to join the press area, which was much closer to a large stage than the public was being allowed to go. As I tried to slip across the street, a policeman caught my arm, gesturing that I needed to get back. I took one of my BBC business cards out of my pocket and held it up. 'Es importante, para un documental para la BBC,' I said, chancing my luck – I knew he couldn't read my card. He let me through, despite the fact that I didn't look like any of the other journalists I was joining, me dressed in my lycras, them in their official press waistcoats. Some looked at me suspiciously as I set up my tiny camera and tripod.

I then got stuck in the press area for over an hour listening to a number of political speeches, none of which I could understand. It may officially have been a celebration of the Blessed Virgin Mary, but the parade was actually a large and lengthy showcase of Peru's military might. Regiment after regiment marched past into the square, mainly in desert camouflage, some with yellow, white and black face paint on, some wearing gas masks, all carrying an array of armaments from bayoneted rifles and machine guns to grenade launchers and bazookas. It was certainly impressive.

Eventually, once the parade had dispersed, I was able to leave. I turned away from my camera on the tripod for just a few seconds to take a photo; I turned back just in time to watch a journalist catch it with his bag as he walked off. I was too slow and too shocked even to call after him. The camera was smashed.

It was lunchtime by the time I reached the Chilean border. In Mexico I had sent home my work carnet, knowing I wouldn't need it again. Except now I was re-routing through Chile, another carnet country, so there was the minor concern of whether I would be allowed in. Thankfully, the British passport had its usual effect and I was waved through without questions.

The border brought quite a few changes (though not in scenery). Firstly there was the two-hour time difference, despite my route continuing to go due south. My 4.45 a.m. alarm call was now 2.45 a.m.; early the following morning I quickly decided this would need rethinking. Also, before heading into the desert everything needed charging, but I now found that Chile was the only country en route that didn't take US-style plugs. I only had one multi-adaptor, which meant charging each of my ten gadgets one after another.

Keen to stock up with food and to rest before heading into the Atacama, I took a day off in Arica, just across the border, famous for being the driest city on the planet. It has an average rainfall of less than a millimetre per year, which in real terms means that it hasn't rained for a very long time. I met up with a university lecturer who ran a local information website, through which production had contacted him. I'd assumed that living in the driest place on earth would mean an extreme existence, but my guide dispelled that myth. With a year-round temperature in the high twenties Celsius – a near perpetual summertime – the Azapa Valley and the city of Arica is an oasis surrounded by vast deserts. It's fed by the San José River which only runs above ground for some of the year, when the rains run off the Andes. My guide claimed that Arica was one of the most comfortable and laziest towns on earth. The latter seemed to me an odd thing to be proud of, but he insisted on the point.

We drove a short distance up the valley to an olive grove whose owners he knew. I was amazed to see the old trees, which were maintained with elaborate irrigation systems. I chatted to the farmer for a long time. He was in his seventies, with a deeply wrinkled face and hands from a life of manual labour in the sun. He explained how he'd emigrated from Croatia in his twenties. He built the farm and had lived there since 1960. He had not seen any rain in nearly fifty years, and spoke about how he missed the rain of home.

Back in Arica we went for some lunch. We sat at a small table with other diners just an elbow jab away and many other kitchens under the same roof: it was a market of working-class eateries. Busking musicians wandered around the narrow passageways. Seeing a tall white man in their midst, they all stopped by us. After we'd ordered, the lady in charge came over with a big smile, offering me a glass of something. It looked like a cold, creamy, lumpy soup. She chatted away, and I thought she was saying that it was good for my health.

'It's good for your health?' I questioned.

'Of course! For everyone, for everyone, for everyone!'

It was on the house, so I drank it. It was very slimy and didn't taste great, but I thanked her. Only later did I get a full translation of her introduction: 'I'd like to offer you the famous Copa Martinez which contains raw eggs with lemon and shellfish. It's the Chilean Viagra, a love potion and . . . what else can I say? It's extremely nutritious to all. Here you go.'

Nearly 98 per cent of all the people who live in Chile's most northerly region live in Arica, which leaves a lot of empty space around the city, into which I was about to ride. After all those days of desert cycling in Peru I was on the brink of another 1,000km of it in Chile. There are some amazing facts about the Atacama, such as it's over 100 per cent drier than Death Valley in California, and some of its riverbeds have been dry for over 120,000 years. With facts like these lodged in my head I set off, well hydrated and prepared for a tough week.

Arica is at sea level and the Atacama is mainly on a high plateau, so I was expecting a decent ascent to start with. What I wasn't expecting was the greenery. The wider landscape was all desert, but shrubs and thorny bushes grew at the roadside in places, and I dipped into deep valleys whose bottoms were irrigated and dotted with more orchards.

It was a few kilometres' fast descent into the first of these valleys, and I was still going fast on the flat, just past a small bridge over a dry riverbed, when I met a cyclist coming the other way. If I had been looking for a further deterrent to entering the Atacama Desert, this middle-aged Norwegian man who proceeded to talk at me for over twenty minutes was it. He was having a rotten time, and made no bones about how lonely he was, how delighted he was to meet another cyclist. He was laden down with a huge amount of water, which made me concerned that I wasn't carrying enough, and lamented at length the emptiness and boredom of the road that lay ahead of me.

I tried to reassure him that after the next climb he was on a gentle downhill all the way back to civilization. I felt sorry for the guy. He had taken off on his cycle to escape his job and life for a while, had started in Europe but found it too cold, so had taken a flight to South America on a whim and just started riding. Yet he hadn't found the space and freedom he was looking for, and he was now desperately lonely. I guess this lifestyle isn't for everyone. It's certainly an intimidating space if you don't like your own company.

By nightfall I had climbed above 4,000ft (1,220m) on to the desert plateau. After some more rice and chicken I snuggled into my sleeping-bag, trying to smooth out the lumps in the sand under me.

I was warm all night, except for my face, which was exposed. The air temperature dropped surprisingly low, due to the altitude and lack of any cloud cover. I stayed in my sleeping-bag the following morning for more cold rice and chicken, watching the sunlight race across the sands from the far hills on the horizon, waiting for it to warm up the day.

Scott Napier had warned me about the huge hidden valleys of the northern Atacama, and I thought he must have meant the ones I had just crossed. In fact these were tiny, mere warm-ups compared to the real show. I was surprised when I came to the first of these valleys. I could look across to the far side and see that the desert continued at the same level, only quite a few miles away; in between was a very deep scar in the sandy landscape and the only way across was a long way down and back up the far side.

For 15km I hurtled downhill and soon dropped out of the sunlight, the deep valley still trapped by the night. At speed it was freezing, the first time I had genuinely felt cold for months. My teeth chattered and my eyes streamed but I wore a huge smile, not wanting to slow down at all. I knew that for the next few hours I would be on the long crawl back up the other side. It was long, but never steep, as the road cut a steady groove into the valley side. To give the Chileans their due, it was a perfect road.

Midway up the climb, the sun was by now high enough to light the strip of green valley floor behind me. There wasn't much traffic, but quite a few trucks had lumbered slowly past, as well as the odd car. I then heard an engine behind me and glanced back to see a small hatchback following me. It hesitated behind me for a bit longer then pulled alongside. A brunette, maybe in her late teens, leaned out of the passenger window and called out in perfect English, 'Hey, you want to smoke weed?'

'No, thank you,' I managed to say with a smile as I sweated away, grinding my way upwards.

'OK, have fun!' she shouted, and the car sped on.

I was left laughing out loud, which made me cycle even slower.

Even if I was a smoker, getting stoned in the driest place on earth while trying to cycle was perhaps the worst idea I have ever heard.

There was another huge dipper before the day was out. My reward was a lonely roadhouse at the top on the other side where they served my favourite *lomo saltado*. Despite the terrain the afternoon winds hadn't appeared as expected and I was feeling much stronger on the bike. My gut was certainly much better after taking the antibiotics over the few days of plentiful food in Tacna and Arica.

Later on I came across a small stall at the roadside selling fresh mangoes. It's hard to describe how random this seemed to me at the time, but it was certainly doing good business with other road users. I had a pint of freshly squeezed mango juice, which was the sweetest nectar to my parched throat, and took a few mangoes for later.

That night I lay in my sleeping-bag, trying to film the night. It was impossible. The only similar skyscape I have ever seen was in the Australian Outback, but I never slept without a tent there. The starry sky was immense, the sense of absolute space stunning. I then took my glasses off, couldn't see a thing, and soon fell asleep.

I woke in a cloud. I couldn't see anything past 10 metres in the early morning light. It took a minute to work out where the road was, by remembering which way my sleeping-bag had been facing in relation to it. Everything was damp, which luckily didn't matter in a Pertex-covered sleeping-bag. I certainly hadn't expected fog in the desert, and once again it was very cold as I started out.

I now know that this is the Camanchaca, a fog caused by inland winds from the Pacific cooling quickly as they rise. It has enough moisture to sustain the odd lizard (I had seen a few) and some lichens.

Despite the harsh environment, the Atacama has long been a rich source of minerals, salts and copper for the Chileans, making it the wealthiest country in Latin America for natural resource exports. Sodium nitrate, a type of salt, was mined extensively in the first half of the twentieth century. Once the mining stopped, there was no reason for the miners and their families to stay in this desolate, windy world, so they left behind ghost towns in the sea of sand. I passed a number of these empty communities and decided to stop and explore the largest, Humberstone.

James Thomas Humberstone was English and founded the mine in 1872, building the ornate town to look very English. It was eerie to cycle down the empty streets, then walk inside the shells of houses. This was no shanty-town: it had a large theatre, a church, a market centre and a parking area, as well as many streets of small houses. My favourite building was the fire station, a large shed with CUARTEL DE BOMBEROS embossed above the heavy wooden doors. It must have been an interesting job being a fireman in a town with no water that was mining explosive nitrate.

I sat on a large sand dune next to the town for a long while, trying to imagine living there. The area is now a UNESCO World Heritage Site, but hasn't yet been turned into a tasteless attraction. Apart from the touristy entrance, I was able to cycle in and explore the town pretty much as it had been the day they deserted it over sixty years ago.

The winds returned with a vengeance, and late on I found myself pedalling through a landscape that looked like nothing on earth. It was more like how I would imagine Mars to be. The Salar de Pintados is a world of cracked red earth as hard as rocks, the remains of evaporated saltpans. For over an hour I scoured my surroundings for anywhere I could shelter that night. It looked like a concrete ploughed field. After stopping to examine a few possible spots, about 50 metres off the side of the road I found a small trough that had been created by the wind. It was only about one and a half feet deep, just enough to be out of the wind when lying down. I was so excited when I found it, even more so when I found some loose sand trapped in the lee of the bank which I could scrape into a flat area so I wouldn't be sleeping on slabs of salt bricks. Lying the bike on its side meant that everything was out of sight from the road.

As I tried to get to sleep, the earth creaked loudly around me as the slabs cooled quickly after a day in the sun. I had never heard anything like it; it sounded like the ground was breathing. It was an eerie noise in a wild place, and I imagine it would freak out many people.

The following night I was asleep in the desert again when I woke to a bright spotlight shining on me. I'd known it was coming, but I was still completely disorientated by it. It was Nick. He had flown out for the third and final stage of filming and had meant to join me earlier that day, but got delayed in Santiago. Having told him exactly where I was in the desert, he'd said he would either find me that night or in the morning.

I looked at my watch, eyes still smarting from the bright spotlight and camera in my face. It was just gone one a.m.

'Welcome,' I managed groggily. 'Pick a spot, there's plenty of space.'

Nick was quite up for sleeping out under the stars, but I got the distinct impression that his Chilean driver hadn't been told that we would be wild-camping: he only had the clothes he was dressed in. I put up my tent and gave him the new sleeping-mat Nick had brought out for me. A few more nights sleeping on the ground wouldn't hurt after a month of it.

It was nearly two by the time I was back in my sleeping-bag. I couldn't sleep now, so I watched a meteor storm, with shooting stars racing across the dark canvas above my bed.

Four hours later I woke to the sound of heavy snoring coming from the tent. Nick was asleep just a few metres away. For all the space and peace of the desert, this wasn't a situation I had foreseen. It was day 200 of the expedition. Nick and I quickly got up to film a time-lapse of the sunrise.

It was a stunning day on the bike, beautifully still to start with, then as the day went on I was pushed along by a cracking tailwind. In the same way that Nick had appeared in Central America and the monsoon rains had stopped, he now heralded the best winds I had experienced for weeks. Great for the cycling, but I once again wished he could experience what I had been through.

In mid-morning we stopped at Quillagua, a small village where many of the houses' roofs were made of sacking and sun-dried bricks. If it rained, they would certainly fall through. The houses were basic but properly built compared to a lot of what I had seen in Peru and Ecuador. Given the place's reputation as the driest community in the world, I was surprised to see trees in the narrow valley floor alongside a riverbed. The main street seemed deserted, but when we did spot a woman she immediately invited us into her kitchen. I never caught her name, but she was very kind, giving us all some cake and coffee. She explained that the river only ran for a few months per year and was undrinkable. The villagers' water arrived by tanker.

'Have you had water delivered by a truck all your life?' I asked.

'Yes, all my life.'

'What is your main reason for, or the appeal of, living in this village?' I continued, unsure how to ask this, but fascinated with the idea of living here.

'In this village? Ah, well, I'm used to it.' She paused. 'I'm used to it and I wouldn't be able to settle anywhere else. The thing is, my situation is that I'm not educated. I mean, above all else I believe in God.'

'And what do people do here for work? What do the men do?'

'For work? Here you get all sorts, but they are lazy and all the men do is drink, they drink alcohol.' She didn't have many positive things to say about life in Quillagua.

As we chatted she looked after her ninety-four-year-old father. She explained with an odd sense of pride how he had been a womanizer in his younger days and that she had been left to look after him now that her mother had left him.

I raced late into the day to make up for lost early miles. After pulling into the desert for the night, the driver insisted on sleeping in the pick-up this time and Nick opted to take the tent, so I was able to get some space and head back into the desert for some more stargazing. I scribbled in my diary, 'I feel like I have been in this desert for ever now. There is little to differentiate the days out here. It's an amazing part of the planet – a near perfect desert.'

The next day the wind turned again, and Nick was able to film and appreciate the painfully slow progress of going at 5mph for hours while being sandblasted. That night we threw the bike in the back of the pick-up and drove an hour back to the coastal town of Iquique; I think we would have had a mutiny from the driver if we had suggested another night in the desert. He was usually a driver for the mining companies in the Atacama and was reasonably friendly, despite the unexpected working conditions. Early on he had expressed an interest in photography, so I gave him my stills camera and suggested he help when not driving. He did manage to take some good shots of the landscape, but I was surprised when I got the camera back to find that a lot of the photos were unsmiling self-portraits. They were very funny, but both Nick and I found it rather disturbing too. They were a set of murderous-looking mugshots.

For the last of three days with Nick the plan was to film at the Paranal Observatory. On closer inspection of the map we discovered that Paranal wasn't actually on my route south so I cycled until mid-afternoon before driving the final section there. It was a relief to be able to cycle without stopping regularly, as Nick had finally run out of new ways to film me cycling through the desert. Taking the more coastal road to Paranal, we climbed to an altitude of over 2,500m (8,200ft), by which time I was very glad that I hadn't attempted to cycle the last bit.

Before going up to the main observatory we were met and shown around the Residencia, a climate-controlled hotel for the scientists. The building was used in the James Bond film *Quantum of Solace* as the bad guys' hide-out, supposedly in Bolivia, when they are trying to hold the government to ransom for its water supply. Inside was a jungle of plants in a space-age building. I was so used to the super-dry desert air that it felt strange and very humid.

We then drove up to the main platform and went inside one of the four huge telescopes to watch its 8.2-metre mirrors open for the night's work. I spent the next hour outside watching the remaining telescopes rotate and open. Seeing these 400-ton devices move silently in the growing darkness as they searched the skies was a beautiful thing.

The actual stargazing, however, was less romantic than I had imagined. We descended into a normal-looking office where astronomers studied computer screens. One of the scientists took the time to show me a black hole he was researching, but as it was a black hole I couldn't actually see anything on the screen. It was probably very interesting and significant, but I'd felt more impressed just standing on the large platform outside, looking up at the sky and down at the desert.

It was one thing spending weeks in this world, but being above it and having the chance to step back from it and observe it was magnificent. I absolutely loved those moments of peace, watching the desert as the darkness enfolded it. I knew that in a few hours I would be sleeping out there again, somewhere.

It was gone one a.m. by the time we got back to where I had finished cycling and unloaded the bike and bags. There was absolutely nothing for miles around, only a few signposts to tell us we were in the right place. After a hug goodbye from Nick, I watched the headlight do a sweeping turn and then the tail-light quickly disappearing. I was alone again in the middle of the night. For just a moment I stood there, wishing they would come back.

I'd had an average of five hours' sleep for four days and I felt pretty tired on the bike the next day. I stopped at the only food place I saw all day, a very rustic roadhouse, and was recognized by the owner. On closer inspection, the only sign of modern life was a big satellite dish on the roof, and it seemed that the owner was an avid BBC documentary follower.

'Your hair was shorter,' he commented, very excited about my visit.

Nick had left me with a number of items, mainly essential supplies. However, I spent that whole day thinking about just one thing: a huge wedge of Christmas cake, wrapped in tinfoil, from Mum. I kept telling myself that I would keep it for Christmas, as it was the only present I'd have. But as I tucked into more cold chicken and rice that evening, sat in the middle of nowhere on my comfy new sleeping-mat, I gave in.

It was utter bliss. I peeled back the tinfoil, then the greaseproof paper, taking my time. It smelled rich and wonderful. I waited a bit longer, enjoying the thought of the cake, anticipating its flavour. Christmas cake always tastes good, but in comparison to my standard diet it was an explosion of flavours. I sat there in the near dark with my eyes closed, chewing slowly. Magic. I forced myself to leave some so I could repeat the ritual for breakfast, and fell asleep the happiest man.

I flew the next morning. Whether or not it was down to a genuine punch of nutrition, I made great miles. Remembering how good the cake had been, I justified eating it with the thought that it would have been very heavy to carry for a week. Once again there was only one place all day to pick up supplies. I ate until I couldn't eat any more and then asked for more to go. As I went to pay, I asked for some bottles of water as usual, only to be told that they were out. There was nowhere else for the next 80 miles. 'Pero tengo Pap,' the lady reassured me. Pap is a Chilean fizzy drink made by Coca Cola but not sold anywhere else, and is bright orange with a fairly indescribable taste. So I set out into the desert again with the litre of water I still had and 3 litres of what would soon be warm fizzy orange cola to keep me going for the next twenty-four hours.

Despite this odd fuel, or maybe thanks to it, I made great miles and the following day covered another 100 miles, making it back to the Pacific. Even before I got there I spotted the very first signs that I was leaving the Atacama. Around me now were earthier-looking rolling hills, like parts of southern Peru had been, instead of wide-open sandy desert. I was also spotting the first hardy plants on the roadside.

Chañaral, the first coastal town I came to, was an industrial place thanks to the nearby copper mines. I felt unaccustomed to so many people. It didn't help that my first stop was at the bus station, which was bustling, before finding a very busy restaurant for some food. On the road heading south I passed a number of small beaches where lots of people were swimming and sunbathing. I watched them in wonder. It seemed to me an utterly bizarre activity. I craved shelter more than anything else, shade from the relentless sun and wind; I had just spent long hours in the desert wondering where my next bit of shade and my next drink would come from. As I pedalled on, I had a laugh at myself. The desert had obviously left its scar on me.

I felt a new lease of life being back in the world of the living, even if it was still very arid. The next day, 19 December, I managed 101 miles from Chañaral to Copiapó. After six months of pushing south I was now within a week of the end of the cycle. I was tired for sure, in a burned-out kind of way, and definitely underweight, but I no longer had any doubt that I could get there.

Aconcagua lies 32.4 degrees south of the equator so I planned to reach that latitude by Boxing Day, or possibly the 27th. This would allow me four or five days' recovery before starting the climb. My girlfriend Nicci was booked to fly out on Christmas Eve, bringing all my climbing gear. I would be climbing with an Argentinian team based in Mendoza, so I planned to spend these rest days there. It now felt tantalizingly close, yet still a long week in the saddle away.

The Atacama officially ended at Copiapó. Just south of there I had a couple of punctures, both thanks to large thorns – something I hadn't seen for a while. Down on the coast, cacti were now every-where. Not the large, iconic Mexican types with a couple of branches, but shorter bushy ones, like the hairy legs of an upturned tarantula. I passed an area that had been fenced into fields using lines of these cacti instead of posts and wire. An ingenious solution.

Like in the far north of Chile, the first signs of arable farming were in the valley bottoms I dropped into. I was now amazed to find vineyards and orchards, before climbing back into a semi-arid world.

After a couple of hundred more miles I reached the coastal city of La Serena, and could have stopped there for a while. The main boulevard is tree-lined, with grand neo-colonial buildings on each side. It was unlike anything I had seen in the Americas; it felt European. A couple of jugglers entertained cars waiting at traffic lights, gentrified ladies strolled together pushing prams, and a group of teenagers skateboarded past as I tried to find a room. I felt like I was being thrust back into another epoch; my mind was still in the desert and a simpler life.

The following day the road south became a dual carriageway and much busier. In mid-afternoon I saw some cars stopped on the road ahead. Even from a few hundred metres off it was clear that the crash had only just happened. Only a few other cars had arrived on the scene, and I could see some people on their mobiles. I kept going, there was nothing I could do to help. One of the drivers was lying a few metres in front of his car, having come through the windscreen. It was an awful sight. All afternoon I couldn't get the image out of my head. Without anything to distract me it went round and round in there, and soon I found myself cycling along with tears rolling down my face.

Back on a hilly coastline, I ended up camped at the back of a truck stop, right next to a building on the only flat land I could find. It was only once I had the tent up that I noticed the smell of sewage. Inside, the roadhouse was a typically basic room with tables, chairs and a small TV in the corner. The news was talking about Michael Schumacher making a comeback to F1. The girl who served me was maybe in her late teens and seemed quite moody. She certainly knew that I hadn't understood all the things she had said. Once I had ordered, she said, 'You look like a lion,' with a completely straight face. I understood that perfectly: the Spanish for lion is *león*. From my surprised glance, she immediately realized that I had understood her. I don't think it was an insult or a chat-up line, it had simply been a case of her thinking aloud. In any case, she seemed embarrassed and raced off. Dinner was delicious, but she didn't serve me again.

The following morning I woke with a horrible raspy throat and head cold. Initially I thought it was caused by the sewage, but it wouldn't shake off. I had a radio broadcast to do first thing, always tricky when it's your first words of the day, pre-coffee, but that morning I sounded particularly terrible. It was a bad time to get ill: in less than a week I needed to pass a complete medical check at a hospital before being allowed to start the climb. I spent the day trying to cycle carefully, keeping my heart rate down, getting a recovery ride.

The BBC team had the idea that I should somehow decorate my bike for Christmas morning. It was a fun idea but I hadn't found anywhere to buy any decorations, and it was now Christmas Eve. Back on the Pacific coast, I stopped at a truck stop for some lunch, hoping for some great fish which I always enjoyed having back in my diet. The place was empty, always a bad sign. If the truckers don't use it, there's normally a good reason. However, I immediately spotted an opportunity. It was not my most honest or Christmas-spirited moment, but I saw that their artificial tree had a huge amount of tinsel on it. While ordering a fried fillet of fish, I asked if I could charge my mobile phone. This gave me the excuse to go behind the tree to find a plug. There was really far too much tinsel; they wouldn't miss a little bit.

The fish was really terrible and I had to leave most of it. Without any other customers to distract the women running the place, I said thanks and waited until they were back in the kitchen before fetching my phone. Slipping my knife under a section of tinsel I was horrified to find that it had a metal wire through it. It wouldn't cut.

The whole tree then shook back and forth as I quickly bent the wire to break it. Once it had severed I stuffed the length of tinsel into my pocket, emerged from behind the tree holding my mobile, and raced out of the door. I am officially the worst thief in the world, with absolutely no sense of calm. My heart was racing as I pedalled away, as if I had robbed a bank, not a few feet of tinsel.

On Christmas morning I woke feeling horrible, with a very raw throat. Lying down felt worse than getting up, but all I wanted to do was get back into my sleeping-bag and go back to sleep. I must have put a hole in my tent as hundreds of ants had moved in and found my breakfast, some empanadas, which are like flat Cornish pasties. I brushed off those I could see, but it was still a slightly crunchy breakfast.

It had been very windy in the night, but it was now calm and I looked out on a misty landscape of cactus and rocks. I managed a groggy 'Merry Christmas' piece to camera, holding my tinsel, before taking the tent down and lifting my bike back to the road to avoid the roadside thorns. I was ready but not very enthusiastic for a Christmas Day spent pedalling down the Chilean Pacific coast.

I hoped to find a good lunch on the road but it was a particularly desolate stretch, so Christmas lunch was some spaghetti and a yoghurt in a garage restaurant. The highlight was going live on Radio 1 for a chat and then speaking to friends and family back in the UK. Two years earlier I had been cycling in the rain on the north island of New Zealand. I remembered having those exact same emotions as I pedalled into the wind that afternoon. I always thought I wouldn't mind being away from home at Christmas, until the day itself, and then it wasn't actually great fun. The roads were very quiet.

Nicci wasn't having much more fun. Having flown out to Buenos Aires and then internally to Mendoza, she had discovered that all my climbing gear had gone missing en route. I hadn't seen her for nearly five months, and felt bad that she had to spend Christmas Day in Mendoza on her own.

Sunset over the Pacific was wonderful, and the very last one I would see. Having planned a journey down the mountains, it had turned out to be as much about following the ocean and getting through the deserts. Throughout Central and South America, the Pacific had been an important compass, a regular companion, always on my right. My spirits soared in the last few hours, and I rode until it was nearly dark.

'That was an odd Xmas!' I wrote in my diary as I sat in my tent that night. 'Loved the whole journey from Alaska but at this point very ready for some time off the bike. Nearly there!'

After all the concerns and lost miles in Ecuador and Peru, I had managed to speed up considerably. The re-route had worked. The Atacama had been wild, but it had also been relatively fast. To the long-distance cyclist, wind direction is everything, and I had had a better run of luck.

On Boxing Day I turned off the main Pan American Highway and headed due east towards the border with Argentina, following the Río Aconcagua upstream into the foothills of the Andes. Cycling up past the towns of San Felipe and Los Andes was a beautiful and fitting way to finish the half-year commute between the two mountains. The Aconcagua River was fast-flowing, the valley very green and wooded, and the villages quaint but surprisingly developed with cycle paths, nice parks and lots of coffee shops – a completely different standard of living to the foothills in Ecuador.

On the late morning of the 27th I met up with Nicci, who had come over the imposing 3,810m (12,500ft) Uspallata Pass from Argentina with a local driver. Aconcagua stood about 30km to the north-east, just behind a wall of lower mountains.

The sense of relief was quite incredible. I felt like a massive weight had been lifted off me. Since June, getting from Talkeetna, via Denali, all the way south to Los Andes and Aconcagua within the climbing season had been my main focus, overriding everything else. And I had done it. The climb ahead remained intimidating, but for now I could only think about getting off the bike for a while and enjoying a short rest.

Admittedly I had been forced to miss both Honduras and Colombia, as well as the route over the Andes into Bolivia, but even so it had been a far tougher ride than I had expected. Not just in terms of terrain, but the experiences off the bike and all the filming and storytelling had made it the most relentlessly intense six months of my life. And, for all that, enjoyable.

The big question now was would I be in good enough shape to climb? After cycling around the world I had found walking around the streets of Paris extremely uncomfortable. I had been incredibly fit, but only for cycling, after spending half a year doing little else. Now, after another half a year's cycling, I planned to put a rucksack on in a few days' time and climb Aconcagua, the western hemisphere's highest peak at 6,926m (22,841ft).

17

I knew Aconcagua would be very different to Denali. After Alaska I had decided that my chances of summiting in Argentina would be improved as part of a smaller team. Andrew Robertson, a good friend who had climbed Aconcagua in 1996, recommended and introduced me to Willie Benegas, whose brother Damian agreed to lead the ascent.

The Benegas brothers are two of the most experienced and respected guides from South America. In 2003 they won the coveted Golden Piton award for the best high-altitude mountaineering route of the year, on Nuptse, a 7,800m (25,600ft) peak in Nepal. They have also both guided Everest, Willie having summited ten times. Between them they have over a hundred summits on Aconcagua, a seemingly unbeatable tally.

But before climbing anywhere I had to get a clean bill of health. Getting up at eight a.m. for a trip to the hospital in Mendoza wasn't my favourite way to spend the first morning off the bike. En route there, the taxi we were in drove straight into the side of another car at a crossroads. Neither of us nor the drivers was hurt, there was just lots of broken glass, bent metal and annoyed Argentinians. Strangely, neither driver got out of his car to speak, instead both just picked up their mobiles. Nicci and I sat there for a minute, not knowing what to do, before letting ourselves out. At this the driver also got out, flagged another cab for us, and we continued our journey. The irony of crashing on the way to the hospital wasn't lost on me.

At the Hospital Español the doctors took blood and urine samples, did some chest scans, and, much to my horror, put me on a static bike with sensors attached to me for a heart check. I thought I had escaped the saddle for a month! I was there until early afternoon, and it cost a small fortune, but I managed a clean bill of health. I was run-down for sure, and underweight, with a nasty cold and blistered lips, but there was nothing wrong with me that some rest and recovery wouldn't cure.

The next day it was the bike's turn for a check-up. It needed a complete service including a new chainset, an oil-change in the Rohloff hub, new cabling, brake pads and tyres. My focus had been so set on just reaching Aconcagua that I had to keep reminding myself that there was still about 2,000 miles to ride to Tierra del Fuego.

My missing climbing gear had been found and delivered to Mendoza the day after it was lost, which was a massive relief. I never found out where it went, but it had done its own mini tour of Argentina. It now took a lot of time to go through this, rechecking, packing, unpacking, then packing again. One concern was climbing in new boots, always a risk, so I went for a long walk around Mendoza wearing my new boots. My feet got horribly hot and I drew a lot of strange looks, but I thought it was worth doing to break them in.

In between all this activity, Nicci and I enjoyed four days of complete rest, although it wasn't much of a sightseeing holiday for her: all I really wanted to do was sleep and eat. Mendoza is a great city, wonderfully relaxed, world famous for its wine and olive oil. Its strong European roots are very evident in everything from the architecture to people's appearances.

The plan was to leave for the climb on New Year's Day, but on the 31st I still had a bad cough so Damian suggested we take another day's rest and that we start on the 2nd. There was no point in going to high altitude if I was unwell. So New Year's Eve was a very quiet affair, followed by Nicci flying home early on New Year's Day. The 1st is also my birthday. It was my 27th in 2010, and I celebrated by spending much of the day in bed, reading the rest of Harry Kikstra's guidebook on Aconcagua.

An event called the World March for Peace was planned for 2 January on the road up to Aconcagua. Damian didn't think this would be a problem, until the news on the 1st reported that fifteen thousand people had turned out and were entirely blocking the route. Our departure was now delayed again, until the 3rd. It felt frustrating after rushing for months to get here, but once I realized that Damian remained optimistic about our window on the mountain, I relaxed as well. I certainly appreciated every extra hour of sleep and meal I could fit in before the climb.

I was excited but also nervous about what lay ahead. My only emotion when I arrived in Mendoza after finishing the cycle had been relief. Then my body had gone into a partial shut-down for the first few days, consumed by a lethargy that was hard to fight out of. I had then started to think more and more about the climb ahead, to mentally prepare for it. Originally I had imagined cycling to the base of Aconcagua, locking my bike up, changing my shoes and starting to walk. That's how the cartoon journey might have looked, but I was grateful for the advice to recover slightly first.

There was a third member of our team, a man called Sebastian Ezcurra, a pizza maker by trade and the dictionary definition of a man who works to be able to play. I was surprised Damian had chosen Sebastian, who was by his own account a fairly in-experienced climber and who didn't speak fluent English. The connection was that both Damian and Sebastian are North Face-sponsored athletes; still, Sebastian's sport was adventure racing, not climbing. Regardless of this inexperience and our limited initial communications, he was immediately likeable. In his late thirties, with shoulder-length dark hair and a lean but muscular build, he was ruggedly handsome and wore a constant smile. Running the length of one forearm was a large tattoo of a gladiator's helmet and sword with the Spanish word 'Espartacus'.

Damian was a similar age to Sebastian, with wild curly hair and the look of a man who has spent his life in the mountains. He seemed to run on a manic energy all the time, speaking quickly, always moving, and was the definitive 'yes' man. Nothing was impossible for Damian. I could see why they were friends. Their passion was the same, but the fact that one was highly strung and the other laid-back made for a good balance.

Until Base Camp we were also being joined by Alice, an English friend of Damian's, who was very welcome for her great humour and her keenness to help with the filming.

Sebastian drove a huge Chevy truck complete with full sponsor's livery – a worthy chariot. The back was absolutely stuffed with cargo bags and rucksacks for the 100-mile drive to the start. It seemed an impossible amount of kit for the climb. At least this time we wouldn't need to pull everything on sleds. In fact, we would never need to carry all of it at once. From the main road until Base Camp at around 4,370m (14,340ft) mules would carry most of our gear, including all the kit for the higher reaches of the mountain.

A childhood friend of Damian's, Fernando Grajales, ran a porters company out of the roadside village of Puente del Inca, at 2,740m (8,990ft), so we spent the evening there packing the expedition food and checking and packing our bags for the mules once more before retiring for our last night in a bed.

Meaning 'Stone Sentinel', Aconcagua was first officially summited in 1897, although an Incan mummy has been discovered at about 5,500m (18,000ft), meaning that people were in its high reaches over half a millennium earlier. Aconcagua is the highest mountain in the world outside the Himalayas, just shy of 7km (4.3 miles) high, yet its normal northern route is considered non-technical and it's reached by walking in from the road. When there is little snow on the upper mountain you can climb the whole route without crampons. For these reasons it attracts a lot of climbers each year, over twice the number who attempt Denali. And for these same reasons it has to be one of the most underestimated of the big mountains, with a lower summit rate than Denali and one of the highest death tolls in the world. Safe to say, it is definitely a mountain whose bite is worse than its bark.

I was hoping that the walk into Base Camp would be as easy as the guidebook suggested. Some days of gentle adjustment would be very welcome.

After being dropped off a few miles further up the road, we signed our registration papers in the rangers' Portakabin station, having completed and paid for our climbing permits back in Mendoza. We each had a daypack, and I wore shorts, a T-shirt and trail shoes. It felt like a day's summer hill-walking in the Alps, except that framed perfectly between the spurs of the valley ahead of us rose the snow-peaked, rocky bulk of Aconcagua's southern flank. She looked hugely imposing and not very far off, yet it was 24 miles (38km) to Base Camp at Plaza de Mulas, from where our route would turn right on to the upper mountain. So she wasn't that close, just so much bigger than anything else around her.

It would take us four days to reach Plaza de Mulas. We had Damian to advise us to stop and rest at certain points along the way, but I could see how easy it would be to fall into the trap of carrying on up quickly. It's frustrating to stop when the trail is simple and beautiful and there are still over 9,000 feet to be climbed. It also takes time for the effects of each new level of altitude to really hit you, so you can climb, feel great and move on, then twelve hours later you realize you have made too big a jump and your body is struggling to adapt.

Only two hours from the road we reached a camp at 3,400m (11,150ft) called La Confluencia. As its name suggests, the place lies at the confluence of two valleys, the Inferior and Superior Horcones Valleys. We had started in a wide green valley with rolling grassy hillocks and moved past a small lake before following the river upstream into rockier terrain. There were a lot of day hikers and even a few people sunbathing by the lake, which didn't at all fit with what I had expected. And I was amazed to find that La Confluencia was a busy semi-permanent village of tents. I was looking forward to reaching quieter parts.

I had forgotten what adjusting to altitude felt like. Even at Puente del Inca I had started having very vivid dreams. Now it felt like I was adventuring all night as well as all day. My first night at La Confluencia I slept very badly and woke with a cracking headache, which went away very slowly.

We took two days to acclimatize before moving up, and tried a few smaller climbs, including up one of the side valleys to 3,900m (12,800ft) on the Horcones Inferior Glacier. It was hard to tell we were on ice as it was covered in a moraine of dirt and rocks. With lots of very loose scree and steep scrambling, it was an excellent test for my climbing strength. Even with a daypack on, my back and shoulders were hurting slightly, but no more than I'd expected, and my legs felt strong. Throughout the six months of the cycle I had finished most days, whenever possible, with stretching and some basic yoga in an effort to maintain flexibility and strength, especially in my lower back. It had probably been the hardest thing to motivate myself to do regularly, especially when tired, but the memory of how sore and broken I had felt at the end of the world cycle was enough to remind me that the climb would be nearly impossible if I didn't do things differently this time.

So far it had been completely clear, warm and still, although as soon as the sun set the temperature plummeted, from a T-shirt to a fleece and thick jacket within an hour. As we packed up to leave La Confluencia for Plaza de Mulas, on day four of the ascent, it seemed that most people in camp had the same idea and were on the same schedule. I guess the peace march had delayed others as well, bunching everyone up. With over four thousand climbers attempting Aconcagua every year, within a limited season, it's a busy place. Like on Denali, this is an odd phenomenon to observe, as mountaineers arrive to experience space and natural beauty only to find many others with the same idea.

Aconcagua, however, is a very arid mountain of rock and dust as opposed to glaciers of endless ice so I could at least wander off and find a view without people, without fear of falling into a crevasse. The other great freedom was my team. In Alaska we had been under strict instructions at all times, for good reason in a large group of mixed abilities in such a dangerous environment. But Damian and Sebastian were both exceptional athletes, that was very clear, and while Damian always took the lead, there was from the start a wonderful warmth and comradeship I have rarely experienced on expedition. It made me think about how much I had done solo in my life, and how as part of the right team I would relish being able to share some journeys.

We were the last to leave camp, by a good margin, and spent the next seven hours overtaking teams. We moved at the same pace, stopping regularly, but never for long. It was a revelation for me to share with others the same mindset, same fitness level and obvious commitment. And there was that wonderfully unsporting joy of passing groups who were crawling along in long lines, staring at their feet. Where the path allowed we walked side by side, especially across the Playa Ancha, literally 'Wide Beach', a 15km (9-mile) flat-bottomed stony section of the valley. All the way we were shut in on each side by steep valley walls that rose in an array of colours from reddish brown through light tan to slate grey. Some rock faces looked like a child had drawn on them, with their stark sedimentary lines. If you were to see them in a painting you would doubt such contrast was possible.

All the way up Playa Ancha we could see Aconcagua getting closer. We were well below even half the summit altitude and it looked wild, spindrift telling the tale of another world up there dominated by the infamous *viento blanco* (blizzard). It was fairly windy where we were, with lots of dust billowing around us, which meant that it must be blowing an utter gale up high – an impossible summit day. It would be the last time we saw the top during the ascent.

All day trains of mules clattered past, incredibly sure-footed and fast. The size of a horse but with the hardiness of a donkey, the mules moved over the rocky, sometimes steep terrain and forded the streams with ease. Each was saddled with a couple of climbers' bags or a couple of large plastic drums containing food and supplies for the team.

We stopped for longer to have some lunch in an area of large boulders in a narrow section at the top end of the Playa Ancha. The whitewater of the Aconcagua River was down a very steep bank off to the left of the path. As we ate, I filmed about a dozen mules being herded down the steep traverse above our spot, slipping with each hoof in the loose scree, but always descending fast. A couple of *assieros* (mule handlers), or gauchos, rode behind in the cloud of dust. Then, suddenly, one of the mules went berserk, bucking and bolting forward. It passed within a few metres of us. Damian ran out and tried to grab it. He was too late, and we watched the mule, still bucking, canter straight off the edge. I couldn't see the fall, but Damian did: the animal rolled twice down the 30-metre bank of stones, ending up on the riverbank. When I got to the top I watched Damian skid downward in an avalanche of small rocks, half skiing, half falling to the bottom. The mule was no longer fighting when Damian managed to catch hold of its collar.

I was amazed that any animal could survive such a fall. Incredibly, it was immediately on its feet, not even lame, though it did have a couple of cuts that would need attention. Its empty saddle bag had completely slipped back, which had caused the animal to spook. It was an accident. Damian, who had been a gaucho in his late teens, was visibly relieved by the outcome, surprised that they hadn't had been forced to put the animal down.

Despite the mules' resilience, further up we passed a number of skeletons, white bones on a bed of rocks. All the animals I had seen, except for the runaway, had looked happy in their work, ears pricked, running loose. But there was a big part of me that wished we were carrying all our own kit, going unsupported. I guess most climbers don't want this extra work so the tradition is now for almost all to use pack animals.

The last hour of the approach was when we did most of the climbing, following steep traverses on a large hill of moraine. As we crested it started snowing very lightly and we arrived quite suddenly in a small tent city in a wide dusty bowl of scree. We had reached the head of the valley, and I looked up at fingers of glaciers pointing towards us. We were one of the first teams of the day to arrive, which gave us the pick of available places for the tent.

I felt the effects of 4,360m (14,300ft) much faster. It was much colder, and putting up the tents meant stopping every few minutes to get a breather. Physically I felt pretty good after the biggest day yet. The only (and slightly amusing) pain was coming from deep in my backside, where I had obviously been working a climbing muscle that is redundant on a bike. I couldn't find any way or anyone to ease this tight ache.

Plaza de Mulas, literally 'Mule Square', was a real eye opener, a veritable town of about five hundred people living under canvas. It's meant to be the second largest base camp in the world, after Everest. There's power from generators, internet access and a public satellite phone, even warm showers, which consist of a bucket with a tap which you fill with some water from the stove.

The most important ingredient to help acclimatization is good hydration. I had been force-feeding myself water since day one, which on Aconcagua has an unexpected side effect. The natural spring and glacial water, which is all we could find to drink, is very high in magnesium, which is hard for the body to get used to. I will spare the details, but it's a well-documented issue. In La Confluencia and Plaza de Mulas you have very basic long-drops, but for the rest of the mountain you use a bag, and nothing can be left on the hill. For a team of three, that's about 15kg of waste during the climb. It's not glamorous.

Water for so many at Base Camp is an even bigger issue, especially as the only supply is a glacier-fed stream running down one side of the camp. In the morning it runs crystal clear, but by midday it's very murky due to the meltwater run-off. We drank it with powdered juice, to make it more palatable and to hide the dirt, but it felt like being back at university being forced to down dirty pints.

I woke the next day with a cracking headache, feeling terrible. I wrote in my diary, 'It's the part of mountaineering you forget in retrospect. The mind is a strange place. If it remembered the true balance of pleasure & pain on expeditions, it should logically stop dreaming of more!' As bad as I felt, Sebastian was suffering more. After forcing down some breakfast and ibuprofen the 'hangover' feeling started to pass, but Sebastian continued to feel nauseous. Twice a day we took our vital readings using a pulse oximeter, the small clip that fits over any finger, like the one we had used on Denali. It showed pulse rate and the level of oxygen saturation in the blood (spO2). When I arrived at Base Camp, at rest my heart rate was 95 beats per minute and my spO2 was 81; twenty-four hours later it was 65 and 86, which showed good acclimatization. It had been a day of complete rest, except for a short walk to film the mules climbing the steepest section of scree below the camp.

That evening the weather report bore bad news. A very low pressure system was moving in from the east, with high pressure from the west bringing 60mph winds on the higher mountain. Damian looked concerned: after Base Camp there are three higher camps, and it's normal to have a day off to acclimatize at one or both of the first two of these; the weather meant that we wouldn't be able to camp and acclimatize at these higher camps for another three days. Damian's new plan made the best of the situation but would mean a longer and tougher climb. We could use the days to ferry kit higher up the mountain, but retreat to Base Camp each

night for safety. Once the storm passed, we could assess how everyone felt and then try moving up the mountain faster than usual.
'Everyone' now included a young Russian climber and
photographer called Oksana Chekulaeva, the final member of our
summit team. Oksana had already summited the week before and
would be a great help filming on the upper mountain.

I woke at six a.m., put on my huge down jacket, hat, gloves and
boots, and pulled my cameras from inside the sleeping-bag.
Sebastian followed, and we climbed far above the camp to find a
spot to film sunrise. It was very cold, and I sat there cradling my
face to keep warm. Very few people were up, and we sat there for
over half an hour before the sun started peering over the high valley
walls.

I had the camera set up for a time-lapse. It was magical, from
the first glint of golden sun on Cerro Cuerno, the mountain to the
north-west; then the light raced downhill, pulling back the dark
curtain over camp. Seb was busy taking photos while cracking jokes
and giggling at the general level of discomfort. The imposing
craggy rocks of Aconcagua's west face cast the last shadow, and it
took much longer for the sun to inch upwards, as if the great mountain had a stronger hold over the night.

Sebastian's limited English still beat my ropey Spanish, especially
my Argentinian Spanish, which has strange pronunciations and
words. With his unbounded enthusiasm there was little issue
communicating, and when there was misunderstanding it was
usually more funny than frustrating. Sebastian had taken it upon
himself to teach me more Spanish, but adopted the unusual
approach of laughing and mocking my every mistake. My faux pas
from the night before soon became the campsite joke over breakfast. In our small tent, snuggled next to each other in our very large
down sleeping-bags, I tried to express that I was hot. 'Estoy
caliente,' I exclaimed. Word for word, this is correct, but in Spanish
this phrase actually means 'I am horny', so it was met by a howl of

laughter that must have woken half the campsite. And so it went on.

After breakfast we were packed. This was the first major test of the climb as I heaved on a rucksack weighing 20kg or more and we set off to Plaza de Grajales at just shy of 5,000m (16,400ft). It was over 600 metres higher, but certainly not as the crow flies, following a series of long traverses on the relentlessly steep scree. The various routes criss-crossed one another, making serious scars in the mountain, and I joined Damian in berating those who felt the need to create more than one path, causing more damage than was absolutely necessary.

Plodding upwards felt painfully slow as my heart raced like a budgie's, but we still overtook other groups on this section. The right speed is a fine balance. While pacing yourself is very important, going too slow risks unnecessary exposure to the elements and wear and tear on the body carrying a heavy pack. Denali had been too slow for me, but with Damian, Sebastian and now Oksana I found a great pace, and it was so much easier to stay in the zone and be positive.

This porterage was to carry food, cooking gear, crampons and extra clothing for summit day, and our heavy full-plastic high-altitude boots. I had spent the whole climb on Denali in these but would hopefully only need them for the summit day here, for the extreme cold and for wearing crampons. We also brought up a couple of small bottles of oxygen which were surprisingly heavy. If all went well we wouldn't need them, but the summit was at about the same height at which climbers on Everest often switch to artificial breathing. If any of us became hypoxic, suffering acute mountain sickness, the oxygen could save our lives.

The return to Plaza de Mulas was brilliant fun, albeit ankle-breaking scree running, the source of the erosion nightmare, and I gulped in what now felt like enriched air as we descended.

The following morning, 10 January, we set out again up the same path, this time carrying 18kg. After pausing briefly at camp one, we pushed on to Needles, camp two. It took nearly five hours, and I felt very weak above 5km. My bag felt more like 50kg, digging painfully into my shoulders and causing a deep ache in my lower back. I climbed with my thumbs hooked, trying to release the pressure. Now it was my turn to stare at my feet. My lungs felt fine, but I could hear my pulse in my ears as my heart fought to beat fast enough to get the scarce oxygen to my aching legs. It was by far the hardest day yet, and I collapsed on to a rock when we finally reached the small plateau camp at 5,400m (17,700ft). After stashing all we were carrying under some rocks, we quickly turned back, once again with empty rucksacks.

I hadn't been at camp two for long enough to get anything worse than breathlessness, but Sebastian continued to suffer from a bad headache. Altitude hits indiscriminately; the fact that he wasn't adapting as well as Damian and me wasn't a sign of anything in terms of fitness. I hazard that Sebastian would beat me over most races of less than a week's duration.

With supplies stashed at two of the upper camps, it was now a case of sitting out the worst of the storm for another day at Base Camp. Others seemed to have had the same idea, a mass exit of higher camps causing Plaza de Mulas to be especially busy. Camping higher would be a miserable experience during the storm, with a good chance of tents being destroyed.

Apart from bruised feet and shoulders, I felt very good. That night I slept dreamlessly for eleven hours – a sure sign that I was fully acclimatized, at least for Base Camp.

I woke to the wind buffeting the tent. We had secured the edges with some extra boulders so it would now break before blowing off. Others weren't so prepared. From outside the kitchen I watched a couple of tents do high cartwheels across the campsite. One went uncaught and disappeared from sight across the rocks. Standing outside was a stinging experience as a torrent of horizontal grit peppered the air. Inside the tent, the canvas only amplified the howling, so I spent the day listening to music and reading a book while eating and drinking as much as I could face.

The 12th dawned clear and still. Packing what little was left, mainly tents and sleeping-bags, we set off. If all went to plan, we wouldn't return until after we'd summited. The climb to Plaza de Grajales was longer than I had remembered, but worth every steep step, for the space of our own camp – just the three tents, with a bird's-eye view back down to Plaza de Mulas. Once the tents were up, it took me over an hour to dam a stream running out of a small glacier above the camp and funnel enough water into bottles for cooking dinner and drinking. I'm not the most gifted engineer, but it was nonetheless wonderfully satisfying.

At sunset we all clambered up on the cliff-top alongside our tents and shared a gourd of *maté*. A national drink in Argentina, the *yerba maté* infusion of green leaves took some getting used to because of its strong grassy herbal taste. It isn't really socially acceptable to climb with Argentinians and not share *maté*, their sur-rogate coffee. Every time we ate, and at several other times each day, some *maté* would be prepared and passed around, everyone drink-ing from the same gourd out of a thin metal straw called a *bombilla*. There seemed to be more etiquette to drinking *maté* than there is to the game of golf, but once accustomed I could see that it was the social centrepiece to the climb. That and Sebastian's singing. It was a great moment to share with friends, sipping *maté* and watching the sun slowly sinking over the mountains to the west, the valley bottom already lost to the night.

I had a fitful sleep again and was awake early, keen to get up. As with a head cold, at altitude you feel better when upright and moving than when lying down. I ate breakfast sitting on a rock, overlooking the amber glow of the glaciers in the dawn light. It was a great perch, looking out over the mountains into Chile.

It was a slow push up to Needles but we made good time. The final stretch traversed a section of glacial snow, cutting through other patches of melt and over huge rock slabs to reach our camp, which overlooked the main camp of Nido de Cóndores. As we set up the tents I had to keep reminding myself to move slowly: we were now higher than High Camp on Denali. Standing up after bending down left me completely light-headed. Carrying small rocks for pinning the guy ropes felt far harder than usual, and even my legs and arms felt leaden.

Sebastian was suffering badly now, and for the first time even Damian mentioned a cracking headache. Sebastian was unusually subdued, and spent a few hours pacing around outside, hood up, trying to make the nausea pass. As we sat inside Damian's tent he got news on the radio of another bad weather front, set to arrive in a few days. With the limited clear weather we had to make some bold decisions. If Sebastian wasn't fit to go higher then we would need to face weathering a storm here or retreat to Base Camp again. Otherwise, if he improved in the night and we all had a reasonable oxygen saturation level, then we could carry on without any rest days. And so, along with dinner, Damian and Sebastian took some Diamox, a drug to aid their acclimatization. I was very tempted, but decided to wait till the morning, to let my body try to adjust naturally.

We were now camped above most of the surrounding mountains, and the views were even better than before. Above the tents on Aconcagua's west flank, opaque fluffy white clouds drifted quickly across the ridgeline. The sense of exposure was far greater up here, not because of any great drops, but in the sense of being up in the clouds, and because of the flux in the weather here. As it got dark, this west face glowed orange, while the western peaks disappeared in ever lightening silhouettes. On the closest mountains I could see white glaciers between dark rock, while on the very far horizon a light-grey ridgeline was framed by a fiery sunset.

The scene was enough to lift everyone's spirits, and Sebastian even managed a few verses of a tango song. His regular renditions of 'Por Una Cabeza' had become the theme tune to the climb. The song's story is of a man lamenting (most tangos lament) about losing a race by 'a horse's head', and how the gambler compares his addiction for horses with the lure of women. I knew the song from the wonderfully evocative scene in *Scent of a Woman* when a blind Al Pacino takes to the dance floor with a young lady. Sung into the growing darkness of our quiet camp at 5,400 metres, it was a wonderful moment of calmness and friendship.

When you sleep your heart rate drops. When unused to being at altitude, the body quickly becomes starved of oxygen, which is called mild hypoxia, and this causes you to wake up gasping for air. This process releases stress hormones which prevent you from going back to sleep. At the same time you get a blocked nose and congested sinuses due to breathing freezing mountain air through your mouth, which dries out and cracks your tongue and lips. All in all, sleeping at altitude is not a lot of fun.

Inevitably it was my worst sleep yet, and I got up at dawn with what felt like a serious hangover. It was the highest I had ever slept. All the team were suffering, even Oksana, who had been here the previous week. I opened my tent to find a thin layer of snow had fallen in the night. What to do was a tough call, but all of our levels were decent so Damian suggested we should keep moving up. This, in essence, was committing us to a summit attempt the next day. There is no way we would move to High Camp at nearly 6,000m (19,700ft) to take a day off. It would be a horrid place to weather any storm and a miserable altitude to sit around at for any longer than was absolutely necessary.

It was a relatively short climb to High Camp, Camp Berlin, but very slow going. The traverses continued up the mountainside like a demented bee dance, never actually pointing in the direction we were going, instead searching out a gradient that was sustainable before making a sharp tack into the mountain for the next. It did the morale no good to search out the route of the path above. I now felt out of breath with every step, but my head was clear, and I hadn't suffered any nausea for a few days.

To reach the craggy grey rocks that create a protective fort around Camp Berlin meant scrambling from the scree hill on to bare rocks, then up a steep, narrow crevasse. It wasn't difficult climbing, but any exertion 6km up is laboured, and I was struggling to juggle the filming. Trying to scramble with only one free hand made me nervous, and I could see that stopping the team so that I could go ahead and film sections was testing everyone's patience.

Surrounded by erratic-looking pinnacles, Camp Berlin is a barren place. Cloud cover shrouded any view, and it felt like a patch of grey lunar landscape. Sebastian and I set about putting up the tent and ended up in fits of laughter, delirious with the breathlessness and our inability to do anything normally. It felt like we were a bit drunk, in control but slightly dazed.

There was no glacial melt up here so once the tent was up Damian and I set off with a sack and shovel to collect snow to melt. Digging into old glacial snow is hard work at any time, but at this altitude I had to stop after each shovelful, leaning on the shovel for support. It was about 100 metres back to the tent, and with Damian's help I swung the full bag on to my back. Still bent nearly double with the weight, I set out at a good pace. It was so heavy that it hurt and I wanted to get it over with. Less than halfway, still staggering, I abandoned the sack on the rocks, gasping for air, eyes watering, head spinning, exclaiming with each rasping breath. My heart had rarely raced faster. Damian laughed at me, picked up the bag, and at a much more sedate pace finished the job.

It had snowed gently all afternoon, but hadn't amounted to much. As we settled into melting the snow for dinner we were greeted by thicker flurries of horizontal snow and a biting cold. We had been so fortunate with the wind-chill so far, and I could immediately feel this change. The forecast was for 3mph winds, almost nothing, but significant cloud cover, which Damian promised was a good thing, as it wouldn't be so cold.

Over some food and *maté* everyone seemed in great spirits. Only Sebastian had lost his appetite. He had eaten one sweet all day. It was a normal symptom of altitude, but Damian was worried about his energy levels and tried to get him to eat. I was happy to dig into the amazing meal of rice, cold meats and cheese. At the highest campsite of my life, it was better food than I have had in many a roadside restaurant.

After checks with the pulse oximeter we all agreed to keep going in the morning. Going from Base Camp to summit without any days off for acclimatization was something Damian had only ever done a couple of times, and only with very strong climbers. His confidence in me was a great boost for my morale. We had already seen a number of teams turn back from camp two and I realized we were in a fight against time to summit before the storm. Somehow, seeing my friends suffer also made my suffering easier to bear and I again refrained from taking Diamox, feeling that my body was adjusting well.

We would leave the tents up, and only packed essential supplies for the summit climb. As we packed, it continued to snow heavily. Holding the camera at arm's length (it felt oddly heavy), I joked that it was midsummer in Argentina, although it was hard to believe here.

It was a wonderfully snug feeling to eventually crawl inside the tent, brush off the snow, take off my boots and wriggle into my huge sleeping-bag. Like every night, my three cameras, all the spare batteries, the satellite phone, my contact lenses, and two bottles of water came inside the sleeping-bag with me, which didn't help with comfort. Sebastian had taken to sleeping propped up on both of our rucksacks, almost upright, to keep his head elevated. I lay awake for most of the night, aware that he was sitting next to me, staring into the darkness.

Long before daybreak I sat up and turned on my head torch, causing a shower of ice particles to fall from the tent. Our frozen breath made every surface sparkle.

'How did you sleep?'

'Mal,' Sebastian laughed – badly.

Outside it had continued to snow, leaving a smooth icing on the jagged world. The camp was still in blackness and the sky above was holding on to the night, but on the eastern horizon a narrow

spectrum of reds and oranges heralded the coming daylight as we
made our last preparations. By the light of our head torches, we set
out for the summit.

'Pole, pole,' Damian called over his shoulder – slowly, slowly.
Pronounced 'poley, poley', it was a traditional climbers' motto.

It was still minus 15 degrees. At this temperature frostbite can be
a real problem, and constant movement of fingers and toes helped
to keep blood circulating. Frostnip and frostbite are normally
caused by poor hydration as much as poor layering so I kept sipping
from a Nalgene of warm water as we climbed. It was too cold to
take off my gloves to film, but I managed some with thin gloves,
swapping hands often. Despite being warmer than Denali at the
start of summit day, it somehow felt colder here, maybe due to
the darkness. All I could see as we climbed was the small pool of
light that illuminated my frozen breath, and Sebastian's back.

Within half an hour we could climb without lights, although it
was still before dawn. When the sun did appear, at seven a.m., we
were in the shadow of a ridgeline, and it was still no warmer.
Looking back I could see our tents, far below us, just coming into
the light. We paused after a while and Damian pointed right to a
line of light and shade that went all the way to the horizon. It took
a second to register. It was Aconcagua's shadow, so vast that miles
and miles of other mountains were still in semi-darkness. We kept
climbing, breaking our own trail for a long section, but I kept glancing to my right, mesmerized by the great shadow.

Everyone had slept badly, for only two or three hours at most,
and everyone mentioned a headache, but spirits were good. We
climbed in silence, each of us tucked into the hoods of our thick
down jackets, lost in our own thoughts. A few teams had left just
before us. Once again, despite what felt like a very steady pace, we
soon overtook them, and after two hours we climbed a ridgeline
and broke into the sunshine. We had reached 6,400m (21,000ft) and
the euphemistically named Refugio Independencia, the highest
refuge hut in the world.

We stopped to eat and rest – except for Sebastian, who was feeling nauseous again and insisted on carrying on slowly while we rested – and I managed the first of a number of calls on the satellite phone, to update the blogs. If possible, I wanted to share the summit as it happened. Despite the forecast, it was completely clear. The views in every direction were magnificent, the fresh snow adding a softness to the harsh, rocky landscape.

The summit, from where I stood, was up a vertical cliff, an intimidating and jumbled rock face, half a kilometre above us. But our route, one that would take us to the rear side of this face, was less direct. The next section was La Travesia, a steep, exposed traverse. The new snow had already been shaped and blown by the wind here, and I slowed further. I was breathing hard through my mouth and the dry air was starting to make me cough. A horrid, dry hack, it hurt my throat and was hard to stop once it got started. I had to keep stopping in a fit of coughs that felt like I was going to be sick. Sipping more water and sucking sweets helped a bit, but it wasn't easy to do while gasping for air all the time.

We were again climbing together as we reached another ridgeline, to start the part every climber I had met spoke about, the seemingly dreaded Canaleta. For the first time I attached crampons to keep my grip on the snowy loose scree. The mountain dropped off to my right, without a break, for many thousands of feet. It was a dizzying view down on to other high peaks. It wasn't dangerously steep, but enough to make you concentrate on each footing, as the route cut a very long line across the side-slope.

From Refugio Independencia, it took another two and a half hours to clear the Canaleta. It was never technical, I was just struggling to control my breathing. Time felt different; I thought I'd been climbing the Canaleta for hours; it seemed never-ending. We finally reached a high section of overhanging rock which created a shallow cave for shelter. From here it was just another few hundred vertical metres to the top. I had been told that this was easier than the Canaleta, but I wasn't feeling strong enough to celebrate yet.

And the weather was turning fast. In the last minutes before reaching the cave large snowflakes had started to fall again, and we soon lost the vast view below us. Sebastian looked grim, but was relentlessly strong. Oksana had also withdrawn into herself, saying very little. Only Damian offered regular words of encouragement, but I could see that he was hurting as well. It was, once again, strangely reassuring to know that we were all suffering, to be able to tell myself that I wasn't being weak.

Whoever said that the last push was easier obviously didn't climb it in the snow. For over an hour we climbed from the cave. It was the steepest section yet, deep in snow that had piled up in the lee of the ridgeline, out of the wind. Along the Canaleta it had simply been a case of putting one foot in front of another – relentless but simple. This was an unstable, uneven staircase up which we had to toe-point and side-step using our crampons. It was worse for Damian who broke his crampons and had to climb on using his bare boots.

We were now breathing just over 40 per cent of the oxygen present in the air at sea level; at this altitude an unacclimatized person would be unconscious in less than twelve minutes. Thankfully another team and Damian had done their best to set a trail because each toe-point for grip and push upwards felt like a one-legged squat; my quads screamed as I rasped for air. I kept muttering to myself, 'Just get to the top, just get to the top.' I could see it through the cloud, far above me, but for a long time, every time I glanced up it didn't seem to be getting any closer.

The team ahead of us, who had successfully reached the summit and were now descending, were a group of soldiers. We shimmied our way past them on the very narrow path just below the final push for the top.

In the last fifteen minutes we all broke into voice, summoning what energy remained to encourage one another. I couldn't believe Sebastian's resilience; he was as strong as an ox. It was me who was left at the back. On two occasions I paused for too long, unable to summon enough energy to go on. The fleeting thought crossed my mind: can I physically carry on? 'Come on!' I shouted out loud to myself.

One step, stop and breathe for a few seconds; two steps, breathe for five seconds, hands on knees for support; another step, gasp some more, pause.

In the final few metres Damian stopped and let me pass. He showed me the widest smile, leaning heavily on his climbing pole. I took the camera out, and pushed on.

As I stepped on to the wide plateau, an incredible sense of relief caught me like a punch. Tears rolled freely. It was elation like I have only felt a few times in my life, the sense of having pushed through something that I knew had nearly failed me.

Sebastian was next, and he met me with a hug, followed by Damian and then Oksana. 'Duro,' Sebastian muttered – hard. I could see he had also been fighting his demons.

Shrouded in cloud, we could have been anywhere, but that didn't matter, it felt like the top. The summit of the Americas.

A small cross marked the very top, and after a few minutes I pulled out the sat phone and called home with the news. Carrying my GPS tracker, Mum and the team had been watching the whole climb, but it had stopped updating just shy of the summit. It was a wonderful call to make, to share the success and hear their euphoric clamour.

I had made it, not just the climb but the half-year cycle to get here as well. As a team, I, Mum and the production guys had beaten the odds on a number of counts and succeeded in sharing a unique journey. As a team on the mountain we had pushed ourselves hard, harder than I have ever gone at altitude.

But there wasn't much time to celebrate, even though it felt like the end. The skies had cleared slightly for about five minutes but the snow continued to fall, allowing me to grab only a few brief clips of the summit and the ridgeline we had just climbed. Then the cloud cover dropped again and Damian warned us that we needed to descend fast. It was still calm, but the storm was clearly on its way.

*

The descent back to the cave was slow going, with little grip in the deep snow. Damian was having a much harder time without crampons. Thanks to his experience, he managed, but I would have been in serious trouble trying to get down that section on my boots alone.

We then regrouped and had a little water and a few sweets before starting down the Canaleta. There was by now a heavy blizzard and I felt utterly exhausted, every so often half catching my crampon spikes on a rock, which startled me back into sharp focus. But my mind was drifting on to autopilot, and it was hard to shake off.

The wind was picking up, causing the snow to drift. I was disorientated, and grateful that Damian knew the route so well. At the top of the traverse, Sebastian, Oksana and I took off our crampons, but soon wished we hadn't. Before reaching Refugio Independencia we had all fallen at least once, including Damian. None of us fell very far, but it was still dangerous. We were in a very vulnerable place if any of us broke a bone or were to be knocked out. We should have stopped and put our crampons back on but we were all so keen to keep going, and to keep warm, that we didn't. By the time we reached the Refugio the snow had eased and we stopped briefly. It wasn't far now back to High Camp for the night.

But Damian had other ideas. He asked each of us how we were, just like he had throughout the day, but I could tell that this was a loaded question. And he didn't need to explain why; we were all thinking the same thing. With the storm closing in, High Camp wasn't a good place to stay.

I felt rubber-legged and exhausted. The last thing I wanted was to keep going. If Damian had suggested it on the ascent I would have said it was impossible. We were so close to our warm sleeping-bags, but now I knew that the right decision was to push on.

So the arrival back at our tents wasn't the celebration I had been looking forward to and we set about clearing camp. Half an hour later, now with much heavier loads, we started off again. Having stopped, my feet felt bruised as we set out again. My leg muscles, which had started to seize up, screamed in protest.

At camp two we stopped and I was able to switch into the lighter boots I had stashed there, pick up some more supplies and carry on. The final hours were a blur. Everything ached and the loose scree path bullied my tired legs. Going downhill for a long time is always sore on the legs, and I had never descended the best part of three vertical kilometres in one go.

From camp one, Damian radioed ahead to the main organizer of Grajales Expeditions at Plaza de Mulas. He was understandably shocked to hear that we were en route, but more than happy to have some food ready.

After eleven hours spent climbing up and down almost four vertical kilometres, we arrived back at Base Camp. The camp team and other climbers came out to clap us in, thrusting a bottle of white bubbly into my hands. I popped the cork and handed it around, receiving hugs and handshakes from everyone. Among them were a few climbers on their way up, and I noticed the way they looked at us, slightly in awe. It was the same envious feeling I had felt when I saw climbers returning triumphantly from the top.

The camp coordinator also had news that only two teams had summited that day, the soldiers and us, and at least three teams had turned back. I was grateful for the news, and the welcome back, but honestly too tired to feel that excited any more.

18

I woke after eleven hours' sleep feeling like I had spent the night in a tumble drier. Everything ached, but it wasn't my muscles that were most painful. My tongue was stuck to the roof of my mouth and my lips were blistered together, while the underside of my nose was red-raw. After rubbing open my eyes and slowly opening my mouth, I managed a sip of water, which was wonderfully soothing.

My lips hadn't fully healed after the deserts of Peru and Chile, but it was the roof of my mouth that was more painful. It's the only place you can't really put sun cream and I had climbed with my mouth wide open, mainly looking down, gasping in the cold, dry air. The reflections off the snow had blistered the top of my mouth.

Once up, I started to feel more human, and managed some breakfast, slowly. Damian, Oksana and Sebastian looked equally weather-beaten, although they had avoided blistering to their lips, nose and mouth. I could easily have gone back to my tent and slept for another day, but it made more sense to muster my reserves for one last big push to get off the mountain, and recover back in Mendoza.

And so, after repacking our main bags for the mules, we set off on the seven-hour descent back to the road. Except Sebastian, who felt it would be more fun to run the 31km, and reach the road in less than three hours. Walking was sore enough so I declined his insane idea.

It was a stunning climb out, and I went at my own pace, lost in the world around me. After the seemingly endless Playa Ancha, some vegetation reappeared at about 3,500m (11,500ft), and I appreciated the details of the quickly changing world around me. I stopped a number of times to look back at the summit behind and far above me. I could see it was a stormbound world up there and, as with Denali, it was hard to believe I'd been up there less than twenty-four hours earlier.

It felt like a long, long way, and by the end I was just willing myself on, promising myself it would be over soon. My feet ached with the constant stubbing, but there was no sense in stopping.

Over the bridge, past the lake, the valley was falling back into shadow as I caught sight of the helicopter station and threw my arms in the air, laughing out loud. It was over – at least for now. There were still 2,000 miles or so to cycle, but I wasn't even thinking about that. I just wanted to get a shower and a sleep in a proper bed in a world of plentiful oxygen.

We shared a great team hug. Even Damian, who had been up Aconcagua so many times before, felt that it had been a climb to remember as we'd all pushed ourselves far beyond the usual schedule.

It was 2.30 a.m. by the time we'd sorted the kit out, driven back to Mendoza and celebrated the climb over a steak and a bottle of Malbec. Luckily, Argentinian restaurants all operate on a late shift. Back at the hotel I wallowed in the luxury of a bath before trying to sleep. Despite my exhaustion, the throbbing pain from my blackened toes kept me awake, so after a while I had to get up and operate using the minibar's corkscrew to release the pressure. It was not glamorous, but very effective, and I slept in the bliss of thick, luxurious oxygen.

I actually felt worse when I woke up. I doubt I could have climbed anywhere, but then again, the convenient fact that I didn't need to proved how much of the climb had been a mental game, about managing targets. It was over, and my body had gone into shutdown. The weight scales claimed that I had lost 8kg (over a stone) on the mountain. Having started the climb underweight, I now looked pretty unhealthy in the mirror. I certainly felt weak, though with the appetite of a bear coming out of hibernation. But my lips and upper mouth were blistered white and bleeding. Eating may have been essential and desirable, but it was painful.

Before reaching Aconcagua I had had grand thoughts of jumping straight back on my bike, but for the next few days in Mendoza I continued to feel utterly wiped out. I got up just to eat, and briefly sort out some blogs, photos and kit, but I mainly slept until hunger woke me again. The hotel had great breakfasts, or so Damian told me, but for the first three mornings I slept straight through.

On day four off the mountain I committed to leaving and starting the final leg south. On the grand scale of the 11,000 miles and half a year's cycling so far, the final push was small. But in real terms it felt like the toughest section to get psyched about. About 2,000 miles away was Ushuaia, the southernmost city in the Americas, and the world. That was just over twice the distance between John O'Groats and Land's End, but it was through Patagonia, a part of the world I had always dreamt about visiting. Put that way, it sounded very doable and interesting.

But, as I went to leave, my spirits dragged. Now in recovery mode, my heart had fallen out of the journey. If this had been a Hollywood movie it would have ended at the mountaintop, the highest point of the Americas. That tingle of utter relief and joy, of deep contentment, hit me every time I thought back to the summit. An indescribable feeling. It wasn't just the climb but the six months of uncertainty, perspiration, pain and hope, always hope, that had preceded it. But this wasn't Hollywood, and the real expedition wasn't over. This was the less glamorous bit, the inevitable low that follows any emotional (and literal) high. It was time to start the search for a new mindset, because I had the very end of the expedition to focus on now.

My production team had been supportive throughout, sharing

the months of pressure to reach Aconcagua on time and then the elation of the summit. Now, just before I left Mendoza, they took the pressure off. As far as they were concerned the documentary would reach its natural finale at the mountain, with just a few minutes on screen after that to tell the story of the final month on the road. So I wouldn't need to film much. I would be left to my own devices, in my own world from now on.

It took a few days to find my rhythm again on the bike, but it was hard not to be charmed by the flatlands stretching south-east of Mendoza. My first impressions of rural Argentina were that it was similar to Mediterranean Europe, particularly Italy. It was the many old cars, the vineyards, even the laid-back attitudes that gave the region its wonderful charm, that sense of stepping slightly back in time. The girls were pretty, many people cycled and every village sold ice-cream. What more is there to life?

And it was quite a shock speaking Spanish again. Aconcagua may be in Argentina, but it's not the real Argentina. Like all major mountains, it's a melting pot of cultures where English becomes the main language. Back on my own during those first days on the bike I often had dialogues in shops and cafés where I bumbled away in Spanish and they replied, yet I didn't understand them and they looked blankly back. They might as well have been speaking Portuguese.

Physically I felt pretty good, but it was a strange kind of reverse acclimatization. In theory my body was oxygenated, but I felt remarkably weak. Thankfully there were almost no hills to climb and I felt like I could go on for ever, just not very fast. My legs felt fresh, just lacking energy. It was certainly enjoyable not to have any saddle sores to make me wince. It felt like I hadn't been cycling for months.

It was midsummer in Argentina and therefore light till gone nine p.m., and I soon relaxed into long, well-spaced days on the bike. It was certainly tempting to take longer breaks in the middle of the day, when the temperature hovered around 40 degrees. A 55-degree temperature swing in a week takes some getting used to.

I was on a week-long tack east then south to the Atlantic, where I would join the coastal Ruta 3. I knew that it wasn't going to be the most scenic road, but it was the only way south on tarmac all the way. The inland and more mountainous Ruta 40 sounded spectacular, but involved long miles of dirt roads.

Before long the villages grew fewer and further apart. Three days into the ride I passed just one place all day where I could buy some water, but no food. There was another town, but everything was shut: the Argentine siesta seemed to stretch for most of the afternoon. The sea of farmland was slowly giving way to plains of scrub. The sense of space was huge; empty horizons were only punctuated by the odd radio mast.

After a clear hot day I spent the last few hours trying to outrace a storm I could see building on the horizon. I was zipping along, feeling like I was surfing in front of a huge breaker, except my wave of momentum was the wind that signalled the full might of what came behind. I knew that as soon as I stopped I would have just a few minutes before the full storm was upon me. Choosing my spot carefully, I dived off the road in the growing dusk and raced to get the tent up. The plan worked, except the soil was parched and once again wouldn't hold pegs. There were no branches or stones to be found so I laid the bike down and tied one end of the tent to the frame, using a few pannier bags stacked together to peg the other. It was a sorry, sagging home for the night but I dived into it just as the storm hit. It was a real sky-splitter. I lay in my tent, aware that I was the only thing keeping it on the ground. I was buzzing from the exhilarating finish to my first 100-miler since the climb. At that speed I would finish in three weeks. I was back in the moment, loving the bike.

I was also loving the flatlands, after my vertical world, as long as the winds stayed kind. But I knew they wouldn't. Damian, who'd grown up in the Valdes Peninsula midway down Patagonia, had

warned of the infamous *viento zonda*, the winds that scour the
plateau east of the Andes leaving it an almost treeless and dusty
world. It seemed fitting that the last great challenge on my ride
down the Americas would be the wind and not the mountains. Like
most endurance cyclists I would choose big hills over a headwind
every time. There is nothing more sapping or unrequited as battling
a big headwind. But for now the going was good and I made a
conscious note to myself to savour the thrill of fast miles.

The going stayed good for the next few days, but it was just as
well that production had eased the pressure on filming as there was
literally nothing to point the camera at. Roadside altars were my
only regular and intriguing distraction, some with piles of bottles,
obviously left by travellers, and some with small memorials, often
surrounded by red flags.

Sitting outside my tent one evening, I tried to research online
what these were. But the computer screen was the only light source
for many miles and I could barely see the screen for flying bugs. It
was a mini plague and quite incredible, but using my hand as a
screen wiper, I managed to complete my research. The memorials
with red flags, I learned, were in honour of Gauchito Gil, a rather
odd nineteenth-century folk legend. There seem to be a number of
accounts of his life, some saying he was a Robin Hood character
who robbed from the rich to feed the poor, but the more popular
account says that he joined the army to escape an illicit affair he was
in trouble for. He then deserted the army, was caught and killed. All
rather unheroic, except that posthumously he had been credited
with saving the life of the son of the policeman who killed him. It
was all slightly confusing, and some might say unlikely, but he is
now revered by many Argentines, who ask the 'saint' for similar
miracles.

The bottle shrines often looked like big piles of litter, less than
impressive except in their scale, but I was equally fascinated by the
story behind them. This legend, also set in the mid nineteenth
century during the Argentine civil war, concerns a lady called Maria

Antonia Deolinda Correa who decided to follow her husband who had gone to war. But she didn't have enough water with her and died of thirst in the desert. Only her baby son survived, by suckling her breast. Other miracles were also attributed to her post-humously, and she is meant to protect travellers and bring good fortune. This is why passers-by leave empty bottles by her many shrines, to quench her thirst. Like piled stones on Scottish cairns, these travellers' tokens had in some cases become very large mounds.

The folklore and tradition of these stories added hugely to the identity of these vast spaces. I loved them for that. They created a mystery and sense of history in an otherwise fairly wild but feature-less landscape.

On a more twenty-first-century theme, I was finding that Argentina had some surprising communication issues. On the positive side, I found myself cycling through a village that had been turned into a wifi zone. I sat at the roadside with my laptop open, able to use the internet with no mobile phone signal for miles around. On the not so brilliant side, when I did get a phone signal I often got crossed lines with other calls. It was hard to fathom how this happened, but apparently it's a well-known and accepted reality of the archaic phone networks. I would be chatting away to Mum or the team back in Scotland and then suddenly I was listen-ing to some random Argentine conversation for a while, before switching back. And so it went on. If I'd been able to understand Argentine Spanish better I'm sure it would have been amusing. As it was, I didn't dare say anything unless they could hear me, but it was nonetheless a strange thrill to eavesdrop.

I woke the next morning with 70 miles to complete till the next food stop, so I ate some cold beef and biscuits before setting out. It was a famine-and-fast technique I had quickly got used to since ditching my stove. I would ration food for the big gaps, then eat like a king whenever I could. My eating was becoming more lion-like as well.

After two and a half hours I had covered over 40 miles, an almost unprecedented push, thanks to a blissful northerly. Long may it last, I hoped. By nightfall I had cleared another century and met up with Mike and Alanna in their Russian contraption for the fifth time. I decided to treat myself to a room and got a lift on the back of the motorbike, with Alanna still in the sidecar, into the town of Santa Rosa for a pizza. I was fairly used to people having a good look as I cycled past, but this eccentric form of transport was another level. Most people stopped and many looked equally amused and confused. Even those in cars looked dangerously distracted. Stopping at traffic lights attracted an uncomfortable amount of attention. I just sat there wishing for green.

Mike and Alanna had got stuck in Bolivia for a month due to mechanical issues and bizarrely I had managed to pedal through Ecuador, Peru and Chile, climb Aconcagua and pedal across the Argentinian pampas and stay ahead of them. It was a fact that did nothing to dampen their well-humoured rant about their long run of bad luck, and then their grievances at the hands of unhelpful Bolivians. Now that I was used to Alanna's sisterly bullying she and Mike had become my best friends on the road, and meeting them was a welcome chance to come out of my own world, laugh out loud and think about something other than the expedition.

The next day didn't go so well, and I covered a less impressive 23 miles. It was very hot again but it was more comfortable to be riding, which created a slight breeze, than to rest. Even early in the day it was a battle to get myself to leave the air-conditioning of a garage I'd stopped at. And then I broke a spoke. A nuisance, but fairly easy to fix. I found some shade under a tree with a Gauchito Gil memorial and started taking apart my back wheel. The spoke had broken right at the rim of the wheel, by the 'nipple', the oddly named nut that joins the two. I then discovered that I had thrown out my bag of spare nipples by mistake, probably during my frenzied weight-saving efforts. I could put the wheel back together but it would have a wobble, which would put a strain on other spokes, eventually causing more to break. I called Mike and Alanna, and they again saved the day by driving back to Santa Rosa, searching for a bike shop, and eventually waking a man from his siesta to find me the spare parts.

From there it was a 200km stretch without food or water supplies. Thankfully, my rebuild worked well – there was only a slight wobble – and I was only slowed the following day by three punctures thanks to the ubiquitous thorns. Garage workers and travellers alike nodded in sympathy when I mentioned these *pinchas*. Everyone in Patagonia seemed to know about the vicious 'rosata' thorns. Even the Ural had been punctured.

At the town of Bahía Blanca I reached the Atlantic for the first time in South America. From there I turned south and finally met the Ruta 3, the road that would take me all the way to Tierra del Fuego. Having followed the Pacific for so long, it felt like a significant milestone to make it across the continent. It also felt satisfying actually to be cycling due south and heading for the finish line, still nearly 1,500 miles away. I wouldn't reach the coast properly for a few more days, but I could see it, normally just a few miles off to my left.

The thick thorny bushes that scattered the roadside gave poor shelter, and each night I camped fairly openly to the road, but out here I wasn't worried. It felt safe, and the traffic on those long straight roads was so fast and blinkered, like the vehicles in the Australian Outback, that behind the curtain of darkness I was all but invisible. I certainly felt like a wild man of the road, with limitless places to sleep, few communications and the most dishevelled appearance I have ever had in two decades of adventures. My hair had not been cut for seven months now and had gone from dark and short to sun-bleached and like a *león*, as the Chilean waitress had commented. Maybe like a scarecrow would have been closer.

On the afternoon of the first day out of Bahía Blanca, the wind changed direction and I pedalled into a horizon of storm clouds. Later, it was uncomfortably hot inside the tent, but I didn't dare open the door as a dust storm was swirling around outside. I fell asleep to the first patters of rain on the tent – my first proper rain since Panama.

With 120km to go to the next food stop I made a keen start the following morning and was soon rewarded with my first signpost for Ushuaia – just 2,190km (1,360 miles) to go. And then another spoke broke. It was already getting dark so I set up camp and left it for the morning. My only chance of finding someone to properly rebuild it for the empty miles of Patagonia ahead of me was in the Welsh settlement town of Trelew.

Wheel-building before breakfast is character-building stuff, and my diary from later that day captures the mood well: 'In the end did 95 miles into the wind & passed nothing. Endless scrub, no houses or supplies all day. Haven't taken any photos for two days. Back wheel is fixed but it has a nasty wobble that made me nervous.'

As I pedalled along, it occurred to me how very different to the world cycle this finish was feeling. I had been chasing a world record then, and the last thousand miles moved through the constantly changing landscapes of Spain and France. I'd also been cycling back into the welcoming arms of family and friends and I'd been blinkered and obsessed till the last pedal strokes in Paris. Here, the urgency had passed. I had reached and summited Aconcagua in time. I was now riding through an almost unchanging landscape towards a finish line where I would be alone, many thousands of miles from anyone I knew. And for those reasons it felt like an even greater test of my resolve. It wasn't a lonely place, but I fought with myself every hour of every day to maintain momentum. There was little stopping me from cycling much slower until the end, except maybe a lack of other things to do in this barren landscape.

It felt like a grind, counting down the hours and the miles, but that's not meant to be a negative point. There was something wonderfully cathartic about getting lost in this world, pitting myself against the now almost constant headwind, blanking out any other emotion save the desire to keep going.

A few days later this changed and a whisper of a northerly gave me all the encouragement I needed to reach Trelew. At a garage some way shy of the town I counted fourteen workers, one on the till, the rest standing around chatting, and a long queue of customers. It epitomized how I had come to feel about rural Argentina: charming but hopelessly inefficient. The tyre and wheel issues took a bit more sorting out than I had expected and I ended up stopping for the day in Trelew.

Established by the Welsh in the late nineteenth century, it's still a community where many residents speak the language. I liked Trelew, slightly lost in time as it was; my hotel had a tiny metal-grate lift that stopped at uneven levels to each floor, and my room had a telephone with a circular dial. I wandered unknowingly into a very nice restaurant, still dressed in my dirty cycle top. The waiter tried his best to extend his usual welcome, but I could tell he wanted to ask for a deposit, or better still for me to leave. This was the downside to looking so windswept and organic.

The bike fixed, the next day I resumed my journey and continued to pass 'nothing, nada, zilch, except one petrol station', as I blogged the following night. 'I know Patagonia is stunning (I have seen the pictures) but this part didn't make the brochure. It is windy though!' The next day's account was slightly more interesting: 'Today went well, but was largely the same, so will spare you the (lack of) details! Cool to see some more wildlife.' I was sure I had spotted some emu, but was soon corrected by one blog follower that no such birds existed in Argentina, and that they were in fact rhea, which I hadn't heard of. But the king of the plains was without doubt the majestic guanaco. A wild version of the llama, it had a spirited lollop and ranged the roadsides in small herds. Some might say guanaco are daft-looking animals. I was certainly surprised when I first spotted one – some sort of cross between a camel, a deer and a sheep. But once used to them I liked their proud, alert stance and the way they streaked effortlessly through the scrub.

One night I was sitting outside my tent in the near darkness, eating by the light of my head torch, when I heard a scuffling close behind me. Turning with a fright, my headlight caught an armadillo, just a few feet from me. It had no fear at all, but I guessed it had few predators here. Its name means 'little armoured one' and I studied the amazing shell of this alien-looking beast. I can't remember many times when I've been so close to a wild animal and neither it nor I felt threatened. It scuffled around, considering me, as I sat still, watching it back. I chatted away quietly, asking him where he lived and what he was up to, but he ignored the conversation and continued scuffling. After a while he wandered off, leaving me to finish my food.

19

On 6 February I finally and properly reached the Atlantic at the town of Comodoro Rivadavia. It was approached by a glorious 12-mile descent which was all the more exciting after having been blown into the road all morning by the relentless gusts. It was the first town I had reached in three days, yet because it was mid afternoon, everywhere was shut. I had been dreaming of my first hearty meal since Trelew, but had to make do with another garage diner.

However, not everyone was on siesta. While I was climbing the road out of town, a car pulled alongside and gestured for me to stop. They then raced ahead a bit, pulled in, and a cameraman and reporter jumped out. They introduced themselves so fast that the words blended into a seamless sound. I smiled blankly, going back to basics: '¡Hola! ¿Cómo estás?'

I would love to have a literal translation of what happened next. I realized that they were reporting for the local TV news, and the reporter did a very good job of using slow, baby Spanish so that I understood his questions perfectly. However, my answers, like all my conversations, were limited to the 'I' and 'you' form of the handful of verbs I knew, and only in the present tense. And what I couldn't say I made up in an unexpected surge of confidence, the sort I would normally only experience after a few pints. Rising to the challenge with complete disregard, I watched the reporter's expression visibly flinch as I bulldozed his language with straight-faced bravado. Eventually they bid me 'Feliz viaje' ('safe travels') and I pedalled on, laughing out loud as soon as they were out of earshot. It would have to be a desperate day of local news for them to use that interview, but I have no doubt that it made their 2010 outtakes.

The following day I received news that Mike and Alanna had reached Ushuaia. They had beaten me in the end and also reassured me that between us lay some of the windiest and most boring roads they had ever experienced. I chose to ignore that warning as I had no viable alternatives, and enthusiastically started what I hoped would be my last week on the road.

They weren't exaggerating. As soon as the road left the coast just after Caleta Olivia it got very, very windy. At this force it was quite dangerous. Constantly blowing from my front right, the wind pushed me into the narrow road. I developed a technique of cycling while leaning right, shouldering the wind to stay upright and straight. I twice had to put my foot down to steady the bike, which also demonstrates how slow I was going.

The forecast was for even stronger winds, which I was dreading. By now I was running out of new ways to blog about this issue, and becoming acutely aware that the followers might not be enjoying the repetition. But, if anything, my descriptions played down the true mind- and body-sapping force of being wind-blasted all day, and if the reading was becoming uncomfortable then it was at least honest, if not exciting. My mild obsession wasn't simply for the lack of anything else to mention, but for the fact that the wind was my best friend and worst enemy in one. It tried to dictate my mood and it most definitely dictated my speed.

It was a relatively rubbish day's mileage, but on balance, I don't think most people would have been cycling at all in those conditions.

I set up camp by a tunnel under the road. I'm not sure why it was there as it was unlikely to be for flooding out here; maybe to let sheep cross under the road. I hadn't seen any sheep on the plains, but there was a dead one near the tunnel mouth so I placed the tent further out, while still close enough to benefit from the windbreak afforded by the steep banks up to the road.

At just gone one a.m. I woke with the tent canvas slapping my face. The cracking noise of the material whipping in the wind was all around me as I felt around in the dark for my glasses and head torch. The full gale had hit and the tent had collapsed. There wasn't the slightest chance it would stand up to these winds, and I knew there was no point in trying, so I lay still for about twenty minutes, trying to go back to sleep. It was impossible with the tent in my face and the noise.

After grabbing everything loose that I could feel for and stuffing it back into pannier bags, I waited for a lull before making a break. Opening the zip, I piled the pannier bags together, jumped out, picked up the entire tent and ran for the tunnel. Its entrance had been used as a toilet by passing drivers so I explored deeper, stopping about midway, directly under the road. I was bent double, and it was quite narrow and concrete-hard. I pulled my sleeping roll and bag out from my tent, used it for extra padding, and tried to get back to sleep. Whether it was the faeces or the dead sheep, a nasty smell was being blown in. Even so, I managed to sleep fitfully until six a.m.

The wind had calmed slightly and I packed everything away fairly easily. The tent had ripped and I couldn't find all the pegs, but I felt fine and was happy to move on. The first few hours were tough, but reasonable going.

Then it got silly.

Winds hammered in from the south-west, blowing me backwards and again into the road. It was impossible to cycle. I simply couldn't go more than ten pedal rotations in a straight line, and that felt like climbing the steepest of hills, hammering it. So I started walking along the verge, head bent, leaning forward, pulling the bike along beside me.

For four hours I walked like this, very slowly. It felt on my face like I was driving a convertible very fast, without a windscreen. Even behind sunglasses I was squinting, and I pursed my lips to keep out the whirling dust. It was magnificent, and intimidating. Lost in my own world, I swung from thoughts about how long it would take to walk to Ushuaia to the almost manic joy of facing up to all that Mother Nature could throw at me. I was still moving south, just very slowly.

LA CABAÑA said the large white sign. It wasn't on the map, and I have never been so delighted to see a lonely building. It seemed deserted, almost no one was on the road, but a lady appeared and agreed to make a meal for me. We didn't discuss what, I was just so elated to be out of the wind. My skin felt numb to the touch. I left my bike lying on the ground to save it from blowing over, getting blasted with grit.

A few hours later I cycled away with renewed energy, got about half a kilometre down the road, got off and started walking again. I spent the next couple of hours walking, but was also at times huddled down behind my bike. I looked up at the sound of a siren to see an old white van coming towards me. AMBULANCIA was emblazoned across the bonnet. The van stopped and four men got out, all dressed in police uniform.

'Are you all right?' one man asked, in Spanish.

'Sí, gracias. ¡Hay mucho viento!' I gestured towards the wind, as if it needed pointing out.

'Sí, está peligroso en bici,' he agreed – it was dangerous for cycling.

It transpired that someone had passed me in a car then stopped at the community of Tres Cerros, where I was trying to get to, and reported an emergency. It was a kind gesture, but I wondered why he or she hadn't stopped to help personally if I had seemed in so much trouble. I tried to explain that I was fine, that 'voy a estar en Tres Cerros antes la noche'. But they weren't convinced, although they clearly understood that I wanted to keep walking and that I planned to reach Tres Cerros by evening. They insisted they couldn't leave me out here, and after some more debate I worked out that I was much closer than I had thought, only a few kilometres away, so I conceded. I didn't mind missing a few kilometres, all things considered.

Inside, the ambulance looked more like a workman's van, lined with cutting tools and boxes. It looked like the police, fire and ambulance all worked out of the same vehicle. We covered the distance in a few minutes, and to my utter joy they told me that there was a motel I could stay at. But not before I was held at the police station for an hour as they filed out reports about me. I have no idea what these reports said as they asked me no questions, just fed me tea. I got the distinct impression that they had nothing better to do than stretch out my little adventure and extend their authority for as long as possible. I didn't mind. They were very friendly and, again, I was just grateful to be out of the wind.

I had made 38 miles, dusk till dawn – not great considering I had made half that total in the first few hours. But it was a night and a day to remember, a tough battle with the elements which I had ultimately lost, partly thanks to the insistence of the police.

It was a charming roadhouse, and I relished the great meal and a bed. My 'rebel without a cause' side also got the better of me here: I 'borrowed' a coat hanger to make some new tent pegs.

I set my alarm for 4.30, keen to win the next round. When I walked outside, still half asleep, I was nearly knocked off my feet. I had a wee laugh at myself and went back to bed.

By seven things were a bit calmer and I started out again. I hardly stopped until eight p.m. and covered 90 miles. They were hard won, and I felt battered but elated.

The next day, the 11th, was calmer still and much more scenic as I passed lots of wide salt lakes with Chilean flamingos wading in the shallows and Coscoroba swans and other water birds swimming and flying around. Now midway through the Santa Cruz region, I had less than 500 miles (800km) to go.

After lunch on the 12th the storm had well and truly passed and there was silence. It felt very odd. Constant noise and buffeting had become the norm, but now the world was calm again. I rode along, amused by a message from production reminding me to keep filming the 'changing' landscape. Tricky: I couldn't think of any significant changes over the last 1,000 miles.

There were signs, though, that I was nearing the tip of the Americas. Many of the cars on the road were now Chilean, going to and from the town of Punta Arenas, as the fjords and glaciers on their side of the border prevented any roads making it all the way south without crossing into Argentina. These were my last days on the mainland and I felt stronger and more focused by the day. This last leg from Aconcagua may have had moments that dragged endlessly, yet the days and weeks were flying by.

'Hello Tailwind, welcome to the show! Your ugly sister was here a few days ago giving me a hard time,' I wrote happily in my notes as I neared Río Gallegos, the last major town before Tierra del Fuego. Before reaching the town I stopped at yet another garage to stock up again and got into a conversation with an older man, maybe in his sixties, his face weathered with dark wrinkles. He stopped by the back of his truck and asked me where I was going. He then explained very slowly, as if time meant nothing to him, that he was a gaucho, a cowboy, who had lived here his whole life. He then took ten minutes to explain the wind direction in relation to the moon phases. Peering at me closely, he spoke unlike anyone I had met, mainly in Spanish with the odd word in English. I felt like he was passing down great wisdom, and, unlike most Argentinians, I understood every word. It's rare that you meet anyone who is so utterly and obviously at peace with themselves, unrushed by life. He smiled warmly as I explained my journey from Alaska. 'Keep your heart big,' he said in English, and shook my hand before walking off. It was in every sense one of the nicest comments of the journey.

On Valentine's Day I crossed back into Chile. The islands of Tierra del Fuego are split between Chile and Argentina and the

ferry leaves from the Chilean side. It had been a tough day, 65 miles
at an average of 8mph in leg-sapping conditions. The last few hours
were easier going but it stayed windy, and I was worried about
camping as the tent just wouldn't take it. The border was easy, and
I rode until nine p.m., using all the daylight, looking for somewhere
sheltered to stop.

There was nowhere, literally no convenient hollows, walls or
tunnels that I could use to hide. Then I saw a small wooden bus-
stop standing alone in the landscape, the only building for miles
around. Normally I wouldn't have looked twice as it was right on
the roadside, but needs must and I pulled in to investigate. It was
ideal insofar as it had a door at the front instead of being completely open. On each end and at the front were small windows, and
it had a peaked tin roof, making it look like a little house. Inside
wasn't so quaint: there was a wooden bench above a floor of bottles
and other litter, and it smelled of urine. It would have to do as there
was literally nowhere else, but it wasn't a place I would have chosen
to spend Valentine's night.

The bike fitted perfectly inside, which meant that if I rolled off
the narrow bench I would be propped up by my panniers rather
than hitting the floor. It was actually quite warm, once I had
boarded up the broken window with some cardboard. I put on all
my clothes and wedged my knees against the wall, as the bench
wasn't long enough; I hoped that would stop me rolling off. It
stank, but I was pleased with my ingenuity and soon dozed off.

At 2.30 a.m. I woke to the sound of a truck engine idling just a
few metres away, headlights streaming in the doorway. I stayed still,
but got ready to react. The truck doors opened and I could hear two
men talking. One came to the door and paused. I didn't look up,
pretending to be asleep. He then said something to his friend and I
heard them walking round the back. They were soon back, and
I heard both truck doors shut before the vehicle pulled away, with a
hiss of air brakes. I was left in darkness again, my heart rate going
like the clappers. I soon fell asleep again.

In the morning, after a short ride, I couldn't have been happier when I came across a roadhouse where they served me a mug of coffee and scrambled eggs. If only I had known it was here the night before I would have cycled on. It had got very cold in the night in my bus-stop and I enjoyed the feeling of warming up over breakfast.

PUNTA ARENAS STRAIGHT ON, TIERRA DEL FUEGO LEFT the next road sign said, and I turned off the road I had been on for weeks and headed for the ferry.

It was a short hop across the Straits of Magellan and I arrived just as the ferry ramp hit the dockside. The queue of cars and lorries was invited to load up first before I was waved onboard. Climbing on to the viewing level, I gazed back at the land as we pulled away. That was the end of mainland South America, quite a thought after over three months journeying through it. Once in the Straits I was far too distracted by the rough ride and amused by the many green-looking passengers around me to become too nostalgic.

When we arrived at the far side I was ushered off first, somehow having missed the part where you pay. It didn't seem right to go back and insist on it. Between this and my stolen coat hanger and tinsel, I had a growing criminal tally for South America.

Ahead of me lay just over 100km of dirt tracks before reaching the Argentine border again (I guess that the Chileans don't see the point in paving a road for the Argentines to use). But before leaving I had a big meal at the small port café and bought a stash of chocolate. Apart from long daylight hours, the greatest benefit of now being so far south was being able to carry chocolate again without it melting.

The road was much better than I'd expected to start with, perfectly compacted and smooth, actually an enjoyable change from tarmac. But as I reached the first undulating hills it became rougher, mainly stones without the smooth filling of fine dirt. The land was covered in the same coarse grasses as the last few hundred miles of the mainland. Lots of guanaco dotted the landscape, standing out due to the lack of anything else. No rocks, no trees, no anything.

Patagonia had amazed me. It was as wild as its reputation suggested, but I hadn't seen any of the scenery I had dreamt of. I had now cycled a couple of thousand barren miles from the grassy pampas to the scrubby wastelands of northern Patagonia, and was into the ranchlands of the far south.

I cycled until ten p.m., by which time it was completely dark, but there was nothing else on the road so it didn't matter. After covering 60km of gravel road I'd got the hang of picking the smoothest line, wandering all over the road to avoid rocks. Every time I got it wrong my heavy bike protested; it felt clumsy and unforgiving over the stones. When I stopped I had that jelly feeling in my arms and wrists that you get at the end of a long day's mountain biking from the constant bumping.

I put the tent up right on the verge, no longer worried about security. It felt like being on an island off Scotland's west coast, far away from the cares of the busy world. Almost nothing passed in the night, I am guessing because the ferries stopped running.

The morning was calm and I set out for another 50km of dirt road until second breakfast at the Argentine border. It took longer than I thought and towards the end I started riding with greater disregard, hammering over the bumps in my urgency to get back to smooth tar. This cavalier style caused a puncture, but it was a slow one, so I kept going, stopping every few miles to pump it back up rather than fiddle with the repair while still on the rough stuff.

There it was, the sign I'd been waiting for: REPUBLICA ARGENTINA. PROVINCIA DE TIERRA DEL FUEGO ANTARDIDA E ISLAS DEL ATLANTICO SUR. I crossed a cattle grid, skirted by a fence line and was back into Argentina some kilometres short of the actual border crossing. The gravel road had been hot work, and the passport checkpoint turned out to be inside a very crowded building. I felt very self-conscious. I could smell myself, which meant I had to be fairly unacceptable to the clean people around me. My clothes hadn't been washed for three weeks.

Once through, I stopped for an hour, got some food and changed my puncture. That was my last border crossing, and that was the last of the gravel. I punched the air and laughed with relief as I pedalled back on to tarmac. There couldn't be many more tests ahead now. I was on the last 200 miles (320km).

It was exactly two years since I had finished the world cycle, and that's what I was thinking about as I cycled away from the border. Those racing thoughts, combined with the perfect roads and a cracking tailwind, put me into time-trial mode, and I absolutely flew. From seven p.m. I covered 50 miles, eventually reaching the town of Río Grande at 10.30. It was a beautiful ride, skirting the coast through a stunning sunset and into the chill of the night. I would have sung out loud if I'd had breath to spare.

Thankfully I quickly found a room, and as it was Argentina, the restaurant was still full. I feasted and studied the map to check out the remaining miles of the journey.

Those late, fast miles that had felt so good at the time hurt a lot in the morning and I gingerly got back on my bike and pedalled slowly out of town. I was mentally all over the place. Again, in stark contrast to the world cycle, on which I had been focused until the very last miles, here I was the day before the finish daydreaming. I couldn't wait to see everyone back at home, but there was also a part of me that didn't want the journey to end. Nine months was a long time to have been on the go, and it was strange to imagine waking up and not having the journey to focus on.

Alaska to Tierra del Fuego. The more I thought back, the more I got lost in the hundreds of people I had met, the range of sceneries I had cycled through, and the many battles against the elements. It had been less about the mountains than I had originally planned, far more about the people than I had imagined it would be. I was pedalling along thinking of playing with the monkeys, drinking tequila, about meeting Maria in Pisco, and embracing Damian and Sebastian on top of Aconcagua. I was thinking back to leaving Scotland, moving out of my flat in Edinburgh, waving goodbye to my girlfriend and family and then flying to Anchorage, staring down at the Rockies from the plane. There was far too much to remember, many lifetimes of experiences in a single journey. I felt immensely content and grateful.

I was dreaming too early. From feeling strong and totally motivated, I now found myself sitting at the roadside struggling to find the will power to complete the hundred or so miles to the finish. It was utterly bizarre. I had just finished an interview with Greg James on Radio 1, and rather than pack the satellite phone away and keep going I'd just sat down and considered going for a sleep in the grass. It was an internal battle. A part of me was celebrating, reminiscing, relaxing, while the rational side was screaming for me to keep the focus, to keep going. It was a torn feeling, a momentary loss of self-control after nine months of focus.

Once I'd got back on the bike I had a laugh at myself and found the flow again. As the road climbed inland, trees appeared in large numbers for the first time in over a thousand miles. Pine trees and old hardwoods changed the landscape entirely, so that by the time I reached the small town of Tolhuin it felt like a different country. Having started the day in coastal grasslands, I could now see snow-peaked craggy mountains ahead. It looked kind of like Alaska again.

Tolhuin has a fantastic bakery, and I stopped there for my last stash of supplies. The owner greeted me warmly and insisted that I take a room for the night. At any other time it would have been a random act of kindness I couldn't have refused, but I was determined to keep going and to spend my last night in the tent. As I packed my panniers and got ready to leave, he ran out with a box of chocolates, wishing me good luck for the end of my journey.

I was thrown back into a weird world of jumbled emotions, assailed by thoughts of this time tomorrow. Forcing myself back into the moment, I attacked the next hills with an unsustainable gusto, sweating profusely and hurting, but enjoying the distraction.

The scenery was now completely beautiful, everything I had imagined Tierra del Fuego to be. I passed Lago Fagnano, where deadwood tangled the shoreline, a high ridgeline of mountains on the far bank. The roadside was now thick grasses and mosses, an entirely different ecosystem from the world I had just emerged from. After the day's confusion I pitched my tent near the road and fell asleep instantly. It was a luxurious green mattress, and I remember waking up in the night thinking how comfortable I was.

The morning started overcast with a heavy dew. I packed away a wet tent for the last time and set out early. Quite a few people back in the UK who had been following the blog throughout were committed to joining me virtually for my last 50 miles, so when I set out I let them know. I really appreciated their gesture.

It started to drizzle and the road continued to climb, far more than I had expected. Up past another lake, it then clung to the mountainside with sheer rock on my left and a drop to the right. I found a safe place to pull in and looked back down the length of Lago Escondido to the surrounding forested valley. Over the col I screamed downhill, forgetting that I wasn't yet descending to the coast.

Around a sharp U-bend the road started to follow a new valley, and I was back in a tunnel of trees. I was cruising now, climbing more gradually until I reached the ski station at the base of the most southerly resort in the world. It wasn't that high, but considering I needed to get back to the coast I knew the remaining miles had to be mainly downhill. To my surprise I kept going up for another half an hour. It had now stopped raining and the clouds were moving off.

The road was now hugging the valley side, just below the tree line, and climbed up to another saddle between two high peaks. All around were the craggy snowy peaks of the Martial Mountains. My stomach was doing absolute somersaults as I reached the flat. A few minutes later I was zipping downhill again. Still surrounded by trees, I could only get views of the rock faces above and behind me. Then I rounded a corner and ahead of me I could see the water. The Beagle Channel. I couldn't yet see Ushuaia, but I knew somewhere down there was the finish. I didn't want to end the cycle in the middle of a town, I wanted to try to find a way down to the water's edge, across the bay from Ushuaia.

I didn't have a map for this final bit. With complete abandon I flew the final miles on the main road, overtaking a car in my haste. Going on instinct, as I reached the very outskirts of town I pulled on the brakes and took a side road that looked like it led towards the water. It continued downhill and curved back into town so I turned left again, on to a dirt road. Here the slope stopped as I crossed a little bridge and cycled back up a small hill. The road ahead disappeared around a headland, yet the water was so close to my left, just a few hundred metres away. I kept going, and around the point I was even closer, but high above the water now. Half a kilometre further on I came to a small car-park. Footpaths ran from the car-park so I jumped off my bike and pushed it along one of them. The grass continued down between big bushes until I emerged at the top of a wide pebble beach.

There it was, across the small bay, 'El Fin del Mundo' – The End of the World, as Ushuaia is nicknamed. I was smiling, but I felt slightly removed. Was this spot the end of the journey? There was no reason why not. There was no tape to cross this time.

I dropped on to the beach and the bike sank into the pebbles. I dragged it forward. A few metres from the sea I kicked it on to its stand and wandered over to the water's edge, looking around. I couldn't see anyone. I didn't really know what to do. My body was buzzing with adrenalin from the final miles but my mind was pretty blank. So I just crouched down by the water. It was so quiet, just the lapping of the waves on the pebbles.

The sense of relief caught me by surprise. I thought I would just be excited, but in fact I found myself cracking up.

I had made it.

It had always been about finishing the journey, about getting to this point, although it was the mountains that had dominated my hopes and fears. An amazing feeling, impossible to describe.

And what a perfect spot to finish a journey, on the edge of an ocean with snow-peaked mountains looking on. Unforgettable. I stayed there for a long while, enjoying the peace. There was nowhere else to go. It was over. Unlike Paris, I was on my own to savour the bundle of emotions that hit me. I cried and I laughed.

13,080 miles. Two big mountains. 268 days on the road.

It was going to take some time to get used to the odd notion of opening a packet of biscuits and not finishing them.

ABOUT THE AUTHOR

Mark Beaumont grew up in the foothills of the Scottish Highlands. When he was twelve, he cycled across Scotland, then, a few years later, completed the 1,000-mile solo ride across Britain from John O'Groats to Land's End. His next long-distance ride took him the length of Italy, a journey of 1,336 miles, helping to raise £50,000 for charity. After graduating from Glasgow University, he decided against a conventional career and devoted himself full-time to his endurance adventures.

In 2008, Mark completed his Guinness World Record-breaking cycle around the world, having travelled 18,297 miles in just 194 days and 17 hours. He has self-filmed and presented two documentaries for the BBC, *The Man Who Cycled the World* and *The Man Who Cycled the Americas*, and will embark on his next adventure in the summer of 2011. Visit his website at www.markbeaumontonline.com